THEODICY
OF LOVE

THEODICY
OF LOVE

Cosmic Conflict
and the
Problem of Evil

JOHN C. PECKHAM

B
Baker Academic
a division of Baker Publishing Group
Grand Rapids, Michigan

Published by Baker Academic
a division of Baker Publishing Group
PO Box 6287, Grand Rapids, MI 49516-6287
www.bakeracademic.com

Printed and bound by CPI Group (UK) Ltd, Croydon, CR0 4YY

Library of Congress Cataloging-in-Publication Data
Names: Peckham, John, 1981– author.
Title: Theodicy of love : cosmic conflict and the problem of evil / John C. Peckham.
Description: Grand Rapids, MI : Baker Academic, a division of Baker Publishing Group, [2018] |
    Includes bibliographical references and index.
Identifiers: LCCN 2018010830 | ISBN 9781540960269 (pbk.)
Subjects: LCSH: Theodicy. | Good and evil—Religious aspects—Christianity. | God
    (Christianity)—Love.
Classification: LCC BT160 .P36 2018 | DDC 231/.8—dc23
LC record available at https://lccn.loc.gov/2018010830

18 19 20 21 22 23 24   7 6 5 4 3 2 1

In keeping with biblical principles of creation stewardship, Baker Publishing Group advocates the responsible use of our natural resources. As a member of the Green Press Initiative, our company uses recycled paper when possible. The text paper of this book is composed in part of post-consumer waste.

Contents

Contents

Preface

Why do you make me look at injustice?
    Why do you tolerate wrongdoing?
Destruction and violence are before me;
    there is strife, and conflict abounds. . . .
Your eyes are too pure to look on evil;
    you cannot tolerate wrongdoing.
Why then do you tolerate the treacherous?
    Why are you silent while the wicked
    swallow up those more righteous than themselves?

Hab. 1:3, 13 NIV

Since I was a young child—indeed for as long as I can remember—I have been deeply troubled by the suffering and injustice in this world. I have wondered how the evil I saw in this world could be reconciled with my belief that "God is love" (1 John 4:8, 16). Before I knew what it was called, I was wrestling with the problem of evil: If God is all-good and all-powerful, why is there evil? And so much of it? One of the primary reasons I became fascinated with theology was because of this problem, perhaps the most difficult problem that Christian theism faces.

The problem of evil is far more than a philosophical or theological problem. The kind and amount of evil in this world present a deep, sometimes faith-crushing religious or existential problem, which is particularly acute for those who believe in an all-good and all-powerful God. Many people have lost faith for this reason, and others find it difficult, if not impossible, to believe in the God of Christianity in light of the horrendous evil in this world.

Although the religious, existential, and philosophical problems of evil should be distinguished and addressed quite differently, they should not be thought of as entirely unrelated. On the one hand, often the last thing somebody needs to hear while in the midst of acute grief is a philosophical or theological treatment of evil. Often, the best thing that can be done in the presence of someone grieving or suffering is to remain silent relative to attempts at explanation while expressing compassionate love and care for them in meaningful, tangible ways.

On the other hand, many Christians who undergo profound suffering eventually seek answers regarding how to reconcile such suffering with their faith in the goodness and love of God. I often wonder how much the framework one holds prior to undergoing such suffering or grief makes a difference in how suffering and grief are experienced. It seems to me that the very way one conceives of God and God's providential involvement in this world bears significantly not only on how suffering and evil are understood but also on how they are felt and processed. What I think of God's involvement in the cause of evil and suffering, or his lack thereof, will significantly affect the way I experience such evil and suffering, and misunderstanding God's relationship to evil may significantly intensify my psychological experience of suffering.

Although motivated by the relationship between how one conceives of God's relationship to evil and how one experiences evil, this book is not aimed at providing an approach to the religious or existential problem of evil, which demands book-length consideration of its own. Whereas addressing the religious or existential problem of evil concerns how people should deal with their experience of suffering and evil, this book focuses on the philosophical problem of evil (in its logical and evidential forms), which is concerned primarily with how one might understand the problem of evil and reconcile it with the goodness and love of God.

One unhelpful way to deal with the philosophical problem of evil is to attempt to downplay the problem itself, suggesting (even if only implicitly) that evil is not so bad after all. Such an approach tends toward justifying evil, which in my view is unjustifiable. Rather than justifying evil and injustice, even implicitly, we should abhor them and stand resolutely against them. Whatever else we say about the philosophical problem, I believe we should never attempt to downplay the horrendous evil and suffering in this world. Accordingly, it is never my intention to trivialize evil, justify evil, explain evil away, or minimize the magnitude of the problem.[1] On the contrary, my limited

---

1. For this reason I tend to avoid referencing specific examples of people's suffering. I do not want to give even the impression of trivializing such instances of suffering by using them as anecdotes in a theological discussion.

goal in this book is to try to understand, from the vantage point of Christian theism, how to coherently hold that God is entirely good and all-powerful, despite the evil in this world.

No perspective on evil can assuage its devastating impact. Ultimately, only God can resolve the problem of evil in all its aspects. And he will. In the meantime, I pray that some might find the approach and framework laid out in this book to be helpful to their own wrestling with evil and suffering, even though many questions remain. At the same time, with the many voices in Scripture, I wait in hope for God's final resolution while asking in lament, "How long, O LORD?" (Ps. 13:1).

Acknowledgments

This book is motivated not only by my own questions and wrestling with the problem of evil but has also been impacted by many family members, friends, and students with whom I have had numerous conversations on this issue over the years. I am thankful to all who, in good faith, have asked the kinds of thoughtful questions that I attempt to address in this book.

I am deeply grateful to Dave Nelson at Baker Academic for his interest in publishing this book and for all of his excellent support and guidance throughout the process. I also owe special thanks to Melisa Blok, who has expertly guided the manuscript through the editing process. Many thanks are also due to the rest of the Baker Academic team, with whom it has been a joy and a privilege to work on this book.

I'd also like to thank my colleagues in the theology and Christian philosophy department of the seminary of Andrews University. It is my privilege to work with such great colleagues and friends. Thanks are also due to those who read part or all of this work and provided feedback and encouragement and to my students who have shown interest in this work and encouraged me along the way.

I am also thankful to the editors of *Andrews University Seminary Studies* for allowing me to reuse material from my article, "Does God Always Get What He Wants? A Theocentric Approach to Divine Providence and Human Freedom," *Andrews University Seminary Studies* 52, no. 2 (2014): 195–212.

Finally, I am profoundly thankful to my family. I cannot thank my parents, Ernest and Karen, enough for all of their love and support. I would also like to thank my parents-in-law, Lee and Ann, who have also been very supportive of all my work. My seven-year-old son, Joel, provides daily respite from the seriousness of writing. Thanks to him, I get to play like a child nearly every day. Finally, words cannot express my love, gratitude, and appreciation for my wonderful wife, Brenda, the light of my life and my best friend.

Abbreviations

General

ANE	Ancient Near East	MT	Masoretic Text
DSS	Dead Sea Scrolls	NT	New Testament
ET	English Text	OT	Old Testament
LXX	Septuagint		

Old Testament

Gen.	Genesis	Song	Song of Songs
Exod.	Exodus	Isa.	Isaiah
Lev.	Leviticus	Jer.	Jeremiah
Num.	Numbers	Lam.	Lamentations
Deut.	Deuteronomy	Ezek.	Ezekiel
Josh.	Joshua	Dan.	Daniel
Judg.	Judges	Hosea	Hosea
Ruth	Ruth	Joel	Joel
1–2 Sam.	1–2 Samuel	Amos	Amos
1–2 Kings	1–2 Kings	Obad.	Obadiah
1–2 Chron.	1–2 Chronicles	Jon.	Jonah
Ezra	Ezra	Mic.	Micah
Neh.	Nehemiah	Nah.	Nahum
Esther	Esther	Hab.	Habakkuk
Job	Job	Zeph.	Zephaniah
Ps./Pss.	Psalm/Psalms	Hag.	Haggai
Prov.	Proverbs	Zech.	Zechariah
Eccles.	Ecclesiastes	Mal.	Malachi

Apocryphal Works

Sir.	Sirach/Ecclesiasticus	Wis.	Wisdom of Solomon
1 Macc.	1 Maccabees		

Old Testament Pseudepigrapha

1 En.	1 Enoch	Test. Dan	Testament of Dan
Jub.	Jubilees	Test. Levi	Testament of Levi

New Testament

Matt.	Matthew	1–2 Thess.	1–2 Thessalonians
Mark	Mark	1–2 Tim.	1–2 Timothy
Luke	Luke	Titus	Titus
John	John	Philem.	Philemon
Acts	Acts	Heb.	Hebrews
Rom.	Romans	James	James
1–2 Cor.	1–2 Corinthians	1–2 Pet.	1–2 Peter
Gal.	Galatians	1–3 John	1–3 John
Eph.	Ephesians	Jude	Jude
Phil.	Philippians	Rev.	Revelation
Col.	Colossians		

Secondary Sources

AAR   American Academy of Religion

AB   Anchor Yale Bible Commentary

ABD   *The Anchor Bible Dictionary*. Edited by David Noel Freedman. 6 vols. New York: Doubleday, 1996.

ANET   *Ancient Near Eastern Texts Relating to the Old Testament*. Edited by James B. Pritchard. 3rd ed. Princeton: Princeton University Press, 1969.

ANF   *The Ante-Nicene Fathers*. Edited by Alexander Roberts and James Donaldson. 10 vols. Buffalo: The Christian Literature Company, 1885–1887.

BDAG   Danker, Frederick W., W. Walter Bauer, William F. Arndt, and F. Wilbur Gingrich. *Greek-English Lexicon of the New Testament and Other Early Christian Literature*. 3rd ed. Chicago: University of Chicago Press, 2000.

CC   Continental Commentaries. Minneapolis: Fortress, 1986–2004.

CD   Karl Barth. *Church Dogmatics*. Edited by Geoffrey W. Bromiley and T. F. Torrance. 14 vols. Edinburgh: T&T Clark, 1936–1969.

DDD   *Dictionary of Deities and Demons in the Bible*. Edited by Karen van der Toorn, Bob Becking, and Pieter W. van der Horst. 2nd ed. Grand Rapids: Eerdmans, 1999.

DTIB   *Dictionary for Theological Interpretation of the Bible*. Edited by Kevin J. Vanhoozer, Craig G. Bartholomew, Daniel J. Treier, and N. T. Wright. Grand Rapids: Baker Academic, 2005.

EBC   Expositor's Bible Commentary

ECNT   Zondervan Exegetical Commentary on the New Testament

EDNT   *Exegetical Dictionary of the New Testament*. Edited by H. Balz and G. Schneider. 3 vols. Grand Rapids: Eerdmans, 1990–1993.

HALOT   Ludwig Koehler, Walter Baumgartner, and Johann Jakob Stamm. *The Hebrew and Aramaic Lexicon of the Old Testament*. Translated and

	edited under the supervision of M. E. J. Richardson. 4 vols. Leiden: Brill, 1994–1999.
JPS	Jewish Publication Society
L&N	Louw, Johannes P., and Eugene A. Nida, eds. *Greek-English Lexicon of the New Testament: Based on Semantic Domains.* 2nd ed. New York: UBS, 1989.
NAC	New American Commentary. Nashville: B&H, 1991–2014.
NIB	*The New Interpreter's Bible.* Edited by Leander E. Keck. 12 vols. Nashville: Abingdon, 1994.
NICNT	New International Commentary on the New Testament. Grand Rapids: Eerdmans, 1974–2014.
NICOT	New International Commentary on the Old Testament. Grand Rapids: Eerdmans, 1976–2016.
NIDNTT	*New International Dictionary of New Testament Theology and Exegesis.* Edited by Colin Brown. 4 vols. Grand Rapids: Zondervan, 1986.
NIDNTTE	*New International Dictionary of New Testament Theology and Exegesis.* Edited by Moisés Silva. 5 vols. Grand Rapids: Zondervan, 2014.
NIDOTTE	*New International Dictionary of Old Testament Theology and Exegesis.* Edited by Willem A. VanGemeren. 5 vols. Grand Rapids: Zondervan, 1997.
NIGTC	New International Greek Testament Commentary. Grand Rapids: Eerdmans, 1978–2016.
NIVAC	NIV Application Commentary. Grand Rapids: Zondervan, 1994–2012.
PNTC	Pillar New Testament Commentary Grand Rapids: Eerdmans, 1988–2015.
WBC	Word Biblical Commentary

1

The Problem of Evil
and the Free Will Defense

"Life is outrageous. Hardly anyone will deny that conclusion outright. Tragedy, pain, injustice, premature death—all of these and more waste us away. No explanation seems quite able to still our anger, hostility, and sadness."[1] So says John K. Roth in his essay advocating for what he calls a "theodicy of protest."[2] This is not unlike what many biblical authors themselves say in protest against the evil in this world.

Job suffers so much that he wishes he were never born (Job 3). In the midst of his suffering, he questions God's justice, saying,

> The earth is given into the hand of the wicked;
> He covers the faces of its judges.
> If it is not He, then who is it? (Job 9:24; cf. 16:9, 11)

> I cry out to You for help, but You do not answer me. . . .
> You have become cruel to me;
> With the might of Your hand You persecute me. . . .
> When I expected good, then evil came;
> When I waited for light, then darkness came. (Job 30:20–21, 26)

1. Roth, "Theodicy of Protest," 18.
2. Roth explains, "A theodicy of protest believes" that strong emotions of protest against evil "are in many cases justified" and should be expressed as challenges to God's goodness. Roth, "Theodicy of Protest," 18.

Isaiah adds,

> Justice is far from us,
> And righteousness does not overtake us;
> We hope for light, but behold, darkness,
> For brightness, but we walk in gloom. . . .
> We hope for justice, but there is none. (Isa. 59:9, 11; cf. Hab. 1:4)

The author of Ecclesiastes similarly decries injustice in this world, declaring, "I have seen under the sun that in the place of justice there is wickedness" (Eccles. 3:16; cf. 7:15; 8:14). Elsewhere, he repeatedly describes the "grievous evil" that he has seen (5:13, 16; cf. 6:1; 10:5) and declares it would be "better" to have never existed and thus "never seen the evil activity that is done under the sun" (4:3). This world includes "abominable injustice" and corruption; "there is no one who does good, not even one" (Ps. 53:1, 3).

The state of this world raises major questions about God's justice and hiddenness in the face of evil and suffering. "Why has the way of the wicked prospered? / Why are all those who deal in treachery at ease?" (Jer. 12:1; cf. Pss. 10:5, 13; 94:3–7; Mal. 2:17). "Why has the LORD our God done all these things to us?" (Jer. 5:19). "Why have these things happened to me?" (Jer. 13:22; cf. 16:10; Ezek. 18:2). "Why is the land ruined, laid waste like a desert, so that no one passes through?" (Jer. 9:12). "'Where is the God of justice?'" (Mal. 2:17; cf. Ps. 94:3–7). "Why are You silent when the wicked swallow up / Those more righteous than they?" (Hab. 1:13; cf. Job 12:6; 21:7, 9). "Why do You stand afar off, O LORD? / Why do You hide Yourself in times of trouble?" (Ps. 10:1; cf. 10:11; 30:7). Even Jesus himself cries out, "My God, My God, why have You forsaken Me?" (Matt 27:46; cf. Mark 15:34). Why has God not prevented or mitigated evil or at least brought justice in response to it? Evil seems to continue unabated, so much so that psalmists repeatedly ask, "How long, O LORD?" (Pss. 13:1; 79:5; cf. 77:7–10; 94:3). In light of the horrendous evil in this world, where are the providence, goodness, and love of God?

Scripture contains no shortage of depictions of and laments over the problem of evil (e.g., 2 Kings 6:29). However, according to some, there is a severe shortage of adequate solutions to the problem offered by Scripture and, for that matter, by the broad tradition of Christian theism. In his book *God's Problem: How the Bible Fails to Answer Our Most Important Question—Why We Suffer*, Bart Ehrman argues that Scripture provides no adequate approach to the problem of evil. Instead he argues that "the Bible contains many and varied answers to the problem of why there is suffering in the world." Yet he claims that "many of these answers are at odds with one another, and at odds with what most people seem to think today."[3] Because "life is a cesspool of misery and suffering" for so many people, Ehrman finds it impossible to "believe that there is a good and kindly disposed Ruler who is in charge" of this planet.[4] In his view, if there is a God, "he certainly isn't the one proclaimed by the Judeo-Christian tradition, the one who is actively and powerfully involved in the world."[5]

Much has been written toward resolving issues like these and the numerous other enormous problems that evil in this world presents for Christian theism, minimally defined as the view that the triune God is "an omnipotent and perfectly good being."[6] In recent times, the task of addressing the problem of evil has been undertaken primarily by philosophers, with varying degrees of success.[7] Much less has been written that addresses the problem of evil as it is depicted and approached in Scripture.[8] Given the claims of Ehrman and others, however, it seems apparent that more work needs to be done to bridge the realms of philosophy and biblical theology in this regard, with the goal of ascertaining and exploring some avenues for approaching the problem of evil that might be both intellectually satisfying and consistent with Christian theism and its sacred canon of Scripture.[9]

This book aims to set forth and explore one promising avenue in this regard, articulating a constructive proposal for a theodicy of love that is based on a close canonical reading of Scripture.[10] This biblically based, philosophically informed, and theologically systematic treatment builds on and goes beyond

3. Ehrman, *God's Problem*, 15.
4. Ehrman, *God's Problem*, 3. Ehrman writes, "The problem of suffering . . . was the reason I lost my faith" (1).
5. Ehrman, *God's Problem*, 4. He adds, "I can't believe in that God anymore because from what I now see around the world, he doesn't intervene" (16).
6. S. Davis, "Introduction," ix.
7. For one helpful introduction to the philosophical discussion, see Peterson, ed., *Problem of Evil*.
8. Some recent treatments relative to the biblical material include Crenshaw, *Defending God*; Crenshaw, *Theodicy in the Old Testament*; Laato and Moor, *Theodicy in the World of the Bible*. See also the accessible, introductory treatment by Gregg, *What Does the Bible Say about Suffering?* A couple of other notable works that have broken significant ground by approaching biblical material from a philosophical perspective are Bergmann, Murray, and Rea, *Divine Evil?*; and Stump, *Wandering in the Darkness*.
9. Even those who doubt whether any approach could be successful in meeting both of these objectives may find the attempt to set forth such an approach stimulating as a case study.
10. Recognizing that there are many complex avenues within Scripture, this book offers an exploration of one significant stream of Scripture, which does not attempt to resolve all of the issues involved in the problem of evil but aims to complement further study. The canonical approach I employed in researching Scripture for this book involved investigating all of Scripture, approached as the divinely commissioned corpus of writings that God has ordained as the rule or standard of theology. On this approach, see Peckham, *Canonical Theology*.

the basic free will defense, articulating a theodicy that is rooted in the nature of God's love within the framework of a cosmic conflict. This theodicy of love affirms a robust account of God's omnipotence, providence, and involvement in this world that is consonant with Christian theism as described above, while denying that evil is necessary for some greater good or goods. In brief, I argue that God's love (properly understood) is at the center of a cosmic dispute and that God's commitment to love provides a morally sufficient reason for God's allowance of evil, with significant ramifications for understanding divine providence as operating within what I call covenantal rules of engagement.[11]

This theodicy of love is set forth, piece by piece, in the following chapters. This first chapter begins by introducing the problem of evil relative to Christian theism, the basic parameters of the free will defense, and some significant objections and perceived shortcomings of the free will defense, along with some of the more prominent proposals that advocate alternatives or additions to the free will defense. Through this introduction to the problem of evil, it will become clear that while the existing approaches offer considerable resources for addressing the problems that evil presents for Christian theism, significant issues remain, which might be illuminated by closer consideration of the nature of God's love. This introduction thus sets the stage for a constructive proposal of a theodicy of love rooted in the biblical canon and in consonance with Christian theism. This proposal affirms and goes beyond the free will defense toward positing a coherent and morally sufficient reason for God to permit horrendous evil in a broad sense, without suggesting that there are (or need be) morally sufficient reasons for specific horrendous evils in and of themselves or for the proximate impact of such evils.

The Free Will Defense and the Necessary Possibility of Evil

The Free Will Defense

If God is good, why is there *so much* evil in this world?[12] The presence of evil poses a significant problem for Christian theists, insofar as they maintain that God is entirely good (omnibenevolent), all-powerful (omnipotent), aware

---

11. For more on the understanding of divine love employed in this work, see chap. 2 and Peckham, *Love of God.*

12. As David Hume framed it, "Epicurus's old questions are yet unanswered. Is he [God] willing to prevent evil, but not able? Then he is impotent. Is he able, but not willing? Then he is malevolent. Is he both able and willing? Whence then is evil?" Hume, *Dialogues concerning Natural Religion*, 134.

of everything (omniscient), and providentially involved in some significant way in governing the course of history (sovereign). Indeed, if God is both all-good and all-powerful, then he must both desire no evil and possess the power to prevent all evil.[13] Yet there is horrendous evil all around us. Many thinkers contend that this perceived dilemma can be escaped only by concluding that God is not good or that he is not omnipotent or that he does not exist at all.

The free will defense is widely viewed as the most successful defense against the problem of evil to date. Put simply, it claims that God granted creatures a kind of free will that is incompatible with determinism, and it is thus impossible to *determine* that all beings *freely* do what God desires. Tragically, some creatures exercise their free will to do that which God does not desire (i.e., evil), and although God possesses the sheer power to determine all events, doing so would negate the free will that God has granted according to his benevolent purpose. Evil, then, is the result of creaturely misuse of free will.

The appeal to free will in order to address the problem of evil has a long history in Christian theology. As Paul Gavrilyuk explains, "Relatively early among patristic theologians, a broad agreement emerged that the free will of some rational creatures accounted for the actualization of evil. The Creator could not be held responsible for the free evil choices that rational creatures made, since God did not causally determine these choices."[14] Rather, the "misuse of angelic and human free will is the cause of evil."[15] The free will argument is thus in keeping with a significant stream of Christian tradition and is often associated most prominently with Augustine, particularly as put forth in his early work *On Free Choice of the Will*.[16]

In recent decades the free will defense has been set forth in highly influential and rigorous philosophical accounts, most notably by Alvin Plantinga.[17] In the view of many philosophers, including many atheists, Plantinga's free will defense has successfully resolved the *logical* problem of evil. In the words of

13. On divine omnibenevolence, see Deut. 32:4; 1 Sam. 3:18; Ps. 145:9–17; Hab. 1:13; Rev. 15:3. On divine omnipotence, see Rev. 19:6; cf. Jer. 32:17; Matt. 19:26.

14. Gavrilyuk, "Overview of Patristic Theodicies," 4.

15. Gavrilyuk, "Overview of Patristic Theodicies," 6.

16. Some scholars believe Augustine came to embrace determinism after he wrote this work, but others dispute this. Regarding the wide disagreements about Augustine's view of free will, see Stump, "Augustine on Free Will," 124–47.

17. See Plantinga, *Nature of Necessity*; Plantinga, *God, Freedom, and Evil*. Plantinga describes his defense as aiming only at what "God's reason [for evil] might possibly be," in contrast to a theodicy, which "attempts to tell us why God permits evil." Plantinga, *God, Freedom, and Evil*, 28. My theodicy of love, however, uses the term "theodicy" in a weaker sense, akin to that of Stephen T. Davis, who defines it as "any response to the problem of evil from the perspective of Judeo-Christian religious belief, broadly construed." Davis, "Introduction," xi.

William Rowe, a leading atheist philosopher, "The logical problem of evil has been severely diminished, if not entirely resolved," as a "result of Plantinga's work."[18]

The logical problem of evil, as famously set forth by J. L. Mackie, contends that the premise "evil exists" is logically incompatible with the premises that "God is omnipotent [and] wholly good."[19] Plantinga's free will defense, conversely, aims to demonstrate that the presence of evil in the world is not logically incompatible with the existence of an omnipotent and omnibenevolent God.[20] To do so, Plantinga makes use of possible-world semantics, wherein "a possible world is any possible state of affairs that is complete" or "maximal."[21] In other words, a possible world is a comprehensive conception of the way *all* things might be, where "all things" includes the entire history of that possible world. Using this concept, Plantinga summarizes his free will defense as follows:

> A world containing creatures who are significantly free (and freely perform more good than evil actions) is more valuable, all else being equal, than a world containing no free creatures at all. Now God can create free creatures, but He can't cause or determine them to do only what is right. For if He does so, then they aren't significantly free after all; they do not do what is right freely. To create creatures capable of moral good, therefore, He must create creatures capable of moral evil; and He can't give these creatures the freedom to perform evil and at the same time prevent them from doing so. As it turned out, sadly enough, some of the free creatures God created went wrong in the exercise of their freedom; this is the source of moral evil. The fact that free creatures sometimes go wrong, however, counts neither against God's omnipotence nor against His goodness; for He could have forestalled the occurrence of moral evil only by removing the possibility of moral good.[22]

Mackie, conversely, argues that an omnipotent God should be able to create a world in which every creature always and only *freely* does what is good. If God cannot do this, Mackie contends, God is not omnipotent, and if he can but chooses not to do so, God is not entirely good. Mackie's argument hinges on the premises that "a good thing always eliminates evil

---

18. Rowe, "Introduction to Part II," 76. So also, Hasker, *Triumph of God over Evil*, 42. However, J. L. Schellenberg departs from this near-consensus in Schellenberg, "A New Logical Problem of Evil," 34.

19. See J. L. Mackie, "Evil and Omnipotence," in Adams and Adams, *Problem of Evil*, 25–37.

20. I offer only a brief summary of Plantinga's argument here. For his fuller argumentation, see Plantinga, *Nature of Necessity*.

21. Plantinga, *God, Freedom, and Evil*, 36.

22. Plantinga, *God, Freedom, and Evil*, 30.

as far as it can" and that "there are no limits to what an omnipotent thing can do." As such, "it follows that a good omnipotent thing eliminates evil completely."[23]

Plantinga argues, in contrast, that it might be the case that an omnipotent being has a good reason or reasons for not eliminating every evil that he can. Perhaps God cannot actualize the great value of morally significant creaturely free will without also allowing evil.[24] Plantinga argues that it is nonsensical to *determine* beings to *freely* do something, so creatures may choose to do evil, even if God does not want them to do so. As Richard Swinburne explains, "A God who gives humans such free will necessarily brings about the possibility [of evil], and puts outside his own control whether or not that evil occurs. It is not logically possible," then, "that God could give us such free will and yet ensure that we always use it in the right way."[25]

Yet could not God simply create only those creatures that always freely choose good? Plantinga admits that a world in which everyone always and only freely does what is good without being causally determined is theoretically possible. However, he adds, it may not be within God's power to actualize such a world. Rather, it *might* be the case that any world that God could actualize containing significantly free creatures would include evil done by those creatures.[26] If so, this could explain why a God who foreknows the future exhaustively might create *this* world anyway. Perhaps all the alternatives were less desirable in this or some other way.[27] Although Plantinga believes (as do I) that God does possess (exhaustive definite) foreknowledge, his basic free will defense does not hinge on this premise.[28] I will thus set aside (for discussion in later chapters) further questions regarding whether God could have used foreknowledge to actualize only those creatures who always freely do good.

23. Mackie, "Evil and Omnipotence," in Adams and Adams, *Problem of Evil*, 26.
24. See Plantinga, *God, Freedom, and Evil*, 29. See further the discussion of Plantinga's distinction between strong and weak actualization in chap. 2 of the present work.
25. Swinburne, *Is There a God?*, 86.
26. Perhaps "every creaturely essence suffers from transworld depravity," which means "it was not within God's power to actualize any world in which that person is significantly free but does no wrong." Plantinga, *Nature of Necessity*, 189, 186. If so, "it was beyond the power of God himself to create a world containing moral good but no moral evil" (189).
27. Even if God could "actualize a world including moral good but no moral evil," perhaps such a world would include far less "moral good" than this world or would include only a few persons. Plantinga, *Nature of Necessity*, 190.
28. One prominent form of Plantinga's argument presupposes the controversial view that God possesses knowledge of what any creature *would* do in any circumstance (middle knowledge). However, Plantinga has set forth another version of this argument that does not require middle knowledge. See Plantinga, "Self-Profile," 50–52.

Free Will and Omnipotence

Apart from issues regarding foreknowledge, Plantinga's basic line of argument relies on two crucial premises: (1) his libertarian conception of free will, which holds that free will is incompatible with determinism (incompatibilism) and (2) the understanding that, though God is omnipotent, even he cannot bring about just any state of affairs.[29] Both of these crucial points merit further attention.

For Plantinga, "A person is significantly free, on a given occasion, if he is then free with respect to a morally significant action."[30] What is crucial here is *"being free with respect to an action.* If a person is free with respect to a given action, then he is free to perform that action and free to refrain from performing it; no antecedent conditions and/or causal laws determine that he will perform the action, or that he won't."[31] As Rowe explains, "Once given," this kind of free will "is beyond God's direct control."[32] On this view, some of what occurs or does not occur is not up to God alone but genuinely up to the decisions of free creatures.[33] As Richard Swinburne explains, if one has this kind of "free choice between good and evil, that makes him an ultimate source of how things go in the world in a very significant way."[34]

Given such libertarian free will, it follows that there are some states of affairs that God, although omnipotent, cannot actualize. This is not because God lacks any power but because, insofar as God grants creatures libertarian free will, some states of affairs are contingent on the free decisions of creatures. In this regard, philosophers have long understood omnipotence in a way that undermines Mackie's supposition that "there are no limits to what an omnipotent thing can do."[35] On the contrary, Swinburne argues that the assertion "God is omnipotent, that is, literally can do anything" requires the "obvious qualification that to be omnipotent a person need not be able to do the logically impossible."[36]

29. Here Plantinga presents only a defense; he "believe[s] that we do" have libertarian freedom but allows that we might not. Plantinga, "Ad Walls," 337. Jerry Walls argues, however, that Plantinga's argument should commit him to a "free will theodicy." Walls, "Why Plantinga Must Move from Defense to Theodicy," 331–34.

30. Plantinga, *God, Freedom, and Evil*, 30. Here, an action is morally significant if "it would be wrong for [one] to perform the action but right to refrain or vice versa" (30).

31. Plantinga, *God, Freedom, and Evil*, 29 (emphasis original).

32. Rowe, "Introduction to Part II," 76.

33. As Chad Meister writes, "Free choices are truly up to the individual" such that this "type" of freedom "is incompatible with causal determinism." Meister, *Evil*, 18.

34. Swinburne, "Some Major Strands of Theodicy," 250.

35. Mackie, "Evil and Omnipotence," in Adams and Adams, *Problem of Evil*, 26.

36. Swinburne, *Coherence of Theism*, 153. See further chap. 5 in the present volume.

C. S. Lewis explains,

> [God's] omnipotence means power to do all that is intrinsically possible, not
> to do the intrinsically impossible. You may attribute miracles to him, but not
> nonsense. This is no limit to his power. If you choose to say "God can give a
> creature free will and at the same time withhold free will from it," you have not
> succeeded in saying *anything* about God: meaningless combinations of words
> do not suddenly acquire meaning simply because we prefix to them the two
> other words "God can." . . . It is no more possible for God than for the weakest
> of his creatures to carry out both of two mutually exclusive alternatives; not
> because his power meets an obstacle, but because nonsense remains nonsense
> even when we talk it about God.[37]

Omnipotence, then, entails only the "power to do what is logically possible."[38] Yet as Richard Rice argues, insofar as God grants creatures libertarian
free will, the exercise of his power would thereby be self-limited to "anything
logically possible *that does not require creaturely cooperation.*"[39] Insofar as
some good is contingent on the significantly free choices of creatures, it may
not be possible for God to bring it about. In other words, if God is committed to respecting the free will of humans, what God can bring about will
be limited by the free decisions of humans. As Plantinga puts it, "There are
plenty of contingent states of affairs such that it is not within the power of
God to bring about their actuality, or cause them to be actual. He cannot
cause it to be the case that I freely refrain from an action A; for if he does
so, he causes it to be the case that I refrain from A, in which case I do not
do so *freely*."[40]

Plantinga states the matter simply: if God grants free will to Maurice "with
respect to [a particular] action, then whether or not he actually performs the
action is up to Maurice—not God."[41] For this reason, Plantinga's free will
defense does not claim that this world is the best *possible* world. First, the
notion of a *best* possible world might not even be coherent. "Perhaps for any
world you pick, there is a better" one.[42] Second, even if the notion of a best
possible world is coherent, "better worlds than this world certainly seem

37. Lewis, *Problem of Pain*, 18.
38. Swinburne, *Coherence of Theism*, 180.
39. Rice, *Suffering and the Search for Meaning*, 52 (emphasis original).
40. Plantinga, *Nature of Necessity*, 171 (emphasis original).
41. Plantinga, *God, Freedom, and Evil*, 44.
42. Plantinga, *Nature of Necessity*, 168. Perhaps an additional value might be added to
any conceivable world.

conceivable."[43] However, if it is not up to God whether Maurice takes a particular action, then if Maurice chooses to take action x, it is not up to God
to create the possible world wherein Maurice chooses not to take action x,
even if that world is better. As such, if God does not determine the free will
decisions of creatures, only some possible worlds are able to be actualized by
God. Here, "central to the Free Will Defense is the claim that God, though
omnipotent, could not have actualized just any possible world He pleased."[44]
Rather, "the creation of a world containing moral good is a co-operative
venture" involving the significantly free decisions of creatures.[45] If God "aims
to produce moral good, then he must create significantly free creatures on
whose cooperation he must depend. Thus is the power of an omnipotent God
limited by the freedom he confers upon his creatures."[46]

This understanding brings us back to "the heart of the Free Will Defense,"
which for Plantinga "is the claim that it is possible that God could not have
created a universe containing moral good (or as much moral good as this
world contains) without creating one that also contained moral evil. And if so,
then it is possible that God has a good reason for creating a world containing
evil."[47] On this view (contra Mackie), there are "limits on what an omnipotent thing can do," and it is not necessarily true that, as Mackie insists, "a
good thing always eliminates evil as far as it can" or "that a good omnipotent
thing eliminates evil completely."[48] Rather, because of the free will decisions
of creatures, there may be some value or values that God cannot bring about
without allowing evil. Given creaturely free will, Davis writes, "the amount of
good and evil that exists in the world is partially up to us and not entirely up to
God."[49] Indeed, in Plantinga's view all "evil arises from creaturely free will."[50]

The Necessary Possibility of Evil for Genuine Love

If evil is the result of the misuse of creaturely free will, then, as Stephen
Davis argues, "God is not to be blamed for the existence of moral evil. We
are."[51] However, many question whether the value of free will is worth all the

---

43. S. Davis, "Free Will and Evil," 75.
44. Plantinga, *God, Freedom, and Evil*, 34. This is in contrast to what he calls "Leibniz's
Lapse," which claims God could do so (44).
45. Plantinga, *Nature of Necessity*, 190.
46. Plantinga, *Nature of Necessity*, 190.
47. Plantinga, *God, Freedom, and Evil*, 31.
48. Mackie, "Evil and Omnipotence," in Adams and Adams, *Problem of Evil*, 26.
49. S. Davis, "Free Will and Evil," 75–76.
50. Plantinga, "Supralapsarianism or 'O Felix Culpa,'" 4.
51. S. Davis, "Free Will and Evil," 75.

evil in this world. Perhaps, some suggest, God should not have granted free will, particularly if the result is all the horrendous evil in this world.

In my view, the free will defense is strongest when the value that is offered as the morally sufficient reason for God's allowance of evil is not moral freedom alone but love, which I take to be a greater good, perhaps even the greatest good in the universe. Indeed, if "God is love" (1 John 4:8, 16), what value could be greater? Thus I agree with Davis and many others that love was a "main aim" of God in granting free will: "God wanted to create a world in which created rational agents (e.g., human beings) would decide freely to love and obey God."[52] As such, love itself might be God's "overriding reason for allowing the amount of moral evil that exists in the world."[53]

If love requires freedom and if the rejection of God's love is itself evil, then love requires the *possibility* of evil.[54] Davis explains, "Obviously, in making human beings free, God ran the risk that they would go wrong. The possibility of freely doing evil is the inevitable companion of the possibility of freely doing good."[55] Rice further argues that love "requires freedom." He explains, "God's creatures would not be free to say yes to God unless they were free to say no. Sadly, this is just what some of them did."[56] Put another way, love (as defined in this work) must be freely given and freely received. For creatures, this entails the ability to reject God's love and thus directly or indirectly oppose God's desire for love. If opposition to God's desire is evil (as shall be argued in chap. 2), then love itself requires the *possibility* of evil.

The understanding that love requires the *possibility* of evil relates to a number of further issues while also raising additional important questions for exploration throughout this book. First, understanding the possibility of evil as a necessary condition of genuine love provides a potential response to those who suggest that God should not have provided free will to creatures. As noted above, many wonder why free will would be valued so highly as to be viewed as a morally sufficient reason for the permission of evil (particularly horrendous evils). This theodicy of love posits, however, that free will is a functional good, a means to the greater end of love—where love is perhaps the highest intrinsic good. As Lewis puts it, "Free will is what made evil possible. Why, then, did God give [creatures] free will? Because free will, though it makes evil possible, is also the only thing that makes possible any love or goodness or joy worth having. A world of automata—of creatures that

---

52. S. Davis, "Free Will and Evil," 74.
53. S. Davis, "Free Will and Evil," 77.
54. See chap. 2 in the present volume.
55. S. Davis, "Free Will and Evil," 75.
56. Rice, *Suffering and the Search for Meaning*, 47.

worked like machines—would hardly be worth creating. The happiness which God designs for His higher creatures is the happiness of being freely, voluntarily united to Him and to each other. . . . And for that they must be free."[57]

Second, this understanding challenges the view that (actualized) evil is itself necessary for some greater good. Whereas the free will defense is compatible with such a claim, the theodicy of love set forth in this book contends that God never desires or needs evil. Rather, God desires that creatures such as humans enjoy a love relationship with himself and others, which requires the *possibility* but not the *necessity* of evil. Although it is possible that everyone freely chooses to love God, it is also possible that some do not do so. As such, evil is not *necessary* for love, but the necessary context for love requires the *possibility* of evil. As Davis says, "It was not necessary that evil exist. The nonexistence of evil was possible; humans could have chosen to obey God. Sadly, they didn't."[58] Rice adds, "God is responsible for the *possibility* of evil, but not for the *actuality* of evil. The creatures who misused their freedom are entirely to blame for that."[59] If so, the great good of the flourishing of love in this world (particularly in the eschaton) might not have been obtainable by God in any preferable way. This is not because evil is itself necessary but because, in the free will defense, what is obtainable by God is limited by the free decisions of others.

Many additional questions remain, including the much-disputed question regarding whether humans possess such libertarian free will. Mackie, for instance, preemptively argues that appeals to free will as a "solution" are "unsatisfactory primarily because of the incoherence of the notion of the freedom of the will."[60] Further, even if one grants that humans possess such free will, does the extent of free will required by love really provide a sufficient explanation for the evil in this world? It could be argued that there are many evils in this world that God could have mitigated or eliminated without damaging or jeopardizing love.

Objections to the Free Will Defense and a Way Forward

In my view, the free will defense is successful relative to the logical problem of evil, and I will make a case in the following chapter that the biblical data strongly support the minimal parameters of the free will defense, contra

---

57. Lewis, *Mere Christianity*, 48.
58. S. Davis, "Free Will and Evil," 75.
59. Rice, *Suffering and the Search for Meaning*, 47.
60. Mackie, "Evil and Omnipotence," in Adams and Adams, *Problem of Evil*, 33.

Ehrman's claim that free will "plays only a very minor role in the biblical tradition" in accounting for "suffering."[61] In this regard, I agree with Davis that the free will defense "is a theodicy that grows out of the witness of the Christian scriptures."[62] However, many Christian theologians question whether Scripture teaches that humans possess the kind of free will posited in the free will defense in the first place. Alternatively, some theologians claim that God has determined everything that happens in this world in order to achieve some purportedly greater good, such as the manifestation of his power and glory. Before making the case for why I think a libertarian free will approach is preferable to determinism, a number of other objections to the free will defense should be noted, setting the stage for the discussion in the remaining chapters of how a theodicy of love goes beyond the basic free will defense and thus might helpfully address such objections.

The Evidential Problem of Evil

Although most philosophers now view the free will defense as successful relative to the *logical* problem of evil, many philosophers think it improbable that an omnipotent and omnibenevolent God would permit the kind and amount of evil, particularly *horrendous* evil, in this world.[63] They believe the free will defense is insufficient relative to the evidential problem of evil, which claims that the kind and amount of evil in this world counts as evidence against the existence of an all-powerful and entirely good God.[64] In response, some philosophers have made a case for what they call skeptical theism, which doubts the present ability of humans to make sufficiently knowledgeable judgments about why God has acted or refrained from acting as he has. However, others believe that skeptical theism is not adequate to rebut these charges and that more is needed, particularly in light of the positive claims of the Christian faith.[65]

Further, some critics have contended that the free will defense is not able to account for "natural evils" in this world at all, horrendous or otherwise. As William Rowe puts it, "While this theodicy may explain some of the evil in our world, it cannot account for the massive amount of human suffering

61. Ehrman, *God's Problem*, 12.
62. S. Davis, "Free Will and Evil," 89.
63. See M. Adams, *Horrendous Evils and the Goodness of God*.
64. For an introduction to the evidential problem of evil, see Rowe, *God and the Problem of Evil*, 121–233.
65. A great deal has been written recently regarding this approach. See, e.g., the large section in McBrayer and Howard-Snyder, *Blackwell Companion to the Problem of Evil*, 377–506. See further Dougherty and McBrayer, *Skeptical Theism*.

that is not due to human acts of free will. Natural disasters (floods, earthquakes, hurricanes, etc.) bring about enormous amounts of human and animal suffering. But it is obvious that such suffering is not proportionate to the abuses of free will by humans."[66] In response to such objections, Plantinga has suggested the possibility (without claiming it is true) that what we call "natural evils" are actually caused by the free will decisions of "non-human persons," including much evil caused by "Satan and his cohorts."[67] Defining "natural evil" as evil "that cannot be ascribed to the free actions of human beings," Plantinga suggests that "both moral and natural evil" might be "cases of what we might call broadly moral evil—evil resulting from the free actions of personal beings, whether human or not."[68] If this is possible, then the free will defense is also successful relative to the (logical) problem of natural evil.

Some have critiqued this appeal to supernatural agencies as not dealing with "natural evils" at all but rather as claiming that there are no such things. Further, Michael Tooley maintains that "though it is possible that earthquakes, hurricanes, cancer, and the predation of animals are all caused by malevolent supernatural beings, the probability that this is so is extremely low."[69] Plantinga himself recognizes that "many people find this idea [of supernatural agencies] preposterous; but that is scarcely evidence against it. Some theologians tell us that this idea is repugnant to 'man come of age' or to 'modern habits of thought.' Again, this may be so (although it certainly isn't repugnant to everyone nowadays), but it doesn't come to much as evidence."[70] For his part, he considers it

> less than clear that Western academia has much to say by way of evidence against the idea. That beings of these sorts should be involved in the history of our world seems to me (as to, e.g., C. S. Lewis and many others) not at all unlikely, in particular not unlikely with respect to Christian theism. The thought that much evil is due to Satan and his cohorts is of course entirely consistent with God's being omnipotent, omniscient, and perfectly good; furthermore it isn't nearly as improbable with respect to "what we now know" as most philosophers seem to assume.[71]

66. Howard-Snyder, Bergmann, and Rowe, "Exchange on the Problem of Evil," 136.
67. Plantinga, *Nature of Necessity*, 192. See chap. 4 in the present volume.
68. Plantinga, *Nature of Necessity*, 191, 193. S. Davis similarly believes that "the devil exists and is possibly responsible for natural evil." S. Davis, "Rejoinder," 214n12. However, he thinks other responses are stronger apologetically (104).
69. Tooley, "Problem of Evil."
70. Plantinga, *God, Freedom, and Evil*, 62.
71. Plantinga, "Supralapsarianism or 'O Felix Culpa,'" 16. Cf. Lewis, *Problem of Pain*.

In this and other regards, much hinges on the plausibility of appeals to demonic activity within Christian theism. This issue will be taken up further in chapter 3 in light of the claims of Scripture and the Christian tradition.

Even if one accepts Plantinga's defense relative to so-called natural evils, one could argue that the horrendous magnitude of some of these—coupled with the enormity of moral evils in human history (e.g., the Holocaust)—counts as strong evidence that God is not good, not all-powerful, or does not exist at all. According to Plantinga, the "typical atheological claim at present is not that the existence of God is incompatible with that of evil; it is rather that the latter offers the resources for a strong evidential or probabilistic argument against the former."[72] For example, Paul Draper advocates a form of the evidential problem of evil, contending that "our knowledge about pain and pleasure creates an epistemic problem for theists." Because of the horrendous evils in this world, he maintains, "we have a *prima facie* good epistemic reason to reject theism."[73] He believes the weight of the evidence suggests that, even if supernatural beings exist, they are indifferent to human pain and suffering. He calls this the "hypothesis of indifference" and believes it provides a better explanation than theism for the kind and amount of suffering in this world. On this view, "neither the nature nor the condition of sentient beings on earth is the result of benevolent or malevolent actions performed by nonhuman persons."[74]

Whereas free will *might* provide a logical defense for *some* evil in a world created and governed by an all-good (omnibenevolent) and all-powerful God, advocates of the evidential problem of evil contend that it does not adequately account for the amount of horrendous evil that we find in *this* world. They believe that free will by itself does not provide a morally sufficient reason for the kind and amount of evil in this world. In this regard, Davis notes that although the "free will defender" attributes "all morally evil events" to "created free moral agents who chose to do evil," the "question can still be raised whether the moral freedom that the FWD [free will defense] says God gave us was worth the cost."[75] Chad Meister asks further, "Would not a world without free will be better than a world with free will if evil of this magnitude is its result?"[76]

72. Plantinga, *Warranted Christian Belief*, 462.
73. Draper, "Pain and Pleasure," 180.
74. Draper, "Pain and Pleasure," 181. See the further discussion in chap. 6.
75. S. Davis, "Free Will and Evil," 82. D. Z. Phillips, for his part, rejects the free will defense because he thinks it amounts to an "instrumentalism" that "makes creation look like an egocentric exercise." Phillips, "Critique of the Free Will Defense," 90.
76. Meister, *Evil*, 33.

Alternatives and Challenges to the Basic Free Will Defense

Based on the evidential problem of evil and other considerations, John K. Roth sets forth a theodicy of protest, or anti-theodicy, contending that whereas "human freedom has been used as God's defense; in fact, it is crucial in God's offense."[77] In his view, humans "have more power and more freedom than is good for us" such that "history is largely a slaughter-bench."[78] In this regard, William Rowe argues,

> While being free to do evil may be essential to genuine freedom, no responsible person thinks that the good of human freedom is so great as to require that no steps be taken to prevent some of the more flagrant abuses of free choice that result in massive, undeserved suffering by humans and animals. Any moral person who had power to do so would have intervened to prevent the evil free choices that resulted in the torture and death of six million Jews in the Holocaust. We commonly act to restrict egregious abuses of human freedom that result in massive, undeserved human and animal suffering. Any moral being, including God, if he exists, would likely do the same. And since the free will theodicy is representative of the other attempts to justify God's permission of the horrendous evils in our world, it is reasonably clear that these evils cannot be explained away by appeal to theodicies.[79]

Davis offers a series of difficult questions that can be asked in this vein: "Why didn't God create a world of less freedom and thus less murder? Why didn't God place us in an environment that provides fewer opportunities or temptations to do wrong? Why didn't God provide us with a morally stronger psychological endowment? Why didn't God create us with an inability to kill other human beings?"[80] Further, if God possesses foreknowledge, why did he not "opt to create only those" who would be "morally perfect"—or at least only those who would not be "heinous moral monsters"?[81]

One way to reply to these questions is to suggest that all of these evils actually bring about specific greater goods that could not be achieved without them.[82] However, many evil events appear to be what philosophers call gratuitous evils, which Davis defines as "any painful event that makes the world

77. Roth, "Theodicy of Protest," 8.
78. Roth, "Theodicy of Protest," 10, 7.
79. Howard-Snyder, Bergmann, and Rowe, "Exchange on the Problem of Evil," 136.
80. S. Davis, "Free Will and Evil," 82.
81. S. Davis, "Free Will and Evil," 85. This foreknowledge objection is discussed in chap. 6 in the present volume.
82. E.g., Swinburne's higher-order goods defense, discussed below.

worse, all things considered, because it occurs."[83] Meister voices the worry of many when he notes that, whereas the free will defense "may account for some of the moral and natural evils that exist, it does not seem to provide an answer for why there is so much evil, and why there is so much evil which seems utterly horrific and gratuitous."[84]

The problem of gratuitous evils, particularly horrendous ones, is closely related to beliefs about the extent of God's power. As a free will defender, Davis argues that "God has the power totally to control all events and things but does not use it" to do so.[85] Although "God is fully sovereign and omnipotent, [he] voluntarily shares some of the divine power with the creatures."[86] Davis believes that

> God's policy decision to make us free was wise, for it will turn out better in the long run that we act freely, even if we sometimes err, than it would have turned out had we been created as innocent automata, programmed always to do the good. . . . The good that will in the end result from it will outweigh the evil that will in the end result from it. In the eschaton it will be evident that God chose the best course and that the favorable balance of good over evil that will then exist was obtainable by God in no other way or in no morally preferable way.[87]

In his view, even though God temporarily allows horrendous evil in this world, ultimately "God will redeem all evil."[88]

Yet even if the result "outweighs" the evil, it seems that God could have brought forth at least as much good with less evil, which would contradict Davis's view. Does free will alone sufficiently account for God's allowance of all the horrendous evils in this world? Could not some evils have been mitigated without diminishing free will? Even if not, should not one who possesses the power to prevent horrendous evil do so, even if it contravenes free will? What about Christian eschatology? If creaturely free will leads to such horrendous evil now, would it not continue to do so in the eschaton?

Some open theists—who hold that God does not possess exhaustive definite foreknowledge—have argued along the lines of a free will defense similar to Davis's but have added that God may not be culpable for the horrendous evil in this world because, in their view, God did not know with certainty that

83. S. Davis, "Free Will and Evil," 84.
84. Meister, *Evil*, 33.
85. S. Davis, "Critique of Process Theodicy," 136.
86. S. Davis, "Critique of Process Theodicy," 136.
87. S. Davis, "Free Will and Evil," 75.
88. S. Davis, "Free Will and Evil," 83.

such evils would result from his creation of this world.[89] Perhaps God created this world in hope that it would turn out far better than it has but committed to doing all that he can to maximize goodness and love without undermining the free will that is requisite to genuine love.[90] One wonders, however, whether open theism's suggestion that God might not be culpable for that which he does not foreknow actually helps to assuage the difficulty of the problems of evil. Presumably, an omnipotent God with present knowledge of evil could stop any and every evil just before it would occur.[91]

The open theist might reply that, in committing to the context necessary for creatures to enjoy a love relationship with God and one another, God has (morally) limited his own action relative to the mitigation or elimination of evil. As John Sanders puts it, God "does not limit his power or abilities, but does restrain the exercise of his power or the scope of his activities," and this "divine self-restraint" is "the restraint of love in concern for his creatures."[92] Greg Boyd sets forth a trinitarian warfare theodicy of cosmic conflict, wherein the free will and irrevocable power of some supernatural agencies opposed to God help explain why God does not mitigate or eliminate more evils than he does.[93] Both the conception of divine self-limitation and that of cosmic conflict provide helpful avenues for addressing the problem(s) of evil, which shall be further explored in the coming chapters. However, neither of these avenues (nor the emphasis on love) requires commitment to open theism. In particular, they do not require or benefit from the rejection of (exhaustive definite) divine foreknowledge, which stands in significant tension with the majority view of Christian theism and some significant biblical material suggestive of God's exhaustive and sovereign plan for human history. Further, open theism struggles to adequately account for confidence in the final eschatological defeat of evil.

The open theist accounts discussed above and other forms of the free will defense face the considerable challenge of making sense of the view that God could prevent heinous evils but chooses not to do so. In this regard, many

89. As Rice explains it, "open theodicy" maintains that since future "free decisions" are "not there to be known," God not only is "not responsible for these decisions" but also "cannot be blamed for not knowing them, not preventing them or not warning us about them." Rice, *Suffering and the Search for Meaning*, 104.

90. Rice writes, "Suppose the likelihood of rebellion was slight and the results were potentially catastrophic. What then? On this scenario, God did everything possible to minimize the chance that anyone would rebel." Rice, *Suffering and the Search for Meaning*, 102.

91. Unlike many process theologians (see below), most open theists maintain that God is omnipotent.

92. Sanders, *God Who Risks*, 241.

93. See Boyd, *God at War*; Boyd, *Satan and the Problem of Evil*.

thinkers maintain that a God who fails to prevent horrendous evils that he could prevent would not be good at all. If God has limited himself, some maintain, he should "un-limit" himself when faced with such evils.

David Ray Griffin, a prominent proponent of an approach called process theodicy, believes that an omnipotent God *should* prevent evil by intervening whenever necessary to do so and could do so in such a way that nothing would be lost by any creatures. Given omnipotence of the kind defined as the power to do anything that is intrinsically possible, Griffin argues, "God could intervene to prevent any specific instance of evil" without any loss to creatures by determining all events while making individuals think that they possess significant free will.[94] In other words, "God could have created beings identical with ourselves, except that they would not really have been free to sin." Such creatures "could even have believed that they were really acting freely while always doing good. Only God would know otherwise."[95] Since only God would gain from creaturely "genuine freedom . . . granting this freedom, from which most of the world's ills result, would thereby seem to be a very selfish decision."[96] Griffin concludes that since such an omnipotent God would be morally wrong not to prevent or eliminate evil, God must not be omnipotent in the traditional sense.[97] He thus advocates a form of finitism, which avoids the problem of evil by claiming that God is not culpable for the evil in this world because God lacks the power to prevent it.[98]

Thomas Jay Oord sets forth a similar perspective, arguing that God lacks the power to prevent evil because he is love, which Oord defines as utterly uncontrolling. In Oord's view, any "God" who possess the power to override free will to prevent some horrendous evil would be morally obligated to do so. As he puts it, a "God who can veto any specific act should veto acts of

94. Griffin, "Creation out of Nothing," 117.

95. Griffin, "Creation out of Nothing," 118. This would require deception by God. Griffin himself admits that "any kind of deception would be morally problematic." Griffin, "Critique of Irenaean Theodicy," 54.

96. Griffin, "Creation out of Nothing," 118.

97. Griffin believes most "problems of Christian theology" stem from "the traditional doctrine of divine omnipotence." He believes "we must fully surrender this doctrine if we" are to hold that God is "unambiguously loving." Griffin, "Critique of the Free Will Defense," 96. This echoes seminal process theologian Charles Hartshorne's view that the problem of evil is a "false problem" that arises from "a faulty or non-social definition of omnipotence." Hartshorne, *Reality as Social Process*, 41.

98. I use "finitism" as a category that includes any view denying that God possesses the power to prevent evil. Griffin, however, maintains that God has "perfect power, with 'perfect' defined as the 'greatest conceivable,'" claiming "traditional theism's idea of omnipotence" does not provide an adequate standard for saying "the power of process theism's God is imperfect, finite, or limited." Griffin, "Rejoinder," 139.

genuine evil. Not to do so means God is morally culpable."[99] Oord thus argues that any appeal to divine self-restraint, such as that of Sanders, describes a God who "fails to act like a loving human, let alone a perfectly loving God [because] loving parents prevent evil when they can."[100] He maintains instead that "if God does not care enough to prevent genuinely evil occurrences while having the power to do so, God is not love."[101] On Oord's essential kenosis approach, conversely, God's nature is self-emptying love and thus God cannot prevent the horrendous evils in this world. Oord rejects the view that God *allows* evil.[102] If God could prevent any such evils, he would do so. However, as uncontrolling love, God by nature *cannot* mitigate or prevent the evils in this world.[103] Since "God does not essentially possess all power" and cannot coerce, he is not responsible for evil.[104]

Although this view may effectively deny divine culpability for evil, many Christian theists do not find it appealing because it conflicts with the traditional Christian view of divine omnipotence. Indeed, Scripture and the Christian tradition maintain that God has intervened powerfully and miraculously in the past to prevent evils and has thus repeatedly exercised the kind of power that, it seems, could also mitigate or eliminate the evil in this world. As Ehrman puts it, "For the authors of the Bible, the God who created this world is a God of love and power who intervenes . . . [with] answered prayer and worked miracles." Ehrman asks, "Where is this God now? . . . If God intervened [in the biblical narratives], why doesn't he intervene now?"[105] In this regard, while agreeing with Griffin and Oord that God's failure to exercise his power to prevent horrendous evils makes him culpable for such evils, Roth contends that the God of Christianity *must* possess the power to prevent such evils. In his view, the God who raised Jesus from the dead "plausibly had the might to thwart the Holocaust long before it ended."[106]

Finitist approaches that reject the view that God possesses the power to prevent evil have significant problems accounting for the basic claims of

---

99. Oord, *Uncontrolling Love of God*, 141.

100. Oord, *Uncontrolling Love of God*, 135.

101. Oord, "Matching Theology and Piety," 345. Elsewhere Oord writes that a "voluntarily kenotic God is culpable for failing to prevent evil." Oord, *Nature of Love*, 124.

102. Oord gives his approach this label, by which he means God is essentially related to the world in a way that involves "*involuntary* divine self-limitation." Oord, *Nature of Love*, 125 (emphasis original).

103. See Oord, *Uncontrolling Love of God*, 148, 181.

104. Oord, "Matching Theology and Piety," 314.

105. Ehrman, *God's Problem*, 5.

106. Roth, "Theodicy of Protest," 11. Cf. Wiesel, *Night*.

Christian theism. For Davis, although accounts that deny this kind of divine omnipotence deserve a hearing, they are not properly *theistic* responses to the problem of evil.[107] Such views are unacceptable to a traditional Christian theist because they deny what Thomas P. Flint calls "the traditional theological claim that God is the all-knowing, sovereign, providential lord of the universe."[108] In Flint's view, "Scripture seems to speak clearly and repeatedly of a God who knowingly and lovingly exercises detailed control over his creation."[109] Yet if this is so, Roth asks, "Why should anybody bother with a God like this one, who seems so infrequently to do the best that is within God's power?"[110]

If God possesses the sheer power to intervene to prevent evils, as he is depicted as possessing throughout the Bible, then it would seem that he should (at least sometimes) do so. Yet God often appears to be hidden, particularly in times of suffering (see Ps. 10:1; 13:1–4).[111] The value of free will alone seems to fall short in explaining this problem. As Tooley writes, "The fact that libertarian free will is valuable does not entail that one should never intervene in the exercise of libertarian free will. Indeed, very few people think that one should not intervene to prevent someone from committing rape or murder. On the contrary, almost everyone would hold that a failure to prevent heinously evil actions when one can do so would be seriously wrong."[112]

Some approaches avoid this charge by rejecting its main premise. They argue that "failure to prevent [even] heinously evil actions when one can do so" might not be "seriously wrong," particularly if such evils bring about some specific greater good or goods that could not have been achieved without such evils. While a number of prominent proposals take something like this view, for now I will focus on some that do so while also accepting that the free will defense (or something like it) must be part of the equation to effectively address the problem of evil.

One of the most prominent of these is John Hick's soul-making theodicy.[113] For Hick, soul-making takes place "through the evolutionary process"

---

107. For Davis, theism entails "an omnipotent and perfectly good being." S. Davis, "Introduction," ix.

108. Flint, *Divine Providence*, 3.

109. Flint, *Divine Providence*, 17.

110. Roth, "Theodicy of Protest," 11. Although Roth believes in this kind of God, he also protests against what he considers to be God's immorality.

111. Cf. Schellenberg's argument that divine hiddenness justifies atheism. Schellenberg, *Divine Hiddenness and Human Reason*.

112. Tooley, "Problem of Evil."

113. See John Hick's seminal work *Evil and the God of Love*. For a briefer account, see Hick, "Soul-Making Theodicy."

wherein "immature creature[s]" develop by "living in a challenging and therefore person-making world."[114] On this view, genuine morality and spirituality *must* develop freely and at some distance from God, which can take place only in a world like ours with all its religious ambiguity, suffering, and evil. Humans are created morally imperfect and "at an epistemic distance from God," that they might grow into God's children through their own choices.[115] Such "cognitive" or "epistemic distance" from God requires a world that looks "as if there were no God"—that is, "a world which functions as an autonomous system and from within which God is not overwhelmingly evident."[116] Accordingly, "God must set [humans] at a distance from Himself, from which [they] can then voluntarily come to God."[117]

On Hick's account, God's hiddenness, distance from the world, and allowance of evil provide the necessary context for human souls to develop based on their own decisions. In a context of danger, pain, suffering, and religious ambiguity, human souls can develop free from divine interventions, which would purportedly upset the necessary context for utterly free moral development and growth.[118] Indeed, Hick contends, the "capacity to love would never be developed, except in a very limited sense of the word, in a world in which there was no such thing as suffering."[119] Relative to charges against an omnipotent God who fails to prevent horrendous evils, Hick contends that if "we take with full seriousness the value of human freedom and responsibility, . . . then we cannot consistently want God to revoke that freedom when its wrong exercise becomes intolerable to us."[120] Rather, the evils in this world are actually for the greater good of the process of

114. Hick, "Irenaean Theodicy," 39. Hick notes, however, that this theodicy "cannot, as such, be attributed to Irenaeus." Irenaeus is the "patron saint" of this type of theodicy, which is presented by later thinkers, "the greatest of whom [is] Friedrich Schleiermacher" (40).

115. Hick, "Soul-Making Theodicy," 275. Hick thus rejects the view that humans fell from perfection, arguing that it is both implausible, given modern science, and that it is "logically impossible for humans to be created already in [a] perfect state." He claims that the moral development of finite beings requires their "freely choosing the good in preference to evil" and "coming freely to an uncoerced consciousness of God from a situation of epistemic distance" (276).

116. Hick, "Soul-Making Theodicy," 269–70.

117. Hick, *Evil and the God of Love*, 317.

118. Hick explains that soul-making requires that the "environment, instead of being a pain-free and stress-free paradise, be broadly the kind of world of which we find ourselves to be a part." Hick, "Soul-Making Theodicy," 275. Cf. Meister's "theodicy of fulfillment," which "includes the main elements of free will and soul-making [wherein] a challenging environment is necessary," emphasizing "a redemptive component" relative to God's "workings" in "the natural world." Meister, *Evil*, 40. Cf. also Hasker's approach in *Triumph of God over Evil*.

119. Hick, *Evil and the God of Love*, 361.

120. Hick, "Irenaean Theodicy," 49. Although Hick's own theological views have evolved, his soul-making theodicy was premised on divine omnipotence.

soul-making, which allows Hick to affirm the ancient phrase O *felix culpa* (Oh happy fault).[121]

In a somewhat similar vein, recognizing the significant problems facing the free will defender, Richard Swinburne sets forth a higher-order goods defense in addition to the free will defense, which he views as "a central core of theodicy."[122] The higher-order goods defense posits "the good of [freely] performing certain sorts of good action" such as "those done in the face of evils," which "cannot be done unless there is pain and suffering . . . to which they react."[123] Such goods include "showing sympathy, . . . helping the suffering, and showing courage of a certain sort."[124] These are, he contends, part of a "logical straightjacket of goods which cannot be realized without actual or possible evils."[125] Davis appeals to this line of argument in order to deal with "natural evil" as well, saying that "as Richard Swinburne has argued, certain goods are such that God's creating a world in which natural evil exists is the only way, or the morally best permissible way, for God to make them possible."[126]

According to Swinburne, there is "some truth" in "O Felix Culpa. . . . There are good actions of certain kinds which can only be done in the face of good actions of various kinds."[127] Swinburne considers the objection that there are "too many, too various, and too serious evils to justify bringing about the goods which they make possible," to which he replies, "It must be stressed that each evil or possible evil removed takes away one more actual good."[128] He thus argues that each evil is indispensable because "we need a similar amount of evil if we are to have the similar amount of good."[129]

Whereas such a position might be effective as a defense at the level of logical possibility, I have serious misgivings about the adequacy of this kind of

121. See Hick, *Evil and the God of Love*, 400. Further, he argues, the "justification of evil" depends on "the completeness, or universality, of the salvation achieved" such that "in the end all will freely turn to [God] in love." Hick, "Irenaean Theodicy," 52.

122. Swinburne, "Some Major Strands of Theodicy," 250, 251. Notably, Plantinga himself allows that "perhaps some natural evils and some persons are so related that the persons would have produced less moral good if the evils had been absent." Plantinga, *Nature of Necessity*, 192.

123. Swinburne, "Some Major Strands of Theodicy," 250. For a fuller account, see Swinburne, *Providence and the Problem of Evil*.

124. Swinburne, "Some Major Strands of Theodicy," 250.

125. Swinburne, "Some Major Strands of Theodicy," 251.

126. S. Davis, "Free Will and Evil," 79.

127. Swinburne, "Some Major Strands of Theodicy," 253. He does qualify, however, that there is "not as much" truth in *felix culpa* "as the writer of the Exultet supposed" (253). Notably, Plantinga also recently set forth a *felix culpa* theodicy. Plantinga, "Supralapsarianism or 'O Felix Culpa,'" 10. See the discussion in chap. 6 of the present volume.

128. Swinburne, "Some Major Strands of Theodicy," 258.

129. Swinburne, "Some Major Strands of Theodicy," 257.

response and any other that makes the actuality of some evil *necessary* for the achievement of a greater good. As Davis recognizes, "Those theists who hold that all evil helps lead to a greater good deny that 'genuine evil' exists. They implicitly affirm that all evil is only apparent."[130] Such a position appears to make every evil effectively an instrumental good.[131] This appears to contradict Paul's rejection of the assertion, "Let us do evil that good may come" (Rom. 3:8; cf. 6:1).[132] If evil is *never* gratuitous, then why should it *ever* be prevented? If every evil brings some greater good, why not propagate more evil?

Beyond such objections, I question whether the "goods" in virtuous responses to evils are themselves intrinsic goods without which there would be less value in the world. It seems to me far more likely that the intrinsic good displayed in such virtuous responses flows from the underlying disposition of love, which presumably could be maximally displayed in a world without evil. If this is so, there are likely comparable or better virtuous actions and responses in a world without evil that more profoundly display the intrinsic goodness of love.[133]

Another Way Forward

The theodicy of love set forth in the remainder of this book attempts to carefully outline a way forward for those who, like me, affirm divine omnipotence, divine foreknowledge, and a view of providence that includes special interventions, while denying that evil is necessary for (greater) good. However, any path forward will need to address the seemingly plausible claim that an omnipotent God who respects free will would nevertheless be able to do more than he appears to do to mitigate evil in this world.

Perhaps God could make the consequences of bad decisions far less bad than they are, especially with regard to the suffering of innocents. As Meister asks, "Even granting a robust libertarian view of free will, could God not have prevented the consequences of the evil decisions made by free creatures— consequences having to do with both moral and natural evils?"[134]

---

130. S. Davis, "Critique of Process Theodicy," 134.

131. This is notwithstanding Swinburne's view that it "remains the case, however, that evil is evil, and there is a substantial price to pay for the goods of our world." Swinburne, "Some Major Strands of Theodicy," 260. Cf. Hick's discussion of Schleiermacher's "instrumental view of evil." Hick, *Evil and the God of Love*, 239.

132. In this regard, I agree with Karl Barth's protest that "when sin is understood positively" and "when it counterbalances grace and is indispensable to it, it is not real sin." K. Barth, *CD* III/3:333.

133. See the discussion in chap. 6 of the present volume.

134. Meister, *Evil*, 32.

Further, one might wonder why God does not intervene in ways that could prevent or mitigate evil without seeming to impinge on free will at all. For example, perhaps God could have provided some special revelation to the CIA director about the impending terrorist attacks of 9/11, providing just enough information that law enforcement could thwart the attacks. Whereas some perspectives (such as Hick's) might argue that special revelation of this (or any) kind would negate the epistemic distance necessary for free will, the traditional Christian view of God's providence affirms the claims of Scripture that God has repeatedly provided special revelation to selected individuals and groups in the past. If God could warn Pharaoh of an impending famine via a dream (Gen. 41:1–7), why did God not warn the director of the CIA (or someone else in a position to prevent the disaster) of the impending World Trade Center attack or of any other number of atrocities and tragedies?[135]

In this respect and others, the basic free will defense leaves some significant and troubling questions unaddressed. Critics have called for further specific arguments that go beyond defense to theodicy. Accordingly, the following chapters of this book outline a theodicy of love that moves beyond the basic free will defense, addressing the evidential problem of evil within the context of a cosmic conflict over love, aiming to provide an internally consistent and canonically plausible explanation as to why God permits so much evil in this world.

Conclusion

This chapter has introduced the complexity and magnitude of the problem of evil within the context of Christian theology, introduced the free will defense as the most successful approach to the logical problem of evil to date, and noted that the free will defense nevertheless seems insufficient to address the evidential problem of evil. The chapter also briefly introduced numerous proposals that are live options in the current discussion, some competing with the free will defense and some that are compatible with it but move beyond it, including brief examples of protest perspectives, determinism, open theism, finitist approaches, skeptical theism, and some prominent *felix culpa* strategies.

In light of this discussion, it seems that further articulation is needed beyond the basic parameters of the free will defense and perhaps beyond the other live options as well. Although many of these avenues hold considerable

---

135. Here the problems of evil and divine hiddenness converge.

potential, the paths forward discussed in this chapter also leave significant questions unaddressed or raise other significant issues for the Christian theist, especially one who wishes to affirm a view of divine providence wherein God can and does strongly intervene in the history of the world while rejecting the view that evil is *necessary* to bring about (greater) good.

Toward addressing this situation, the following chapters of this book set forth the various components of a theodicy of love. Chapter 2 begins with a canonical account of creaturely free will that might undergird the basic free will defense (thus bridging the gap between philosophical and biblical accounts) and sketches a working model of divine providence wherein God does not always get what he wants. Chapter 3 exposits the reality of the cosmic conflict framework in Scripture, which is robustly supported in the Christian tradition. Chapter 4 unpacks the nature of this cosmic dispute over God's love and moral government, explaining a covenantal rules-of-engagement framework that assists in understanding why God might not intervene or otherwise prevent or mitigate evils, even in cases where doing so would not appear to violate creaturely free will. Chapter 5 turns to the suffering God of the cross as the conclusive demonstration of God's character of unselfish love, which evokes confidence in God's goodness, even as many questions remain unanswered as we await the final, eschatological solution to evil. Chapter 6 concludes the book with an evaluation of the preferability of this theodicy of love and a discussion of the questions that still remain.

2

Love, Evil, and
God's Unfulfilled Desires

As seen in chapter 1, the basic free will defense posits that God might not be culpable for evil in this world because evil might be the result of creaturely misuse of free will. Yet this defense raises a number of questions, including (1) why an omnipotent and omnibenevolent God would grant such free will in the first place or continue to grant it in the face of horrendous evils; (2) whether there are any good reasons to believe God has indeed granted such free will, and, even if so; (3) whether creaturely free will adequately accounts for the kind and amount of evil in this world.

Whereas the free will defense is widely viewed as successful against the *logical* problem of evil, advocates of the *evidential* problem of evil claim that the free will defense does not adequately account for the kind and amount of evil in this world.[1] Further, some claim that there could not be any morally sufficient reason for God to allow the kind and amount of evil that exists in this world.[2]

Conversely, the theodicy of love set forth in this book posits that love, properly understood within the context of a cosmic conflict, provides a morally sufficient reason for God's allowance of the evil in this world. On this view,

1. For an introduction to the evidential problem of evil, see Rowe, *God and the Problem of Evil*, 121–233.
2. See chap. 1 in the present volume.

God gives creatures libertarian free will because it is a necessary condition of love, and God is justified in doing so because of the unsurpassable value of love.

Whether love, free will, and evil are related in a way that supports this supposition is a matter of considerable debate. Whether creatures possess libertarian free will is a live question among philosophers and theologians. Further, one might argue that love does not require libertarian free will, so love could not be the morally sufficient reason for the allowance of evil.

In this chapter I take up these issues in succession, beginning with the issue of whether a Christian theist has good reason to suppose that God grants libertarian free will to creatures and what ramifications such a view might have for divine sovereignty. In brief, I argue that a minimal account of libertarian free will is indicated by Scripture's depictions of God's unfulfilled desires. I then briefly outline a model of divine providence that accounts for God's unfulfilled desires, denying that evil is *necessary* for (greater) good while maintaining a robust conception of God's sovereignty that affirms divine omnipotence, divine foreknowledge, and special divine action.

The Debate over Free Will

Our first question is whether there is any good reason for a Christian theist to believe God grants creatures the kind of free will supposed by the free will defense. Free will is a matter of long-standing and complex philosophical debate, which includes competing conceptions of what "free will" means, disagreements about whether free will is compatible with determinism, and competing views about whether determinism or indeterminism is true. In order to understand the parameters of this debate, some basic definitions are in order.

Basic Definitions in the Debate over Free Will

Put simply, determinists believe every event is caused by prior factors such that every event must occur just as it does,[3] while indeterminists deny this view.[4] One might initially think that determinists deny free will, but this depends on what counts as free will. Determinists who deny free will are often called hard determinists. Determinists who affirm free will are often

3. As Kevin Timpe explains, "Causal determinism is the thesis that the course of the future is entirely determined by the conjunction of the non-relational past and the laws of nature." Timpe, *Free Will in Philosophical Theology*, 8.

4. For an excellent introduction, see Timpe, *Free Will: Sourcehood and Its Alternatives*.

called soft determinists or compatibilists because they believe determinism is *compatible* with free will.[5] Incompatibilists, conversely, believe determinism is incompatible with free will.

The difference between compatibilists and incompatibilists hinges on what qualifies as free will. Many compatibilists define free will as the freedom to do what one wants to do.[6] Here, a necessary condition of free will is that one not be externally compelled to will against one's desires. This definition is compatible with determinism on the view that what one wants is itself determined by prior factors.

The two most prominent incompatibilist (libertarian) conceptions of free will are known as leeway and sourcehood approaches.[7] Leeway approaches contend that free will requires the ability to do otherwise. Such approaches affirm what is sometimes called the "principle of alternative possibility," which means that if a given agent is acting freely in a given instance, that free agent could do otherwise than she does. Sourcehood approaches maintain that an agent may be acting "freely" in a given instance even if that agent could not have done otherwise, as long as the agent is not causally determined by some external factor to act as she does. The agent must simply be the ultimate source of the given action in a way that is not causally determined by any external factors.[8]

One of the most prominent arguments in favor of incompatibilism trades on the widely held intuition that free will requires that what we do is "up to us." The basic elements of this argument, which is known as the "consequence

5. There are, however, different varieties of compatibilism. This description refers to what is sometimes called broad compatibilism, the view that determinism is compatible with free will *and* moral responsibility. Unless otherwise noted, I use the term "compatibilism" to refer to broad compatibilism. Some compatibilists, however, believe that determinism is compatible with moral responsibility whether or not it is compatible with "free will" (e.g., John Martin Fischer). This is semicompatibilism (aka narrow compatibilism), wherein an agent's will may be determined but she nevertheless possesses moral responsibility. On the various forms and contemporary issues regarding compatibilism, see the essays in Kane, *Oxford Handbook of Free Will*, 153–242. See further Timpe, Griffith, and Levy, *Routledge Companion to Free Will*.

6. According to Steven B. Cowan and James S. Spiegel, to say one has "free will" means "that the person has the ability to do what she wants to do" and is "not coerced by external forces against her will." They continue, "The compatibilist defines freedom, then, as the ability to act according to one's desires and intentions." Cowan and Spiegel, *Love of Wisdom*, 237.

7. There are a variety of highly nuanced leeway and sourcehood conceptions, including compatibilist approaches. Here, I focus on the debate's main contours, since the approach offered in this book does not depend on what kind of incompatibilism is adopted. For an introduction, see Timpe, "Leeway vs. Sourcehood Conceptions of Free Will," 213–24.

8. Timpe explains that leeway approaches understand free will as "primarily a function of being able to do otherwise than one in fact does," but sourcehood approaches view free will as "primarily a function of an agent being the source of her actions in a particular way." Timpe, *Free Will in Philosophical Theology*, 7–8.

argument," are explained by Peter van Inwagen: "If determinism is true, then our acts are the consequence of laws of nature and events in the remote past. But it's not up to us what went on before we were born, and neither is it up to us what the laws of nature are. Therefore, the consequences of these things (including our present acts) are not up to us."[9]

Frankfurt-type cases—so called after the seminal article by the philosopher Harry Frankfurt—have been put forth as an argument against (at least one kind of) libertarian free will, aiming to demonstrate that the ability to do otherwise is not a necessary condition of moral responsibility or free will.[10] One simplified case goes like this: Suppose Danny wants to ensure that Rusty robs some bank and thus implants a special device in Rusty's brain that is capable of causally determining that Rusty do so. However, Danny sets this device to determine that Rusty do so only if Rusty does not decide on his own to rob the bank. Suppose further that the device is never activated because Rusty decides to rob the bank on his own. Few, if any, would argue that Rusty did not freely rob the bank. However, it is argued, given the device in his brain, Rusty could not have done otherwise. Hence, the ability to do otherwise is not a necessary condition of free will.

Whether such Frankfurt-type cases successfully demonstrate that free will does not require the freedom to do otherwise is a matter of considerable debate.[11] Incompatibilists who hold to leeway approaches argue that such cases fail in this regard because the device would have to be triggered by some prior signal (perhaps the mental activity of the agent), which would seem to leave room for the agent to at least decide to act in some way other than the manipulator desires—or at least to take some free mental actions sufficient to trigger the device.[12]

9. Van Inwagen, *Essay on Free Will*, 56.

10. See Harry Frankfurt's seminal article "Alternate Possibilities and Moral Responsibility." Whereas Frankfurt argues that *moral responsibility* does not require alternate possibilities, I agree with Timpe's characterization of "free will" as "the kind of control an agent must have over his decisions (choices, actions, etc.) in order for him to be morally responsible for those decisions (choices, actions, etc.)" such that "the alternative possibilities condition for free will and PAP [the principle of alternate possibilities] as defined by Frankfurt stand and fall together." Timpe, *Free Will: Sourcehood and Its Alternatives*, 70.

11. See the various positions in Widerker and McKenna, *Moral Responsibility and Alternative Possibilities*; Kane, *Oxford Handbook of Free Will*, 243–308. Beyond Frankfurt-type examples, some argue that incompatibilist accounts of free will are incoherent insofar as they (appear to) offer an account of uncaused events. There are various responses to this objection. Some appeal to agent causation—the view that free agents themselves are irreducible causes of some events. See Griffith, "Agent Causation." Others believe that agents cause their acts but that such causation is reducible to event-causality. See Ekstrom, "Event-Causal Libertarianism."

12. More specifically, any such signal would either itself be a free action or not. If the signal is a free action, then the case does not preclude PAP. If it is not, the case appears to assume

Whatever one concludes in this regard, this case raises an important distinction between freedom of mental action and freedom with regard to a specific external action.[13] I might not be free to *act* in some way that I *will* to act because I might lack the physical ability to do so, either innately or due to the imposition of some external factors. However, if "willing" consists of mental activity, then a constraint external to mental activity that limits my ability to externally act as I want in some particular way does not remove my free will but merely removes my ability to carry out my will in that particular way. Suppose, for instance, that I am imprisoned against my will. It does not follow that I then lack free will. I may continue to will to run free in the grass outside even as I am unable to run free because of the external constraint of imprisonment.

Further, even if Frankfurt-type cases or some other thought experiments successfully demonstrate that free will does not require the ability to *will* otherwise in a given instance, it does not follow that libertarian free will is defeated. Recall that sourcehood approaches maintain that an agent may act freely in a given instance even if she could not will otherwise in that instance, as long as she is the ultimate source of her willing in a way that is not causally determined by external factors.[14] Incompatibilists who defend sourcehood approaches argue that the requirement for free will is not alternate possibility but merely "the absence of external causal constraints determining one's action."[15]

The Debate over Human Freedom among Christian Theists

Although no consensus is in sight, the outcome of the free will debate holds major ramifications for Christian theism, particularly relative to the problem of evil. Many theologians advocate theological determinism—the view that God causally determines history, including all creaturely decisions and actions. On this view, nothing occurs except that which God

---

compatibilism and thus begs the question. This response is sometimes called the dilemma defense or the Kane-Widerker objection. See Kane, *Contemporary Introduction to Free Will*, 87. See further Widerker, "Libertarianism and Frankfurt's Attack on the Principle of Alternative Possibilities"; Ginet, "In Defense of the Principle of Alternative Possibilities."

13. The freedom to will some action is sometimes called formal freedom, and the freedom to enact what one wills is sometimes called material freedom. Timpe, *Free Will in Philosophical Theology*, 7.

14. E.g., one might have formed her character such that she cannot will otherwise in a given instance, but as long as she formed her character (in part) via earlier free decisions, she remains the ultimate source of her decisions.

15. Craig, "Response to Boyd," 226.

has causally determined.[16] Nevertheless, while Christian philosophers and theologians disagree over whether determinism is true, nearly all Christian thinkers believe humans possess some kind of free will. Theistic compatibilists contend that humans are free to do what they want but that what they want is causally determined by God. Theistic libertarians, conversely, believe that God does not causally determine humans to will just as they do. The crux of the debate hinges on whether humans possess compatibilist or libertarian free will.

Whereas the Christian tradition is thoroughly divided on how to understand human free will, there is broad agreement that such debates should be approached in accordance with Scripture. Yet theologians on all sides of the debate claim biblical support for their positions, prompting some to argue that Scripture is insufficient to advance the discussion.

On the one hand, libertarians appeal to the many texts that appear to support human free will, such as God's proclamation, "I have set before you life and death, the blessing and the curse. So choose life in order that you may live" (Deut. 30:19).[17] Likewise, one might appeal to Joshua's exhortation to "choose for yourselves today whom you will serve," Yahweh or the gods of Canaan (Josh. 24:15; cf. 1 Kings 18:21). Further, one could appeal to Paul's statement in the NT, "If you confess with your mouth Jesus as Lord, and believe in your heart that God raised Him from the dead, you will be saved" (Rom. 10:9).[18]

On the other hand, compatibilists claim that such texts do not exclude determinism but merely indicate that humans are free to do what they want to do, while God causally determines what they want. Further, compatibilists point to texts such as Genesis 50:20, where Joseph states to his brothers who sold him into slavery, "You meant evil against me, but God meant it for good in order to bring about this present result, to preserve many people alive."[19] From the NT, compatibilists often appeal to Paul's exhortation, "Work out your salvation with fear and trembling; for it is God who is at work in you, both to will and to work for His good pleasure" (Phil. 2:12–13). These and other passages, compatibilists claim, evince the

16. On this view, "no event happens without God's willing that particular event," and "God's willing an event" is "sufficient for that event occurring." Timpe, *Free Will in Philosophical Theology*, 9.

17. Cf. Deut. 11:26–28; 2 Chron. 15:2; Jer. 18:7–10.

18. Cf. John 3:16–18; 8:31–32; Acts 16:31; Heb. 3:8–12; Rev. 3:20.

19. See the discussion in chap. 6 on why God might take this circuitous route rather than delivering from the famine more directly.

compatibility of human free will and divine determinism.[20] Libertarians, however, believe these texts support God's providence without indicating determinism.[21]

Both sides claim that texts descriptive of human free will support their view, amounting to an impasse that depends on whether God determines human wills. I propose that instead of first focusing on *human* free will, we should first focus on the logically prior question regarding *God's* will: Does God always get what he wants?[22]

Does God Always Get What He Wants?

God's Unfulfilled Desires in Scripture

Numerous biblical texts indicate that God does not always get what he wants. Humans sometimes will otherwise than God desires. Here it is important to understand that biblical language of desire is closely related to that of will: one tends to will (or wish) to occur that which one desires, and so desire and will are often depicted by the same terminology.[23] Scripture presents a robust conception of God's providence and will, sometimes presenting God as effectively willing that which he desires (Isa. 46:10; Acts 2:23; Eph. 1:11). Other times, however, God's will is unfulfilled because creatures reject or resist God's desires (Isa. 66:4; Ezek. 18:23; Matt. 23:37; Luke 7:30).[24]

Whereas God "longs to be gracious" to his people and "waits on high to have compassion," they are "not willing" (Isa. 30:18, 15). Later, God proclaims, "I will choose [*bahar*] their punishments" because "I called, but no one answered; / I spoke, but they did not listen. / And they did evil in My

20. It is beyond this book's scope to sufficiently address the interpretation of these and other passages offered to support compatibilism (e.g., Rom. 9–11; Eph. 1). On these, see Peckham, *Concept of Divine Love*, 391–98.

21. See, e.g., the brief discussion in McCall, *Invitation to Analytic Christian Theology*, 56–81. McCall contends that the biblical narrative itself "showcases what strongly appears to be a concern for genuine freedom [and] ties moral responsibility to the choices that appear to be genuinely open to human agents," evinced by a "vast range of texts." He believes that the "overarching message of biblical theology seems to be saying that rebellious and unfaithful sinners sometimes are held responsible precisely because they don't (or didn't) do otherwise" (73–74, 76). See also McCall, "I Believe in Divine Sovereignty," 205–6; McCall, "We Believe in God's Sovereign Goodness," 235–46.

22. Here, "want" refers simply to the desire for some outcome, without connoting need.

23. The Hebrew term *hapets* and the Greek terms *thelō* and *boulomai* might signify willing or desiring (among other connotations), depending on the context. See David Talley, "*ḥāpēṣ*," *NIDOTTE* 2:232, and D. Müller, "βούλομαι, θελω," *NIDNTT* 3:1015–18.

24. See the extensive discussion in Peckham, *Concept of Divine Love*, 205–8, 236–41, 372–78, 577–82.

sight / And chose [*bahar*] that in which I did not delight [*hapets*]" (Isa. 66:4).[25] Human rejection of God's will is likewise explicit in Luke 7:30: "The Pharisees and the lawyers rejected God's purpose [*boulē*] for themselves" (cf. Mark 7:24).[26] Further, Jesus frequently references those who do "the will" [*thelēma*] of the Father, indicating that not everyone does God's will.[27]

First Timothy 2:4 asserts that God "desires [*thelō*] all [people] to be saved," but other texts teach that some will not be saved (e.g., John 3:18; Heb. 10:36; 1 John 2:17).[28] Some argue that the terms *anyone* and *all* in passages relative to God's desire to save all may refer to all kinds of people rather than every individual or that such terms may only refer to specific addressees.[29] However, as recognized even by some Bible scholars and theologians who read Scripture in a determinist way (e.g., Tom Schreiner and John Piper), some texts indicate God's desire to save everyone without leaving room for such alternate interpretations.[30] For instance, God states, "I have no pleasure [*hapets*] in the death of *anyone* who dies. . . . Therefore, repent and live" (Ezek. 18:32).[31] Similarly, Schreiner believes that 2 Peter 3:9 "refers to God's desire that everyone without exception be saved," when it states that God "is patient . . . not wishing [*boulomai*] for any to perish but for all to come to repentance."[32] However, not all repent (cf. Rev. 2:21; 9:20–21; 16:9–11), and

25. Cf. Pss. 78:22; Isa. 65:12; Jer. 19:5. Further, God proclaims,

> But My people did not listen to My voice,
> And Israel did not obey Me.
> So I gave them over to the stubbornness of their heart
> To walk in *their own* devices.
> *Oh that My people would listen to Me,*
> That Israel would walk in My ways! (Ps. 81:11–13)

Why would God lament and long for his people to "listen" to him if he himself causally determined that they would not?

26. Evidently, H. J. Ritz notes, "the Βουλή of God can be hindered." "Βουλή," *EDNT*, 1:224.

27. Matt. 7:21; 12:50; 18:14; Mark 3:35; John 6:40; cf. Matt. 6:10; 23:37; John 7:17. I. Howard Marshall comments that if "we freely yield ourselves to God," then "he is able to accomplish his will through us and our prayers. In a very real sense, therefore, the accomplishment of God's will in the world does depend on our prayers." Marshall, *Epistles of John*, 245.

28. Anton Vögtle contends that 1 Tim. 2:4 excludes determinism. Vögtle, *Der Judasbrief, der 2. Petrusbrief*, 231–32. Cf. D. Müller, "θέλω," *NIDNTT* 3:1020.

29. See, e.g., the discussion in Moo, *2 Peter and Jude*, 188.

30. Both Piper and Schreiner believe that 1 Tim. 2:4 and other texts describe God's genuine desire for the salvation of all. Piper, "Are There Two Wills in God?," 108; Schreiner, *1, 2 Peter, Jude*, 382.

31. Daniel I. Block comments, "Without repentance God cannot forgive." Block, *Ezekiel*, 589.

32. Schreiner, *1, 2 Peter, Jude*, 382. Peter H. Davids goes further, claiming that God wants "'everyone'/'all' to come to repentance. . . . God's will may not be done, but it will not be for lack of trying on his part." Davids, *Letters of 2 Peter and Jude*, 281. Similarly, Eric Fuchs and Pierre Reymond believe 2 Pet. 3:9 provides evidence against determinism. Fuchs and Reymond, *La deuxième Épitre de Saint Pierre*, 115–16.

God's very patience evinces unfulfilled desires (cf. Rom. 2:4; 2 Pet. 3:15).[33] It is difficult to reconcile theological determinism with such evidence that God's desires sometimes go unfulfilled.

Why Are God's Desires Sometimes Unfulfilled?

The texts above evince that humans sometimes will otherwise than God desires. This seems to indicate that God does not causally determine human wills (at least in those instances) because, if God did, he could causally determine that humans will precisely what he desires. But God's desires are sometimes unfulfilled and this raises significant questions for determinism. As Piper puts it, "What are we [determinists] to say of the fact that God wills something that in fact does not happen?"[34] Further, Piper adds, "If, as Calvinists say, God deems it wise and good to elect unconditionally some to salvation and not others, one may legitimately ask whether the offer of salvation to all is genuine" and whether "the willing that none perish . . . [is] a bona fide willing of love."[35]

Determinists like Piper address these difficult issues via a distinction between God's revealed and hidden wills. On this view, "God genuinely desires in one sense that all will be saved" while at the same time "he has not ultimately decreed that all will be saved."[36] Here Piper explains that "there is nothing beyond God's own will and nature which stops him from saving people," but "there are people who are not objects of God's electing love."[37] Given compatibilism, God could determine that every individual "freely accept his love and be saved," but, in Piper's view, some are eternally damned.[38] This raises the question of how it could be true that God genuinely desires to save everyone and, yet, everyone is not saved.

Actual and Counterfactual Desires

To avoid equivocation regarding the meaning of "desire," I distinguish between *actual* and *counterfactual* desires.[39] An actual desire is that which one genuinely prefers from any given time onward. A counterfactual desire

---

33. In this and other ways, I do not think universalism comports with the canonical data. See Marshall, "New Testament Does Not Teach Universal Salvation."

34. Piper, "Are There Two Wills in God?," 123.

35. Piper, "Are There Two Wills in God?," 127.

36. Schreiner, *1, 2 Peter, Jude*, 382. Cf. Calvin, *Commentaries on the Catholic Epistles*, 419–20.

37. Piper, "How Does a Sovereign God Love?," 10.

38. Walls, "Why No Classical Theist," 96.

39. In this discussion, I use "desire" and "will" interchangeably.

is that which one *would* prefer *if* other things were different than they are. Whereas humans might mistakenly hold conflicting actual desires, since God has perfect awareness of his desires and never contradicts himself, *all* God's actual desires must be compatible with one another. If God actually desires some state of affairs, God truly wishes for *that* state of affairs to be actual in a way that is compatible with his other actual desires. To actually desire *x* would mean, then, that if God had his way (given the present state of affairs), *x* would occur. As such, if God causally determines every occurrence, God does not, by definition, *actually* desire anything that he does not bring to pass.

Given theological determinism, any divine unfulfilled desire could be only a counterfactual desire—namely, that which God *would* desire if the world were different than it is. Therefore, on the view of determinism, to affirm that God desires that all humans be saved must mean that God only *counterfactually* desires the salvation of all. Here, God does not *actually* desire to save everyone but *would* desire it if the world were different than it is.

Are Divine Unfulfilled Desires Compatible with Determinism?

For God to have counterfactual desires is undoubtedly compatible with indeterminism, but the question is whether such desires are compatible with theological determinism. As omnipotent, God possesses the power to bring about any desire that is compatible with his other desires and his own nature. Unless God desires something opposed to his own nature—which would be absurd—to coherently maintain that any desire of God is unfulfilled, there must be some other desire that God wants more that is itself not compatible with God's "lesser" desire.[40]

Piper claims that "God wills not to save all, even though he is willing to save all, because there is something else that he wills more, which would be lost if he exerted his sovereign power to save all."[41] For Piper, "the greater value is the manifestation of the full range of God's glory in wrath and mercy (Rom. 9:22–23) and the humbling of man so that he enjoys giving all credit to God for his salvation (1 Cor. 1:29)."[42]

For Piper's appeal to a greater value to be effective, the greater value and lesser value must be incompatible in some way that even God *could not*

---

40. Notably here, God "cannot deny Himself" (2 Tim. 2:13).

41. Piper, "Are There Two Wills in God?," 123. Cf. Paul Helm's case that "God ordains evil because it is logically necessary for his goal of the greater good." Helm, "God, Compatibilism, and the Authorship of Sin," 122.

42. Piper, "Are There Two Wills in God?," 124. This has been called the divine glory defense/theodicy. See Johnson, "Calvinism and the Problem of Evil," 43–48.

determine that both obtain. Yet Piper's supposition does not meet this standard. For Piper (as for most Christian theists), God's actual glory cannot be increased. The purported value relative to God's glory, then, could be relative only to the "manifestation" purported to cause creatures to recognize God's glory. Yet if God causally determines the mental actions of humans, then he could make it the case *immediately* that every mind in the universe humbly and joyfully recognize "the full range" of God's glory.[43] There would be no incompatibility, then, between God actually saving everyone and everyone fully recognizing his glory.

Similar to Piper, Paul Kjoss Helseth contends that while "particular evils happen because [God] ordained that they would," God "did so for reasons that, while ultimately inscrutable, nevertheless serve to . . . cultivate in [believers] the Christian virtues of perseverance, proven character, and hope."[44] Here again, though, if God causally determines the mental actions of humans, then he could causally determine that each person directly and immediately possess all Christian virtues, unless such virtues themselves require indeterminism.

In John Calvin's view, at least, God does indeed causally determine the mental actions of humans. He writes that the "internal affections of men are not less ruled by the hand of God than their external actions are *preceded* by his *eternal decree*," and therefore, "God performs not by the hands of men the things which He has decreed, without *first working* in their hearts the *very will* which *precedes* the acts they are to perform."[45]

Given this kind of determinism, nothing could prevent God from instilling in every mind any value, virtue, or characteristic that he desires, unless there is something intrinsic to any such value, virtue, or characteristic such that God cannot determine it to obtain. Any value that intrinsically cannot be determined to obtain in creaturely minds would thereby intrinsically require indeterminism.[46]

Further, if the divine actualization of two values is incompatible in some way, then to claim that God desires both values is to claim that he (counterfactually) desires that the actualization of the two values were not incompatible.

43. Piper, "Are There Two Wills in God?," 124.
44. Helseth, "God Causes All Things," 44.
45. Calvin, "Defence of the Secret Providence of God," 2.23 (emphasis original). Calvin affirms that "the sentiments of Augustine on these momentous points are to be fully received and maintained. 'When God (says he) willeth that to be done which cannot be effected, in the course of the things of this world, without the wills of men, He at the same time inclines their hearts to will to do it, and also Himself does it, not only by aiding their hearts to desire to do it, but also by decreeing it, that they cannot but do it'" (2.23–24).
46. This is just what many free will defenders affirm; God desires some values that he cannot causally determine because something about such values is incompatible with being determined by God.

However, if the incompatibility of the two values is subject to God's will, then God could simply will that the two values be compatible. If, however, the incompatibility of the two values is intrinsic to reality and thus to God's own nature, then for God to desire the compatibility of the two values would be to desire something that is contrary to his own nature. It seems, then, that the God of compatibilism cannot consistently have either unfulfilled actual *or* unfulfilled counterfactual desires. This is because there appears to be nothing that God could desire without self-contradiction that he could not causally determine to be the case.

Consider again Piper's claim that God's glory somehow prevents God from fulfilling his desire to save everyone. If God causally determines the fact that God's glory (somehow) requires that he causally determine some to be damned, then God could determine that this be otherwise. If, conversely, God's glory is intrinsically such that it demands that some be deterministically damned, then for God to (even counterfactually) desire that none be damned would require that God desire something that contradicts his own nature and glory.

Thus, given determinism, if God has unfulfilled desires, God either wills against his own will in a self-contradictory way or possesses desires that conflict with his own nature, amounting to another kind of self-contradiction. Therefore, if determinism is true, God would not have any unfulfilled desires (even counterfactual ones). This conclusion puts determinism in profound tension with the many biblical portrayals of God's unfulfilled desires. To coherently claim that God has unfulfilled desires requires that there is some operative factor beyond God's own will and nature.[47] However, any such factor would by definition be a theologically indeterministic factor.[48]

This line of thought has major ramifications for the problem of evil. If theological determinism entails that God causally determines every occurrence (even the mental events of creatures), then God must have casually determined every occurrence of evil. On this view, even though "God could have created a world in which all persons freely did only the good at all times," God causally determines *every* instance of evil, purportedly *because* God wants to manifest his glory or *because* God wants to achieve some other purportedly greater value.[49] Even if one sets aside the conclusion reached above—that, if deter-

---

47. Recall that Piper explicitly rejected this: "There is nothing beyond God's own will and nature which stops him from saving people." Piper, "How Does a Sovereign God Love?," 10.

48. On indeterminism, divine unfulfilled desires are coherent because nothing intrinsic to God's nature or caused by his will prevents the possibility that humans possess libertarian free will *and* always love flawlessly.

49. Walls, "Why No Classical Theist," 82. John S. Feinberg, an advocate of compatibilism, expresses serious misgivings about such divine glory defenses, noting, "A theology that says

minism is true, God could save everyone and make everyone fully recognize his glory—one wonders how deterministically damning people could bring God glory in the first place.[50] Further, if God needs intervening evil events for his glory or for any other "greater value," then God either needs evil by nature or needs it to accomplish his will. Yet this conclusion would undercut a basic tenet of divine sovereignty.[51] If, alternatively, such evil events are not necessary for some greater value, then (in determinism) all evils are willed by God for their own sake.

A Softer Soft Determinism?

To avoid claiming that God either needs or wills evil, some compatibilists might want to argue that God does not causally determine the mental states or actions of humans. Perhaps, as Ron Highfield claims, God "ordains all events" in some other way without "ordain[ing] evil."[52] Highfield attempts to elude the apparent contradiction here by distinguishing between various aspects of any act—"intention, deliberation, decision, exertion using means, and results"—alongside the claim that, via divine concurrence, "God does not do evil when he works in and through and after stupid, ignorant, and evil human acts."[53] However, mental actions are kinds of events, and if God causally ordains *all* events, then he causally ordains even the evil intentions

---

evil in our world is justified, because God uses it to bring himself glory" may evoke the reaction that God "is morally repugnant." Feinberg, *Many Faces of Evil*, 187.

50. Some claim that God must fully display his wrath. However, divine wrath is not itself an essential attribute of God but is the appropriate display of love against evil. Absent evil, wrath would not be and would thus require no expression. See Peckham, *Love of God*.

51. Walls notes that if God "must display justice by punishing evil in order fully to manifest his glory," then "God needs evil or depends on it fully to manifest his glory. This consequence undermines not only God's goodness, but his sovereignty as well." Walls, "Why No Classical Theist," 75.

52. Highfield, "Response to Paul Kjoss Helseth," 67. Highfield even claims that God "never uses evil as a means to an end."

53. Highfield, "God Controls by Liberating," 161–62. Cf. Feinberg's approach, which rejects the free will defense in favor of compatibilism but maintains that creaturely "desires" are "the ultimate source from which moral evil stems," such that "temptation to evil and the actual willing of evil stem not from God but from man." Feinberg, *Many Faces of Evil*, 171. Feinberg claims that "even with compatibilism, God can't get everyone always to do good, if he wants to maintain the integrity of [nonglorified] humans as created" and, accordingly, "cannot . . . guarantee and/or bring it about that everyone will choose to have a relationship with him" (432). It is not clear, however, why God could not immediately and directly causally determine the very desires of all creatures such that they always "freely" (in a compatibilistic sense) will just as God wants. Feinberg seems to maintain that God cannot causally determine creaturely *desires* without undercutting some outweighing good (nonglorified humans), but this seems to amount to a free desires defense, analogous to the free will defense.

of all agents.[54] Conversely, if God does not causally determine the mental actions of humans, then some things are not causally determined by God. On this view, history is partially determined and partially undetermined by God. This view is, however, a form of indeterminism.

My indeterministic conception of providence affirms that God "determines" some things by his own action (without determining the mental actions or wills of free agents) but does not "determine" the desires or wills of others because he consistently respects the free agency of others.[55] Later in this chapter, I unpack this model of providence, which allows me to affirm indeterminism with the free will defender while also, with the sovereignty defender, affirming that God's (ultimate) purpose will certainly come to pass. While affirming indeterminism, this model affirms (without equivocation) the many strong statements of sovereign providence, such as that God "works all things after the counsel of His will" (Eph. 1:11).[56] Before turning to this model, however, I must first clarify how an indeterministic conception of human free will follows from divine unfulfilled desires.

A Minimal Conception of Libertarian Free Will

A minimal, libertarian account of free will may be derived from the fact of divine unfulfilled desires relative to human actions as follows:

1. Humans sometimes will otherwise than God desires.
2. If humans sometimes will otherwise than God desires, then God has unfulfilled desires.
3. If compatibilistic determinism is true, then God cannot have unfulfilled desires.[57]

54. David Bentley Hart maintains, "If an action is causally necessitated or infallibly predetermined, its indeterminacy with regard to its proximate cause in no way makes it free." Hart, "Providence and Causality," 41.

55. See the distinction between strong actualization and weak actualization below under the heading "God's Ideal and Remedial Wills."

56. Something like this approach might be entertained by those whose primary concern is divine sovereignty, including those open to some form of deviant Calvinism with a robust conception of creaturely freedom. See Crisp, *Deviant Calvinism*; Crisp, *Saving Calvinism*. See also, however, Richard A. Muller's case that there is more complexity in modern Reformed thought (not to mention earlier philosophical and theological traditions) than the compatibilism-versus-libertarianism distinction encapsulates. Muller, *Divine Will and Human Choice*, 31.

57. This is so because God would causally determine the occurrence of his actual desires, and counterfactual desires would contradict either that which he voluntarily determined or his own nature.

4. If humans sometimes will otherwise than God desires, then, compatibilistic determinism is not true (from 2 and 3).

5. Therefore, compatibilistic determinism is not true (from 1 and 4).

Further:

6. If humans sometimes will otherwise than God desires, then humans are free to will otherwise than God desires (on at least some occasions).

7. If humans are free to will otherwise than God desires (on at least some occasions), then human wills are free in some theologically indeterministic manner.

8. Therefore, human wills are free in some theologically indeterministic manner (from 1, 6, and 7).

Based on the argument above, the biblical evidence of unfulfilled divine desires confirms that (at least some) humans (at some times) have libertarian free will, minimally defined as free will that is incompatible with causal determinism such that humans may will otherwise than God desires.

What Kind and Extent of Free Will?

Notably, the model set forth here maintains only that some humans have exercised some kind of free will that is incompatible with theological determinism. It does not specify which incompatibilist account of free will must be maintained (e.g., leeway, sourcehood), and the theodicy of love set forth in this book does not hinge on one's preference in this regard. However, this model does posit that God *consistently*, rather than selectively, grants libertarian free will to free agents—that is, God consistently refrains from causally determining humans to will as he desires.[58] This supposition is based on the view that God desires genuine love relationship with creatures, which requires consistently granted free will. This model holds that love, by nature, must be freely given, freely received, and freely maintained.

58. Notably, even in OT narratives such as those of Balaam and Jonah, we find evidence that God is not causally determining human wills. For instance, if God was determining Balaam's will, it does not seem to make sense that Balaam angered God by trying to curse Israel after God told him not to (e.g., Num. 22:12, 22) or that Balaam later provided Balak with a successful plan to lead Israel into corruption (Num. 31:16; cf. Rev. 2:14). Similarly, if God controlled Jonah's will, he could have made Jonah go directly to Nineveh in the first place. Both cases include strong divine interventions, but the wills of the prophets themselves do not seem to have been determined by God.

Does Love Require Libertarian Free Will?

If libertarian freedom is by nature a necessary condition of *genuine* love, then even God could not make it otherwise. Why should a Christian theist accept this view, however? There are many reasons beyond those that I can briefly adduce here, which I have offered elsewhere in more expansive treatments on the love of God.[59] For our purposes here, I offer just two lines of evidence.

First, Scripture consistently depicts love as freely given and freely received. God himself loves freely (e.g., Hosea 14:4) and commands humans to love him and others in a way that indicates they can do so freely.[60] To take just one prominent depiction, *hesed* (steadfast lovingkindness) is always freely given in Scripture but also creates expectations of free reciprocation.[61] In this regard and others, Scripture consistently treats love as a matter of covenantal faithfulness in a way that requires moral responsibility and freedom.[62]

Second, one relatively straightforward way to arrive at the conclusion that love requires freedom runs parallel to the earlier arguments relative to God's unfulfilled desires. Put simply, the fact that God *actually* desires love relationship with free creatures who are capable of love *as an end in itself* but does not enjoy love relationship with all such free creatures indicates that love relationship cannot be determined by God.[63] The reasoning runs as follows:

9. If God *actually* desires (as defined above) that everyone love him as an ultimate end in itself, and if it is logically possible for God to causally determine that everyone love him, then he would causally determine that everyone love him.

10. God actually desires that everyone love him as an ultimate end in itself.

11. Some do not love God.

12. Therefore, God does not causally determine that everyone love him (from 9, 10, and 11).

13. Therefore, it is not logically possible for God to causally determine that everyone love him (from 9, 10, and 12).

---

59. See Peckham, *Love of God*; Peckham, *Concept of Divine Love*.

60. E.g., Deut. 6:5; 11:13; 13:3; Matt. 23:37.

61. On *hesed*, see Peckham, *Concept of Divine Love*, 300–319; Peckham, *Love of God*, 81–86. Relative to other lines of evidence, see Peckham, *Concept of Divine Love*, 204–35, 372–99, 577–82; Peckham, *Love of God*, 89–115, 257–63.

62. Here I mean "covenantal" in the broad sense relative to a bilateral agreement.

63. As Vincent Brümmer states, "Love is by definition free." Brümmer, *Model of Love*, 175. Eleonore Stump adds, regarding the "mutual love," that God desires with humans: "What is mutual cannot be produced unilaterally." Stump, *Wandering in the Darkness*, 138.

If God actually desires what he commands in the great love command-ments, we can be confident that premise 10 is true. Not only does Christ des-ignate love as the greatest commandment (Matt. 22:38) and thus an ultimate end, but also "God is love" (1 John 4:8, 16), and Paul places love at the top of the taxonomy of values that he lists.[64]

Genuine Love Requires Epistemic and Consequential Freedom

If it is not logically possible for God to causally determine that everyone love him, then the love relationship God desires requires libertarian freedom. Further, the kind of libertarian freedom necessary for love to be freely given and freely received by finite beings entails epistemic freedom—that is, freedom with regard to what one believes and does not believe.

For finite beings, love relationship involves faith and trust, which involve one's epistemic faculties.[65] Further, love relationship is bound up with what one thinks about the object of love. Genuine love, then, is not only volitional but also evaluative and emotional; it takes account of, and is affected by, the other. If this is so (as I have argued extensively elsewhere), then the totality of what we "think" about God—volitionally, evaluatively, and emotionally—governs whether and to what extent we love him.[66] This would explain why God shows such great concern for his name throughout Scripture.[67]

If what we think about God governs whether and to what extent we love him, then God could not causally determine what humans think about him without undermining the freedom necessary for love. This conclusion might explain why creaturely epistemic freedom is emphasized in many biblical passages, not least at the outset of Genesis, wherein Eve possesses epistemic freedom to believe God or the serpent (Gen. 3:1–6).[68]

Further, since genuine love relationship entails more than merely mental action, genuine love requires what I call consequential freedom—that is, lib-ertarian freedom to externally effect in the world what one internally wills

---

64. E.g., Rom. 13:8–10; 1 Cor. 13:13; cf. 1 Cor. 13:1–12; 16:14; Col. 3:14; cf. James 2:8; 1 Pet. 4:8; 1 John. The ultimate value of love entails other values essential to love's flourishing, including faithfulness, righteousness, and justice.

65. In human relationships, there is no way for one to be *absolutely certain* that her spouse loves her and will continue loving her. Further, love and faith/trust are closely associated in Scripture. See Peckham, *Concept of Divine Love*, 468, 523–24.

66. See Peckham, *Love of God*, 89–189. Accordingly, the greatest commandment is to "love" God "with all" one's heart, soul, mind, and strength (Mark 12:30).

67. See chap. 4.

68. See chap. 4. See also many other texts that suggest epistemic freedom or responsibility (e.g., Num. 14:11; Pss. 14:1–4; 26:1–3; Prov. 3:5–7; Jer. 9:6, 24; 13:25; 14:14–15; John 7:17; 8:24; 10:37; 14:11; Rom. 14:5; 1 John 3:23–24; cf. Exod. 4:1–5, 8–9; 13:17; Dan. 4:32; 5:2).

(to some limited extent). For genuine love relationship to be effective, a *loving partner* in relationship must not negate the link between internal willing and external action. As such, God consistently grants not only freedom to will but also freedom to effect one's will in the world (within noncapricious limits).

Each creature's freedom to affect the world is essentially limited because creatures are not omnipotent, and each person's freedom of external action is unavoidably impinged on by the way others exercise their freedom to affect the world. I am not confident about what degree of consequentiality is required for genuine love relationship, but I am confident that God knows and grants whatever degree is required for the flourishing of love. This conclusion seems to require at least freedom to act within some noncapricious limits in a context where relatively predictable effects follow from causal actions.[69]

Insofar as God grants creatures consequential freedom, God's own freedom is thereby limited. If God makes promises and invariably keeps them, God's action would be morally limited by whatever promises and covenants he has made. As Terence Fretheim states, "For God to promise never to do something again, and to be faithful to that promise, entails self-limitation regarding the exercise of divine freedom and power."[70] From a rather different perspective, Michael Horton adds that God "has bound himself to us . . . by a free decision to enter into covenant with us" such that "God is not free to act contrary to such covenantal guarantees."[71] Insofar as God covenants to grant creaturely freedom, God's own consequential freedom is (morally) self-limited, without in any way limiting God's power itself.[72]

Consider, in this regard, the exponential impact of (at least) billions of free agents exercising consequential freedom. Even small causes can have huge effects. Consider the famous example in chaos theory: the flapping of a butterfly's wing could set off a chain of events that eventually produces a tornado far away (called the "butterfly effect"). Insofar as God respects the consequential freedom of myriad creatures, God's own consequential freedom

---

69. Cf. Michael Murray's conception of "free and effective choice." Murray, *Nature Red in Tooth and Claw*, 136–41. Such free, effective choice requires "nomic regularity"—that is, a "natural order" that "operate[s] by regular and well-ordered laws of nature" (7). This provides the context needed "to form intentions to bring about states in the world" with "reason to believe that by undertaking certain bodily movements we make it likely that those states of the world will come about." (139–40).

70. Fretheim, "Book of Genesis," 1:396.

71. Horton, *Lord and Servant*, 33.

72. As Karl Barth stated, "Loyally binding Himself to this work [of creation, reconciliation and redemption] He does not cease to be omnipotent in Himself as well as in this work." Barth, *CD* II/1:527.

is correspondingly limited, and creaturely decisions have an enormous impact on history.

Providence of Sovereign Love: An Indeterministic Model

With the conception of free will explained earlier in this chapter in mind, we now turn to the concern that libertarian freedom might undermine divine sovereignty, particularly as depicted in Scripture. The defender of divine sovereignty affirms, in Thomas Flint's words, "the traditional theological claim that God is the all-knowing, sovereign, providential lord of the universe."[73] The question for those committed to libertarian free will is whether they can consistently uphold the traditional theological commitment to divine sovereignty at the same time.[74]

The theodicy of love aims to uphold both sets of commitments, positing a providence of sovereign love that not only affirms robust divine sovereignty and special divine action but also accounts for unfulfilled divine desires. Below I outline the core working parts of this model, with an eye toward assuaging the free will defender's concern that divine sovereignty might undercut genuine freedom, and the sovereignty defender's concern that libertarian freedom undercuts divine sovereignty.

God's Ideal and Remedial Wills

This providence of sovereign love explains God's unfulfilled desires, without undermining divine sovereignty, by distinguishing between God's ideal and remedial wills. God's ideal will refers to that which would occur if all agents acted in perfect accordance with God's desires from any point onward. God's remedial will refers to God's will that has already taken into account *all* other factors, including the wills of free creatures, from any point onward.[75]

---

73. Flint, *Divine Providence*, 3.

74. Both claims have a significant foothold in the Christian tradition. Richard Swinburne even believes that "all Christian theologians of the first four centuries believed in human free will in the libertarian sense, as did all subsequent Eastern Orthodox theologians, and most Western Catholic theologians from Duns Scotus (in the fourteenth century) onwards." Swinburne, *Providence and the Problem of Evil*, 35. Cf. Paul Gavrilyuk's claim that "the common core of patristic theodicy" included the view that God "could not be held responsible for the free evil choices that rational creatures made, since God did not causally determine these choices." Gavrilyuk, "Overview of Patristic Theodicies," 6, 4.

75. On the traditional distinction between antecedent and consequent wills, Stump explains, "God's antecedent will is what God would have willed if everything in the world had been up to him alone," and "God's consequent will is what God actually does will, given what God's creatures will." Stump, *Wandering in the Darkness*, 385.

God's remedial will includes not only what God will directly cause but also that which other agents *freely* cause. This corresponds to Plantinga's helpful distinction between "a stronger and a weaker sense of 'actualize.'" He explains that "in the strong sense, God can actualize only what he can cause [by himself] to be actual," whereas weak actualization is that which God actualizes in a way that depends on the free decisions of others.[76]

For our purposes, relative to divine agency, let strong actualization refer to cases where God's causation alone brings about some event or state of affairs, and let weak actualization refer to cases where God's causation along with that of some other free agent (or agents) brings about some event or state of affairs. Given these definitions, any occurrence that depends on the libertarian free decisions of others cannot be strongly actualized by God; whether God can weakly actualize any such occurrence depends on those libertarian decisions of others.

Anything caused directly by God, without the contribution of another free agent, is strongly actualized. God might weakly actualize some state of affairs, however, by directly causing some things that he knows, together with the contributions of other free agents, will bring about that state of affairs.

Affirming Exhaustive Definite Foreknowledge

The distinctions between ideal and remedial wills and strong and weak actualization are closely related to divine foreknowledge. In order for God's remedial will to take into account *all* other factors, God must have knowledge of what free creatures *would* do. Although a basic free will defense can be affirmed without it, I believe a model of exhaustive and complex foreknowledge best accounts for the biblical data as a whole.[77]

Whereas some who reject exhaustive definite foreknowledge argue that it is logically impossible that God could know the future (libertarian) free decisions of agents, there is no apparent logical or ontological incompatibility between the assertion that God knows the future exhaustively and that humans possess libertarian free will. The intuition that there is some contradiction between them depends on the fallacy of confusing necessity of consequence with necessity of the thing consequent—that is, it confuses the

---

76. Plantinga, *Nature of Necessity*, 173.

77. E.g., Ps. 139:16; Isa. 41:21–24; 44:28–45:1; 46:9–11; Mark 14:13–15, 27–30; John 13:18–19; Acts 2:23; 15:16–18; Rom. 8:29–30; Eph. 1:9–11. It is beyond this book's scope to address the various interpretations of Scripture on this topic, but I believe the biblical material overwhelmingly supports exhaustive definite foreknowledge, especially via passages regarding God's determinate plan or purpose. See the discussion in Peckham, *Doctrine of God*. On the objections of open theism, see chap. 6 in the present volume.

necessity that whatever God believes will come to pass with the claim that whatever God believes will *necessarily* come to pass. The former is true but the latter is false.[78]

Although divine omniscience entails that God cannot hold incorrect beliefs, God's belief about what an agent will do does not determine or necessitate what that agent does. To refute the oft-cited claim that God's belief that Jones will mow his lawn on Saturday entails that Jones could not do otherwise than mow his lawn on Saturday, one need only affirm the additional premise that if Jones were to do otherwise than mow his lawn on Saturday, God would not have believed that Jones would mow his lawn on Saturday.[79]

In order to affirm *that* God knows the future free decisions of creatures, I need not claim to know *how* he does so (any more than I need to know *how* God is omnipotent, eternal, and so on). I need only be able to affirm that God does so without any actual contradiction. Having said that, I do think God has "hypothetical" or "middle knowledge," meaning that God knows not only what any creature *might* do but also what any creature *would* do in any given circumstance.[80] This kind of counterfactual knowledge appears to be supported by numerous biblical passages.[81]

If God knows what any creature *would* freely do in any given circumstance, then God could factor such knowledge into his own decisions. By "adding" his own decisions to his knowledge of what any creature would do (along with his knowledge of all other factors), God can know and indeterministically plan the entire history of the world.[82] Something like this might be indicated by

---

78. As Plantinga explains, "*If I know that Henry is a bachelor, then Henry is a bachelor* is a necessary truth," but "it does not follow that [it] is necessarily true" that "Henry is a bachelor." Plantinga, *God, Freedom, and Evil*, 67.

79. Plantinga, *God, Freedom, and Evil*, 67–73. Cf. Pike, "Divine Omniscience and Voluntary Action."

80. What an agent would do in some given circumstance is often called a "would counterfactual" or a "counterfactual of creaturely freedom." For an introduction to middle knowledge, see Flint, *Divine Providence*, 11–71. See also Perszyk, *Molinism*.

81. E.g., 1 Sam. 23:8–13; Matt. 11:23; 1 Cor. 2:8; cf. Exod. 3:19. Whereas such texts may show only counterfactual knowledge of human decisions without indicating whether such decisions are (indeterministically) free, such evidence coupled with a persuasive case for indeterminism provides evidence for middle knowledge. One might also argue that omniscience entails that God knows whether any given proposition is true or false, including propositions regarding what any agent would do.

82. This complex account of foreknowledge is not affected by commitments to any particular Molinist system but tentatively affirms the minimal concept of indeterministic hypothetical or middle knowledge. Yet, the main elements of the theodicy offered here do not depend on acceptance of middle knowledge. Notably, Plantinga arrived at his conception of this independently from Luis de Molina, the sixteenth-century Spanish theologian after whom the Molinist theory of middle knowledge is named. Plantinga, "Self-Profile," 50.

the sequence in Romans 8:29–30: "For those whom [God] foreknew, He also predestined to become conformed to the image of His Son, so that He would be the firstborn among many brethren; and these whom He predestined, He also called; and these whom He called, He also justified; and these whom He justified, He also glorified" (cf. 1 Pet. 1:1–2).

On my reading of this passage, God foreknows the future free decisions of creatures, *then* "predestines" or "plans" what will occur by deciding what he will do in a way that takes account of creaturely free decisions, and then providentially executes this plan in history via strong and weak actualization.[83]

If God possesses middle knowledge, why does he not use it to actualize only those creatures who would always freely choose good? Recall that, given indeterminism, God cannot actualize just any world he desires. In an indeterministic world that operates according to some established order of cause and effect, which appears to be necessary for consequential freedom of the kind necessary for love, the actualization of any creature is bound up with countless antecedent factors (including the decisions of any ancestors) and holds potentially enormous ramifications for future events (particularly given the butterfly effect).[84]

Given this complexity, even though we might think it would be simple for God to, say, make it such that some brutal dictator was never born, we have no idea whether that option was available to God without ramifications that were worse *in the end* (that is, with regard to the entirety of history—including all future states of affairs). It might be that all other worlds that God could (weakly) actualize, inclusive of the free decisions of creatures, were worse *overall* or less desirable than this one. Other possibilities in this regard will be discussed in chapter 6. For now, suffice it to say that I believe God actualizes the most preferable world available, given his commitment to love.

Testing the Accounts

Something like the model above is vital to adequately treating all that Scripture says with regard to God's foreknowledge, God's providence, and human freedom. This includes instances of God's unfulfilled desires on the one hand and, on the other, the many strong statements of divine providence—such as, God "does whatever He pleases" (Ps. 115:3; cf. 135:6). This approach to

83. Although this passage can be read otherwise—e.g., "also" might be understood other than sequentially (logically or otherwise)—I take this to be the best reading in both the immediate and wider canonical context.

84. Consider, e.g., the (counterfactual) cases of George Bailey in the film *It's a Wonderful Life* and Marty McFly in the film *Back to the Future*.

providence is in contrast to others that emphasize free will or divine sovereignty at the expense of the other.

On the one hand, the free will defender worries that determinism makes God culpable for all evil in the world and cannot do justice to the vast biblical material that depicts creaturely free will and God's unfulfilled desires, including striking depictions of divine sorrow and relenting (e.g., Gen. 6:6; Jer. 18:7–10). On the other hand, sovereignty defenders worry that libertarian free will undermines God's sovereignty and cannot adequately account for biblical assertions such as that Christ was "delivered over by the predetermined plan and foreknowledge of God" (Acts 2:23) and that God

> declar[ed] the end from the beginning,
>> And from ancient times things which have not been done,
> Saying, "My purpose will be established,
>> And I will accomplish all My good pleasure." (Isa. 46:10)

Because this model of providence affirms that God's remedial will already takes account of the free decisions of creatures via complex foreknowledge, it can coherently affirm that God "predestined" or planned all things "according to His purpose" and "works all things after the counsel of His will" (Eph. 1:11). This model simply understands God's "will" and "purpose" in this context to be God's *remedial* will and purpose, which already includes creaturely decisions that depart from God's ideal will. The phrase here that God "works all things after the counsel of His [remedial] will" is compatible with the fact that some creatures reject God's ideal will, such as when "the Pharisees and the lawyers rejected God's purpose [*boulē*] for themselves" (Luke 7:30; cf. Isa. 66:4; Matt. 23:37).

Further, instead of claiming either that God did not actually harden Pharaoh's heart as Scripture portrays (e.g., Exod. 9:12) or that Pharaoh was not genuinely the source of hardening his own heart as Scripture also portrays (e.g., 8:15, 32), this model might suggest that Pharaoh exercised libertarian free will as the genuine source of hardening his own heart while God also acted in some ways that weakly actualized this outcome without violating Pharaoh's free will. In this and other instances, God is not passive. He not only permits what others freely will but also takes his own actions, greatly affecting the results in history without infringing on the will of the free agent.

This model can likewise account for instances wherein God is deeply grieved and displeased (e.g., Hosea 11:8–9), including instances of divine sorrow and relenting (e.g., Gen. 6:6; 1 Sam. 15:11; Jer. 18:7–10). On this account, God is genuinely sorrowful over evil and regrets that it has occurred, but he does not regret what he himself has done, since the evil that occurred was not up to him, given his commitment to the consequential freedom requisite to love.[85]

Consider one final example. Scripture affirms both that God was "pleased [*hapets*] / To crush Him [the Messiah]" (Isa. 53:10; cf. Gen. 3:15) and that God has no "pleasure" [*hapets*] in the death of anyone (Ezek. 18:23, 32; 33:11) and "does not afflict willingly" (Lam. 3:33). On this model, God did not ideally desire or sadistically take pleasure in the excruciating suffering of the Son, but it was God's "pleasure" or (remedial) will in the wider context of the plan of salvation. Accordingly, Christ desired to avoid the cross, if it were "possible" (Matt. 26:39), but he desired to save humans more and thus "for the joy set before Him endured the cross" (Heb. 12:2).

Whereas determinism does not adequately account for God's unfulfilled desires in Scripture, and some indeterminist approaches cannot account for strong biblical statements of God's providence, the distinction between God's ideal and remedial wills allows both streams of texts to speak without muting either. On this view, God indeed "does whatever he pleases" (Ps. 115:3; cf. 135:6), but he is not always pleased by what occurs because part of what pleases him is to respect, for the sake of love, the free decisions of creatures, which often displease him. God's ideal desires are often unfulfilled, but he will nevertheless bring about his ultimate (remedial) purpose.

This understanding itself reveals a minimal working definition of evil that is implicit throughout Scripture. Evil is that which is opposed to God's (ideal) desires (cf. Ps. 5:4).[86] Broadly speaking, the biblical terminology of evil refers to that which is undesirable from some vantage point, whether or not it is morally wrong or unjust.[87] Since God's vantage point alone is comprehensive and infallible, that which is undesirable in God's view provides the absolute

---

85. See chap. 6 in the present volume; Peckham, *Love of God*, 153–55, 185; Peckham, *Concept of Divine Love*, 266–68.

86. This *minimal* definition does not mean that evil is reducible to that which opposes God's ideal desires.

87. E.g., David W. Baker speaks of the primary OT root translated "evil" (*ra'a'*) as "a uniting into one word of what in English is expressed by two words, physical (bad) and moral (evil)." "*ra'a'*," *NIDOTTE* 3:1155. Sometimes, Baker says, "the evaluation expressed by the word is relative, as, for example, when something is 'bad in the eyes (opinion) of someone' (Gen. 28:8; Exod. 21:8; Num. 22:34; Josh. 24:15; Jer. 40:4) . . . in implicit contrast to the only truly absolute standard, the good in the eyes of God (cf. Deut. 6:18; 12:25)." On a canonical reading, those texts that attribute *ra'a'* to God (Ps. 44:2; Isa. 45:7; Jer. 25:29; 31:28; Mic. 4:6; Zech. 8:14) are not attributing moral wrongdoing to him (which would contradict other texts, such as Hab. 1:13) but use *ra'a'* in the sense of disciplinary calamity/affliction, undesirable from the perspective of those experiencing judgment but not *morally* evil.

standard of what is evil; what God considers morally undesirable is morally wrong.[88]

This understanding of evil illuminates the deep connection between love, free will, and the necessary possibility of evil. If love requires libertarian freedom such that humans may will otherwise than God desires, and if evil is that which is opposed to God's (ideal) desires, then love requires the *possibility* of evil. However, evil need not have been actualized. God's ideal desire (for love) would have been fulfilled if no creature had ever actualized evil, but since love requires libertarian freedom, the actualization of his ideal desire was not up to God alone.[89]

Whereas God cannot actualize just any world he desires, God is not passive in the events of history but actively and strongly works in ways that best achieve his ultimate purpose of love's flourishing. God can and does intervene and work miracles, strongly actualizing many events while also respecting the consequential freedom of creatures that is necessary for love. God is always active to bring about his remedial will or purpose, which is the most preferable outcome that God can actualize while upholding his moral commitments for the sake of love.[90]

This model of providence of sovereign love thus offers a coherent account of God's unfulfilled desires alongside a robust account of divine sovereignty and foreknowledge, affirming both that God prefers that no evil ever occur *and* that God's purpose ultimately triumphs.[91] God does not always get what he wants (his ideal will), yet God will certainly accomplish his all-encompassing providential purpose (his remedial will).

Are Love and Free Will Sufficient to Account for Evil in This World?

The question remains whether God's granting and respecting the kind and extent of free will necessary for love accounts for the kind and amount of evil in this world. It seems that an omnipotent God could have thwarted many evils that occur without in any way damaging free will. To revisit a previous example, it does not seem that the kind of free will necessary for love would

---

88. This is not to say that if God desired some evil *x* that *x* would cease to be evil, but, rather, it presupposes that God desires only what is congruent with his perfect character.

89. Hart notes that "an indispensable condition of what [God] wills is the real power of the creature's deliberative will to resist [God's] work of grace." Hart, "Providence," 47.

90. As Stump puts it, "Many of the things that happen in the world are not in accordance with God's antecedent will." What God "wills in his consequent will, what is the best available in the circumstances, might be only the lesser of evils, not the intrinsically good." Stump, *Wandering in the Darkness*, 428.

91. Cf. Bruce R. Reichenbach's helpful treatment in his *Divine Providence* of how divine sovereignty, creaturely freedom, and love might interrelate.

by itself prevent God from specially revealing to law enforcement just enough information to thwart the attacks of 9/11. Given the many instances of special revelation in Scripture, it cannot be that such revelation by itself undermines the kind of free will necessary for love. Whereas some degree of epistemic freedom is required for love, humans typically experience far more epistemic distance from God than appears to be necessary for genuine love relationship.

Love requires some degree of consequential freedom. Nevertheless, according to John K. Roth, "our freedom is both too much and too little"—too much in that humans can commit so many atrocities, and too little in that humans who would prevent such evils (and others) if they could, very often lack the ability to do so.[92] If God could reveal things in dreams to Nebuchadnezzar and strip Nebuchadnezzar of his "sovereignty" and make him live like a beast for seven years (Dan. 4:31–34), could not God also have stripped power from other brutal dictators of history?[93]

Critics such as J. L. Schellenberg and others have argued that supposing God is love actually exacerbates the problems of evil and divine hiddenness.[94] God often appears to be hidden from those who cry out to him, but would not any good parent respond to the calls of their distressed young child if they could? As Thomas Jay Oord puts it, "Loving parents prevent evil when they can."[95]

Even if love itself is valuable enough to function as the morally sufficient reason for God's allowance of evil, the kind and extent of free will necessary for love, by itself, does not appear to be able to account for the amount and kind of evil in this world.[96] Toward addressing this significant problem, the following chapters look to the wider context of the God-world relationship, expositing a cosmic dispute over divine love that provides a larger framework toward understanding why God might justly permit *so much* evil.

Conclusion

This chapter addressed the question of whether there is any good reason for a Christian theist to suppose that God grants libertarian freedom to creatures

92. Roth, "Theodicy of Protest," 9.

93. Lest one think the Nebuchadnezzar incident is inherently deterministic, the fact that the king was stricken "until" he would "recognize" God as ruler (Dan. 4:32) indicates that Nebuchadnezzar retained some degree of epistemic freedom.

94. See Schellenberg, *Hiddenness Argument*.

95. Oord, *Uncontrolling Love of God*, 135.

96. Robert M. Adams avers that "the necessity of permitting some evil in order to have free will may play a part in a theodicy but cannot bear the whole weight of it." R. Adams, "Middle Knowledge," 125.

and the ramifications of such a view for divine sovereignty. Biblical accounts of God's unfulfilled desires provide evidence that humans can will otherwise than God desires, thus supporting a minimal conception of libertarian freedom. Further, this chapter made a corresponding case that genuine love relationship requires consistently granted epistemic and consequential freedom.

Toward addressing the worries of free will defenders and sovereignty defenders alike, the chapter outlined a providence of sovereign love that distinguishes between God's ideal and remedial wills and strong and weak actualization, thus accounting for creaturely freedom and God's many unfulfilled desires while maintaining a robust account of divine sovereignty and foreknowledge such that God will ultimately achieve his (remedial) purpose.

By itself, this account of the kind and extent of free will necessary for love does not seem to account for God's allowance of the amount and kind of evil in this world. Toward addressing this, the next chapter introduces the wider context of a cosmic conflict over God's love.

3

The Cosmic Conflict Framework

The previous chapters have explored the relationship of love, free will, and evil—particularly in light of God's unfulfilled desires—suggesting that God permits evil for the sake of love. However, by itself, free will of the kind and extent necessary does not appear to account for God's allowance of the kind and amount of evil in this world. Could not God could grant us free will sufficient for love without allowing such horrendous evils? Would not a God of love do at least as much as a good parent would to mitigate or even eliminate horrendous evils?

Whereas many approaches to such questions have been offered, most have neglected the prominent biblical theme of conflict between the true God and false gods or demons. Perhaps the main reason for this relative neglect is the supposed implausibility of such a conflict. Although the vast majority of Christians throughout the ages have believed in a conflict between God and demonic agencies, since the rise of Enlightenment modernism this view has often been dismissed or overlooked. Further, some wonder how any such conflict could be compatible with the omnipotence and sovereignty of God.

In order to address whether and how such a conflict might provide significant insights into the problem of evil, we must first understand the framework and the nature of the cosmic conflict as depicted in Scripture. Accordingly, this chapter offers an introductory survey of the framework of the cosmic conflict, followed in the next chapter by a discussion of the nature of this conflict and its ramifications for the problem of evil.

Introducing the Cosmic Conflict

An Enemy Has Done This

If God is sovereign and omnipotent, isn't he ultimately to blame for the evil in this world? If not, who is (see Job 9:24)? Scripture depicts evil as the work of an enemy of God. In Christ's words, "An enemy has done this!" (Matt. 13:28). This understanding appears in Christ's parable of the wheat and the tares, wherein a landowner sows *only* good seeds in his field. However, tares spring up among the wheat, prompting the owner's servants to ask, "Sir, did you not sow good seed in your field? How then does it have tares?" (v. 27). This parallels the question so many ask today: If God is the sovereign creator of this world, why is there evil in it?[1]

To this the master replies, "An enemy has done this!" The servants then ask, "Do you want us, then, to go and gather them up?" (Matt. 13:28). Their question parallels the question many ask today: Why not eradicate evil immediately? "No," the master replies, "for while you are gathering up the tares, you may uproot the wheat with them. Allow both to grow together until the harvest" (vv. 29–30; cf. Mark 4:29). Later Christ explains that he is "the one who shows the good seed" (v. 37), that "the field is the world," that "the good seed" are "the sons of the kingdom," that "the tares are the sons of the evil one," and that "the enemy who sowed them is the devil" (vv. 38–39).[2]

Here Christ explicitly depicts a conflict between himself and the devil, who sows evil and sets God up to be blamed for it. Such devil-sown evil is temporarily *allowed* because to prematurely uproot evil (tares) would result in irreversible collateral damage to the good (wheat). As John Nolland comments, the tares "are to be removed with as much urgency as is consistent with the protection of all the wheat."[3]

For some good reason, the enemy must be allowed to work—the wheat and tares must be allowed to temporarily grow together—in order for evil to *finally* be defeated while minimizing collateral damage. "Though Satan's interference is an affront to God," writes Nolland, "he will not act decisively yet to root out the problem" lest the "good seed" be "disturbed." Eventually "what has been sown by Satan is to be rooted out and destroyed."[4] In this regard, W. D. Davies and Dale C. Allison Jr. comment that "the parable of the tares addresses the

---

1. Donald A. Hagner states that the people's "immediate, natural reaction" is "to wonder about the continuing presence of evil in the world." Hagner, *Matthew 1–13*, 382.

2. The "reapers" are "angels," who thus play some intermediate role in judgment.

3. Nolland, *Matthew*, 546.

4. Nolland, *Matthew*, 547. Nolland adds that the "figure of 'his enemy' suggests that standing feud is involved" (544).

question of theodicy by putting evil in eschatological perspective, by reminding one that the bad endures only for a season" but that "it shall not always be so."[5]

As we've observed, the servants' two questions raise issues of theodicy that are often voiced today: (1) If God is good, why is there evil in the world? (2) Why does God allow so much evil rather than eradicating it immediately?[6] The minimal responses given by Christ in Matthew 13 resonate throughout Scripture: (1) "An enemy has done this," and (2) the premature uprooting of evil would also uproot the good.

As Davies and Allison note, this parable evinces "a wider problem, namely, the cosmic struggle between God and Satan."[7] Grant R. Osborne adds, "In this world the war between good and evil cannot be avoided, and there is no middle ground. One either belongs to the kingdom [of God] or the powers of evil, and the two forces exist side by side in this world."[8]

The cosmic conflict framework set forth here by Christ raises many questions about its nature, including how there could be any conflict if God is omnipotent and why God would allow so much suffering. These issues are taken up in the following chapters, after we've seen the broad contours of the cosmic conflict, wherein, as N. T. Wright comments, "God's sovereign rule over the world isn't quite such a straightforward thing as people sometimes imagine."[9]

The Temptation of Christ

The cosmic conflict summarized in Matthew 13 is especially prominent throughout the Gospels. At the outset of his ministry, "Jesus was led up by the Spirit into the wilderness to be tempted by the devil" (Matt. 4:1). After Jesus fasts for forty days, "the tempter" comes and tempts Jesus three times. First, the devil tempts Jesus to assuage his hunger by turning stones into bread (v. 3). Second, he challenges Jesus to throw himself from the "pinnacle of the temple" to test God's promised protection via angels (vv. 5–6). Third, "the devil took Him to a very high mountain and showed Him all the kingdoms of the world and their glory." He tempts Jesus, saying, "All these things I will give You, if You fall down and worship me" (vv. 8–9; cf. Luke 4:6–7).

This last temptation highlights two prominent themes of the cosmic conflict. First, the devil desires and seeks to usurp worship (cf. Rev. 13:4); second,

5. Davies and Allison, *Matthew 8–18*, 431.
6. These questions correspond, somewhat, to the logical and evidential problems of evil.
7. Davies and Allison, *Matthew 8–18*, 431. Further, the "'sons of the evil one' helps underline the power of the devil in the world" (428).
8. Osborne, *Matthew*, 533.
9. Wright, *Matthew for Everyone*, 168.

Satan claims to have the jurisdiction to give Christ "all the kingdoms of the world and their glory" (Matt. 4:8–9). In Luke's parallel account, the devil states, "I will give you all this domain and its glory; for it has been handed over to me, and I give it to whomever I wish" (Luke 4:6). Joel B. Green comments, "We discover that the world of humanity is actually ruled by the devil."[10]

The narrative further indicates that the temptations are set up according to particular parameters known by both sides. Jesus is "led up by the Spirit" in order "to be tempted by the devil" (Matt. 4:1). Jesus fasts for forty days; the angels refrain from ministering to Jesus until after the conflict is over (v. 11). And after "the devil had finished every temptation, he left Him until an opportune time [*kairos*]" (Luke 4:13; cf. Matt. 8:29; Rev. 12:12). In this striking conflict, Satan is allowed to antagonize Christ at a set time and place and within established parameters. This is one of many instances that evince what I call "rules of engagement" that govern the conflict between the two parties, which are explained further in chapter 4. Here and elsewhere, as R. T. France notes, the devil "is understood to have real power in the present age," though it is restricted within limits.[11]

The Enemy of God: A Profile of Satan in the New Testament

The New Testament depicts the devil as the archenemy of God and his people. Revelation describes this creature as "the great dragon," "the serpent of old who is called the devil and Satan, who deceives the whole world," and the "accuser of our brethren" (Rev. 12:9–10; cf. 20:2; Gen. 3:1–5). These verses serve to summarize Scripture's depiction of Satan as the original

accuser and slanderer[12]

deceiver and tempter of the whole world from the beginning,[13] and

usurping ruler of this world[14]

Below I treat each of these depictions in order.

10. J. Green, *Luke*, 194. François Bovon notes that the devil is "saying that God has given him the political authority over the kingdoms of this world." Bovon, *Luke 1:1–9:50*, 143. Cf. Deut. 32:8–9, discussed below. Although some think the devil is bluffing, Nolland comments, "The reality of this influence of Satan is not to be doubted" but is "co-extensive with the influence of evil." Nolland, *Luke 1:1–9:20*, 180. Millard Erickson concurs, noting, "Satan actually is the ruler of this domain," though a "usurper." Erickson, *Christian Theology*, 588.

11. France, *Matthew*, 135.

12. Rev. 12:10; 13:6; cf. Job 1–2; Zech. 3:1–2; Jude 9.

13. Matt. 4:3; Rev. 12:9; cf. John 8:44; Acts 5:3; 2 Cor. 11:3; 1 John 3:8; Rev. 2:10.

14. John 12:31; 14:30; 16:11; cf. Matt. 12:24–29; Luke 4:5–6; Acts 26:18; 2 Cor. 4:4; Eph. 2:2; 1 John 5:19.

The Diabolical Adversary, Accuser, and Slanderer

In the NT, "Satan" (*satanas*) basically means adversary,[15] and "devil" (*diabolos*) basically means "slanderer."[16] The devil is repeatedly called the "evil one,"[17] and Christ's work of redemption is repeatedly framed as against this adversary. According to Hebrews 2:14, Christ "partook" of "flesh and blood" so "that through death He might render powerless him who had the power of death, that is, the devil" (cf. John 12:31–32; Rev. 12:9–11).[18] Likewise, 1 John 3:8 explains, "The Son of God appeared for this purpose, to destroy the works of the devil."

Satan is not an equal or eternal force against God. Colossians 1:16 rules out any hint of eternal cosmic dualism, declaring that by Christ "all things were created, both in the heavens and on earth, visible and invisible, whether thrones or dominions or rulers or authorities—all things have been created

15. H. Bietenhard, "Satan, Beelzebul, Devil, Exorcism," *NIDNTT* 3:468; L&N, 144, 829. The noun *satanas* appears thirty-six times in thirty-three verses in the NT, being used "only as a title or name" (BDAG, 916) and most often (twenty-nine times in twenty-seven verses) with the article, which always refers to the devil. Without the article, *satanas* appears in six verses, all of which also appear to refer to the devil (with the possible exception of the address to Peter). These include three instances of personal address (in the vocative): Jesus's command, "Go, Satan!" (Matt. 4:10) and the rebuke to Peter, "Get behind Me, Satan!" (Matt. 16:23; Mark 8:33). The other three are Mark 3:23; Luke 22:3; 2 Cor. 12:7. The noun *satanas* appears only once in the LXX Apocrypha in reference to a human adversary (Sir. 21:27), and *satan* appears twice in 1 Kings 11:14 (never in the NT) in reference to human adversaries.

16. Bietenhard, *NIDNTT* 3:468; L&N, 144. In the NT, *diabolos* appears thirty-seven times in thirty-five verses. It appears thirty-one times with the article to describe *the* devil as, among other things, a false accuser, slanderer, usurping ruler, and enemy. *Diabolos* appears once without the article (Rev. 20:2), but it is capitalized: "the devil [*Diabolos*] and Satan [*ho Satanas*]." It appears once in a genitive construction preceded by a vocative, addressing Elymas the magician as "full of all deceit and fraud, you son of the devil [*huie diabolou*], you enemy of all righteousness" (Acts 13:10). Elsewhere, *diabolos* appears without the article referring to Judas (John 6:70) and to "malicious gossips" (1 Tim. 3:11; 2 Tim. 3:3; Titus 2:3).

LXX translators use *diabolos* twenty times in eighteen verses. Fifteen instances include the article and translate *satan* as *hasatan*, which depicts an adversarial accuser in the heavenly council (Job 1:6, 7 [twice], 9, 12 [twice]; 2:1, 2 [twice], 3, 4, 6, 7; Zech. 3:1–2). One instance is a vocative in direct address (Zech. 3:2), two instances are without the article and are translated as *satan* (1 Chron. 21:1; Ps. 108:6 LXX), and two instances are without the article of Haman (translated as *tsar* and *tsorer*, Esther 7:4; 8:1). It also appears twice in the LXX Apocrypha without the article, once in reference to a human adversary (1 Macc. 1:36 NRSV) and once saying, "Through the devil's envy death entered the world" (Wis. 2:24 NRSV). The word *diabolē* never appears in the NT and appears only twice in the LXX OT in reference to the "angel of the LORD" (Num. 22:32) and to the "slander of a strange tongue" (Prov. 6:24), but it appears eight times in the LXX Apocrypha.

17. Matt. 13:19, 38; John 17:15; Eph. 6:16; 2 Thess. 3:3; 1 John 2:13–14; 3:12; 5:18–19; cf. Matt. 5:37.

18. Notably Wis. 2:23–24 states, "God created us for incorruption," yet "through the devil's envy death entered the world" (NRSV; cf. 1:13).

through Him and for Him" (cf. 1 Chron. 16:25–26).[19] Although the NT does not clearly describe the devil's origin, it explicitly teaches that God is the creator of everything that is not God (e.g., John 1:1–3) such that the devil must be a created being.

The devil opposes Christ by slandering God's character, continually raising accusations against God's people and, consequently, God's moral government. As seen earlier, the devil sowed the bad seeds in Christ's field (Matt. 13:39) yet turns around and accuses and slanders God and his people. Revelation 12:10 depicts him as something like a malignant prosecuting attorney, calling him the "accuser of our brethren" who "accuses them before our God day and night." In this vein, Jude 9 presents a striking example wherein the devil "disputed" and "argued" with "Michael the archangel" over "the body of Moses" (Jude 9; cf. Job 1–2; Zech. 3:1–2).[20]

Further, 1 Peter 5:8 depicts "the devil" as our "adversary" (*antidikos*)—a term often used of one's opponent in court (Matt. 5:25; Luke 12:58; 18:3)—who "prowls around like a roaring lion, seeking someone to devour" (cf. Gen. 4:7). Not only does Satan slander and oppose God but he also works through other agencies to do so. For instance, the devil "gave his authority to the beast" and "a mouth speaking arrogant words and blasphemies," and the beast "opened his mouth in blasphemies against God, to blaspheme His name and His tabernacle" (Rev. 13:4–6; cf. 2 Thess. 2:4, 9).

The Deceiver and Tempter

Not only is Satan the slanderous accuser of God and his people but he also is the one who deceived and tempted humans into sin in the beginning. Revelation 12:9 directly alludes to the fall of Adam and Eve in Genesis 3, identifying Satan as the "serpent of old" who "deceives the whole world" (cf. 2 Cor. 11:3; Rev. 20:2) and who, just before his final defeat, will "deceive the nations" once more and "gather them together for war" (Rev. 20:8; cf. 20:10). The devil "sinned from the beginning" (1 John 3:8) and is a "murderer from the beginning" who "does not stand in the truth because there is no truth in him" and "speaks a lie" from "his own nature, for he is a liar and the father of lies" (John 8:44; cf. Rev. 2:9; 3:9; 1 John 2:22). A master of trickery and the arch-deceiver, "Satan disguises himself as an angel of light" (2 Cor. 11:14; cf. 4:4; 11:3; Gal. 1:8).

19. F. F. Bruce comments, "If all things were created by Christ, then those spiritual powers" in Colossians "must have been created by him." Bruce, *Colossians, Philemon, and Ephesians*, 63.

20. Thomas R. Schreiner notes that the "terms used [in Jude 9] suggest a legal dispute over Moses' body" and "allude to Zechariah 3," which is "another incident in which Satan attempted to establish the guilt of one of Yahweh's servants." Schreiner, *1, 2 Peter, Jude*, 458.

Closely related to the devil's work as arch-deceiver is his work as "the tempter" (Matt. 4:3; cf. 1 Thess. 3:5). He tempted Jesus,[21] cast people into prison to be "tested" (Rev. 2:10), and tempts married individuals to commit sexual immorality (1 Cor. 7:5). Here and elsewhere, via repeated deceptions and temptations, the devil works to persuade humans to believe wrongly and choose against God's desires. Not only does the devil's activity suggest that humans possess freedom with regard to belief (epistemic freedom), but the devil's free will is also apparent in that he plots and schemes to oppose God and his people (2 Cor. 2:11).[22] The devil has "desires" (John 8:44) and a will of his own that is opposed to God's; indeed, Satan attempts to hold people "captive . . . to do his will" (2 Tim. 2:26).[23] Against such "schemes of the devil," the believer is counseled to put on the "full armor of God" (Eph. 6:11).

Although the devil snatches God's Word from some hearts so they will not believe,[24] puts betrayal in hearts (John 13:2), fills hearts with lies (Acts 5:3), and traps people in his "snare," humans might "come to their senses and escape" (2 Tim. 2:26; cf. 1 Tim. 3:7) and need not "give the devil an opportunity" by anger or otherwise (Eph. 4:27). Believers are thus to "be on the alert" and "resist" the "adversary" (1 Pet. 5:8–9). If resisted by one who submits to God, the devil "will flee" (James 4:7).[25]

The Usurping Dragon Ruler

Satan has a limited and temporary domain wherein he wields significant power and jurisdiction. The NT depicts him as the "great dragon" who is the "ruler" behind earthly kingdoms that oppose God's rule (e.g., John 12:31; Rev. 12:9; 13:2). This "dragon and his angels" waged "war" against God's kingdom, "Michael and his angels" (Rev. 12:7; cf. Matt. 25:41). However, this is no battle between equals; Satan and his angels "were not strong enough, and there was no longer a place found for them in heaven. And the great dragon was thrown down" to "the earth, and his angels were thrown down with him" (Rev. 12:8–9; cf. Luke 11:22). Thus the "accuser of our brethren has been thrown down" (Rev. 12:10). Similarly, Christ declares that he "was watching Satan fall from heaven like lightning" (Luke 10:18). The devil wages war against God's people, "knowing that he has only a short

21. Matt. 4:1; Luke 4:2; cf. Matt. 4:5, 8; Mark 1:13; Luke 4:3.
22. Human freedom, however, is limited and severely affected by sin.
23. This depiction of Satan's will provides evidence of the devil's personhood and meets the minimal definition of libertarian freedom discussed in chap. 2.
24. Luke 8:12; cf. Matt. 13:19; Mark 4:15; John 10:10.
25. Cf. Matt. 4:10–11; 16:23; Mark 8:33; Luke 4:13; 1 Pet. 5:9.

time" (Rev. 12:12). Here and elsewhere, the devil's domain is limited, and he knows of these limits.

The multiheaded dragon (*drakōn*) of Revelation is reminiscent of the multi-headed sea serpent, Leviathan, an enemy of God in the OT, which is translated by the same term (*drakōn*) in the LXX.[26] This dragon opposes God's kingdom in heaven and on earth; he "swept away a third of the stars of heaven and threw them to the earth" (Rev. 12:4; cf. Dan. 8:10), waited to devour the child of the woman (Rev. 12:4), waged war along with his angels against Michael and his angels (v. 7), "persecuted the woman [God's people] who gave birth to the male child [i.e., Christ]," (v. 13; cf. v. 16) and "was enraged with the woman" and "went off to make war with the rest of her children" (v. 17).

This dragon exercises his rule on earth through earthly rulers; "the dragon gave" the beast from the sea (symbolic of earthly rulers or kingdoms) "his power and his throne and great authority" (Rev. 13:2). The earth "worshiped the dragon because he gave his authority to the beast" (v. 4) to blaspheme and "make war with the saints and to overcome them, and authority over every tribe and tongue and nation was given to him" (v. 7; cf. 13:5–6; 2 Thess. 2:3–4, 9–10).

This depiction of Satan's desire for worship and his authority to give authority to earthly kingdoms complements Satan's tempting Jesus to worship him and Satan's claim, "I will give You all this domain and its glory; for it has been handed over to me, and I give it to whomever I wish" (Luke 4:6). Similarly, 1 John 5:19 declares that "the whole world lies in *the power of* the evil one" (cf. 2 Thess. 3:3). Accordingly, the devil is repeatedly called the prince or "ruler [*archōn*] of this world" (John 12:31; 16:11; cf. 14:30; Dan. 10:13).

Further, Jesus identifies Satan as "Beelzebul, the ruler [*archōn*] of the demons," who possesses a "kingdom" (Matt. 12:24–26)[27] and portrays Satan as a "strong man" who must first be bound in order for Jesus to "plunder his house" (Matt. 12:29).[28] There is, then, a significant "dominion [*exousia*] of Satan," opposed to God's dominion (Acts 26:18; cf. Col. 1:13). Within this domain Satan wields his limited but significant power to oppress people. Satan afflicted a woman with "sickness caused by a spirit" (Luke 13:11). Jesus

---

26. Pss. 74:13–14 (LXX 73:13–14); 104:26 (LXX 103:26); cf. Job 26:13; 41:1; Ps. 148:7; Isa. 27:1. The word *drakōn* appears thirteen times in twelve verses in the NT, all in Revelation and always in reference to the devil—except once in reference to the sea beast who spoke "as a dragon" (Rev. 13:11).

27. Cf. Matt. 9:34; Mark 3:22–26; Luke 11:15–20.

28. Cf. Mark 3:27; Luke 11:21–22; Rev. 20:2. See also the reference to Belial (*beliar*, 2 Cor. 6:15). Clinton E. Arnold notes that Satan possesses "wide-ranging power and authority," including "over all the kingdoms of the world (Matt. 4:8–9; Luke 4:6)." Arnold, *Powers of Darkness*, 80.

healed this woman, "whom Satan [had] bound for eighteen long years," and she was "released from this bond" (Luke 13:16). Indeed, Jesus healed many "who were oppressed by the devil" (Acts 10:38).

The extent of Satan's jurisdiction is apparent in that he "demanded permission to sift" Peter "like wheat" (Luke 22:31; cf. 22:3; Matt. 16:23; Mark 8:33), and Peter fell, even though Christ prayed that Peter's "faith may not fail" (Luke 22:32). Earlier "Satan entered into Judas" (Luke 22:3; cf. John 6:70; 13:27), and John recounts that "the devil . . . put [betrayal] into the heart of Judas" (John 13:2).

Likewise, "Satan filled [Ananias's] heart to lie to the Holy Spirit" (Acts 5:3). Paul decides "to deliver [someone] to Satan for the destruction of his flesh, so that his spirit may be saved" (1 Cor. 5:5), and he speaks of two he "handed over to Satan so that they will be taught not to blaspheme" (1 Tim. 1:20; cf. 5:15). Paul even reports, "There was given me a thorn in the flesh, a messenger [*angelos*] of Satan" (2 Cor. 12:7). Further, Paul wished to visit the Thessalonians, but he writes that "Satan hindered us" (1 Thess. 2:18; cf. 2 Tim. 4:17). Paul even refers to the devil as "the god of this world" who "has blinded the minds of the unbelieving so that they might not see the light of the gospel" (2 Cor. 4:4).[29]

However, the "condemnation" of the devil has already been "incurred" (1 Tim. 3:6). Apparently alluding to the serpent in Eden, Paul states, "The God of peace will soon crush Satan under your feet" (Rom. 16:20; cf. Gen. 3:15). John adds that "the ruler of this world has been judged" (John 16:11) and "will be cast out" (John 12:31; cf. Luke 10:18; Rev. 12:10). Ultimately, because of the cross "the devil" will be "render[ed] powerless" (Heb. 2:14; cf. 1 John 3:8). But the devil possesses significant authority for a limited time to wreak havoc in this world until he finally meets his end (cf. Matt. 25:41; Rev. 20:7–10).

Celestial Rulers of this World in the New Testament

The Domain of Darkness

As seen above, the NT depicts Satan as the "ruler of this world" (John 12:31; 16:11; cf. 14:30; 1 John 5:19) who wars against God's kingdom with his own "angels"[30] and is "Beelzebul, the ruler of the demons" (Matt. 12:24; cf. 9:34). Acts 26:18 sets the "dominion of Satan" in direct opposition to

---

29. Nearly all commentators view "god of this world" as a reference to Satan. See, e.g., Harris, *Second Epistle to the Corinthians*, 327; Barnett, *Second Epistle to the Corinthians*, 220.
30. Matt. 25:41; Rev. 12:7, 9; cf. Rom. 8:38; 1 Cor. 6:3; 2 Cor. 12:7; 1 Pet. 3:22.

God's dominion (cf. Luke 4:6). Paul similarly depicts conflict between the "kingdom" of Christ and "the domain of darkness" (Col. 1:13–14) and notes that Christ "gave Himself for our sins so that He might rescue us from this present evil age" (Gal. 1:4).

However, not only does Satan have significant jurisdiction in this world during "this present evil age"; other celestial rulers also possess real power and jurisdiction. Indeed, the NT depicts an entourage of Satan in the conflict against God. Beyond the instances above, the NT uses a host of terms to refer to celestial beings opposed to God's kingdom, including "demons" (e.g., Matt. 8:31), "unclean spirits," "evil spirits," fallen "angels" (2 Pet. 2:4; Jude 6; cf. Matt. 25:41; 1 Cor. 6:3; 1 Pet. 3:22; Rev. 12:7–9), "rulers" (*archōntes*), "principalities" (*archai*), "powers" (*dynameis*), "authorities" (*exousiai*), "thrones" (*thronoi*), "lordships" (*kyriotētes*), and "world rulers" (*kosmokratoras*).[31] While these terms might not all refer to the same kinds of beings, for simplicity's sake I use "demons" as an umbrella term to refer to celestial beings who oppose God's kingdom.[32]

Clash of Kingdoms: Light versus Darkness

While entirely ruling out eternal cosmic dualism, the NT sets forth a titanic clash between kingdoms of light and darkness (e.g., Col. 1:16). The Gospels are replete with instances of conflict between Christ's kingdom and that of the devil and his demons, often referred to as "evil spirits" (e.g., Luke 8:2) or "unclean spirits."[33] Christ repeatedly "cast out demons by the Spirit of God," declaring that "the kingdom of God has come" (Matt. 12:28; cf. Luke 11:20) against Satan's "kingdom" (Matt. 12:26; Mark 3:23–24; Luke 11:18). As David George Reese puts it, these passages "clearly depict the power of Jesus over demons as the evidence that God's kingdom had broken into the present world order"; God's "kingdom was confronting more than a loose confederation of hostile forces. It faced an opposing kingdom of evil spirits ruled by Beelzebul."[34]

31. Arnold makes a compelling case that all of these terms, and also the disputed reference to *stoicheia* ("elemental spirits"), "denote supernatural beings." "Principalities and Powers," *ABD* 5:467. See, further, Arnold, *Powers of Darkness*; Reid, "Principalities and Powers."

32. In my view, the biblical data are underdeterminative regarding the precise categorization of these celestial beings. This work is concerned more with the power/jurisdiction of such celestial beings than their ontology/taxonomy. For more on biblical angelology and demonology, see Page, *Powers of Evil*; van der Toorn, Becking, and van der Horst, *Dictionary of Deities and Demons*; Arnold, *Powers of Darkness*; Noll, *Angels of Light*.

33. E.g., Matt. 10:1, 8. Cf. Matt. 4:1–10; 9:33; 17:18; Mark 1:13; 3:15, 22–23; 5:13–15; 7:25–30; 9:17–30; Luke 4:33–36; 8:27–33; 9:38–42; 10:18; 11:14; 13:16; John 8:44; Acts 5:3; 26:18; Heb. 2:14; 1 John 3:8; Rev. 16:13–14.

34. Reese, "Demons," 2:141.

Accordingly, Christ gave *select* followers some jurisdiction over the enemy's domain, including "authority to cast out the demons" (Mark 3:15; cf. Matt. 10:1) and "authority to tread on serpents and scorpions, and over all the power of the enemy" (Luke 10:19; cf. Gen. 3:15; Ps. 91:13). Indeed, Luke writes, "The seventy returned with joy, saying, 'Lord, even the demons are subject to us in Your name'" (Luke 10:17), to which Jesus responds, "I was watching Satan fall from heaven like lightning" (v. 18).[35]

According to 2 Peter 2:4 at least some evil spirits are fallen "angels" who "sinned" and whom "God did not spare" but instead "committed them to pits of darkness, reserved for judgment." Likewise, Jude 6 refers to "angels who did not keep their own domain, but abandoned their proper abode," whom God "has kept in eternal bonds under darkness for the judgment of the great day." There are a variety of theories about the nature of the sin of these angels, but for our purposes it suffices to note they somehow sinned by overreaching their "domain" and thus fell.[36]

Although Scripture has little to say about the origin of demons, such references, along with others—such as the depiction in Revelation 12 of Satan and "his angels" being "thrown down" out of heaven "to the earth" (vv. 8–9; cf. Luke 10:18)[37]—have led many to conclude that Satan and his demons are fallen angels (cf. Ezek. 28:12–19; Isa. 14:12–15; Rev. 12:4). Indeed, Christians have traditionally viewed Isaiah 14:12–15 and Ezekiel 28:12–19 as depicting Satan's fall from perfection. While this interpretation has fallen out of favor, particularly since the rise of modernistic antisupernaturalism, I believe a close

---

35. Noting the widely recognized allusion to Isa. 14 here, Joel Green comments that Satan's "claim to glory and allegiance (cf. 4:5–7; cf. Isa. 14:13) is antecedent to, even mandates, his fall." J. Green, *Luke*, 418. See Garrett, *Demise of the Devil*, 50. Here "Luke identifies 'the enemy' as the cosmic power of evil resident and active behind all forms of opposition to God and God's people." J. Green, *Luke*, 420.

36. Most recent commentators see Jude 6 and 2 Pet. 2 as alluding to "the story of the fall of the Watchers, which was well known in contemporary Judaism," particularly 1 En. 6:1–9 and its interpretation of Gen. 6:1–4. Bauckham, *2 Peter, Jude*, 248. Cf. Schreiner, *1, 2 Peter, Jude*, 447–51. Other scholars (particularly in previous generations) have seen Jude 6 and 2 Pet. 2 as references to a fall of Satan and his angels prior to the human fall. Whatever is said in this regard, Page notes that other texts appear to "allude to fallen angels," such as Paul's statement that humans will "judge angels" (1 Cor. 6:3). Further, Page believes the "dragon and his angels" (Rev. 12:7) warring against God presupposes "a number of fallen angels," perhaps also referenced via the "stars" swept from "heaven by the dragon" as "widely held" (v. 4). Page, *Powers of Evil*, 258. He believes these "fallen angels" underlie OT references to "evil spiritual agencies." Page, *Powers of Evil*, 82.

37. Many NT scholars see Rev. 12:8–9 as a reference to Christ's victory at the cross but some see it as also containing imagery of an earlier fall. I. Howard Marshall comments that "behind the picture" of Rev. 12:8–9 and Luke 10:18 "lies the myth of the fall of Lucifer from heaven (Isa. 14:12; cf. the allusion to this myth in Luke 10:15)." Marshall, *Luke*, 428.

canonical reading supports the traditional interpretation.[38] However, the cosmic conflict approach of this present book does not hinge on this interpretation of Isaiah 14 and Ezekiel 28.

Whatever the precise origin of demons and evil angels, Paul explicitly states that the constituents of the "domain of darkness" are created beings, as are all things other than God "in the heavens and on earth, visible and invisible, whether thrones or dominions or rulers or authorities" (Col. 1:13, 16).[39] Insofar as one accepts the premise that "God is Light, and in Him there is no darkness at all" (1 John 1:5) such that God cannot even look on evil (Hab. 1:13), "cannot be tempted by evil," and "does not tempt anyone" by it (James 1:13), it follows that the constituents of the "domain of darkness" were created entirely good by God but fell into evil of their own accord.

Echoing Deuteronomy 32:17, Paul explains that in sacrificing to idols, the gentiles "sacrifice to demons and not to God" (1 Cor. 10:19–20; cf. 2 Cor. 6:14–15; Rev. 9:20).[40] Whereas 1 Corinthians 10:19 makes it clear that idols

---

38. Ezekiel 28:12 appears to refer beyond the human "king of Tyre" since the addressee is called the "seal of perfection" (v. 12), identified as present "in Eden" (v. 13) and "the anointed cherub who covers" on "the holy mountain of God" (v. 14; cf. 16)—that is, a covering cherub alongside God's throne (Exod. 25:19–20). Twice the text declares this cherub was "perfect," the second time declaring, "You were blameless in your ways / From the day you were created, / Until unrighteousness was found in you" (Ezek. 28:15; cf. 12). These descriptions suggest the addressee is a celestial being who fell from perfection. This cherub became "filled with violence" by the "abundance of [his] trade [*rekullah*]" (Ezek. 28:16; cf. 18); *rekullah* derives from the root *rakil*, which refers to "slander" (cf. Lev. 19:16), the devil's *modus operandi*. This cherub's "heart was lifted up because of [his] beauty" and he "corrupted [his] wisdom" (Ezek. 28:17).

Similarly, Isa. 14 describes the attempt of *helel* (translated "Lucifer" in the Vulgate) to exalt himself above God, saying "I will ascend to heaven; / I will raise my throne above the stars of God" (Isa. 14:13) and "I will ascend above the heights of the clouds; / I will make myself like the Most High" (Isa. 14:14). Michael Heiser comments that this "reads like an attempted coup in the divine council." Heiser, *Unseen Realm*, 85. Given what we know of Satan from elsewhere in Scripture, I believe the most plausible identity of *helel* (Isa. 14) and the cherub (Ezek. 28) is the devil, the celestial ruler behind the earthly rulers who are also addressed.

Relative to Ezek. 28, Lamar Eugene Cooper Sr. makes a strong case that "Ezekiel presented the king of Tyre as an evil tyrant who was animated and motivated by . . . Satan," noting that most "elements associated with the king of Tyre" here also appear relative to "the king of Babylon" in Isa. 14. Cooper, *Ezekiel*, 268. See, further, Bertoluci, "Son of the Morning"; Boyd, *God at War*, 157–62. Heiser believes these passages refer to a celestial being (the devil) because the "divine rebellion motif accounts for all the elements in both biblical passages (which have clear touch-points to the *nachash* [serpent] of Gen. 3), but the same cannot be said for appeals to Adam or the Keret Epic." Heiser, *Unseen Realm*, 83n1; cf. 75–91.

39. James D. G. Dunn believes that "all four terms" here—thrones, dominions, rulers, authorities—"refer only to the invisible, heavenly realm" and dovetail with "repeated emphasis on Christ's supremacy and triumph over the 'principalities and powers' in 2:10 and 15" who are "hostile to God's cosmos." Dunn, *Epistles to the Colossians and to Philemon*, 92.

40. Gordon D. Fee comments that Israel "had rejected God their Rock for beings who were no gods, indeed who were demons" (see Deut. 32:17), perhaps a development of "Israel's realization

are nothing, Paul indicates that behind the idols are real demons (v. 20; cf. 1 Cor. 8:4–6; see also Acts 17:18).[41] Like their ruler, Satan, these demons usurp worship (cf. Col. 2:18; Rev. 9:20). Accordingly, Paul warns against those who will pay "attention to deceitful spirits and doctrines of demons" (1 Tim. 4:1; cf. Rev. 6:13–14).

Evincing the genuine ruling authority of evil celestial beings, Ephesians 2:2 refers to "the prince [*archonta*] of the power [*exousia*] of the air, of the spirit that is now working in the sons of disobedience."[42] Ephesians 3:10 references "the rulers [*archais*] and the authorities [*exousiais*] in the heavenly places" (cf. 1 Cor. 4:9; 1 Pet. 1:12). Further, Ephesians 6:11–12 exhorts: "Put on the full armor of God, so that you will be able to stand firm against the schemes of the devil. For our struggle is not against flesh and blood, but against the rulers [*archas*], against the powers [*exousias*], against the world forces [*kosmokratoras*] of this darkness, against the spiritual forces of wickedness [*pneumatika tēs ponērias*] in the heavenly places."[43] Notice, this language of "rulers," "powers," "world forces of this darkness," and "spiritual forces of wickedness in the heavenly places," which are not "flesh and blood" (Eph. 6:12). It is difficult to imagine how a cosmic conflict wherein celestial rulers have real power and authority could be stated more forthrightly.

Nevertheless, the activity of angels and demons is often unrecognized. As Hebrews 13:2 puts it, "Some have entertained angels without knowing it."

---

that the 'mute' gods of the pagans did in fact have supernatural powers." Fee, *First Epistle to the Corinthians*, 472.

41. Reese explains that this refers to "pagan gods," the "spiritual reality behind the apparent nothingness of idols." "Demons," 2:140, 142. So also Arnold, *Powers of Darkness*, 95; Noll, *Angels of Light*, 81. As such, all of the *many* references to the gods of the nations and idolatry are references to cosmic conflict.

42. Although some believe this refers to another demonic ruler, Bruce has "little doubt that the devil is the being described as 'the ruler of the domain of the air.'" Bruce, *Colossians, Philemon, and Ephesians*, 282. Likewise, Lincoln, *Ephesians*, 95; M. Barth, *Ephesians 1–3*, 214; Page, *Powers of Evil*, 185.

43. Cf. Rom. 8:38; 13:12; 2 Cor. 10:3–5; Col. 2:15. Whereas the terminology relative to Satan, demons, and principalities and powers has been taken by some to refer to merely human systems of power or world systems with inner spirituality (on the latter, see Wink, *Walter Wink: Collected Readings*), Eph. 6:11–12 explicitly references "the spiritual forces of wickedness in the heavenly places." Bruce sees this wording as referring to Satan's "host of allies, principalities and powers." Bruce, *Colossians, Philemon, and Ephesians*, 404. Page adds that to "demythologize the powers and equate them with sociopolitical structures . . . fails to do justice to the historical context of the New Testament" and "to the explicit statements about these powers in the New Testament itself." Page, *Powers of Evil*, 240. Similarly, see Noll, *Angels of Light*, 119. Robert Ewusie Moses notes, "Paul shows that the powers" actually "operate across all levels simultaneously—cosmic, personal, political, social." Moses, *Practices of Power*, 209. See also Arnold's strong case for the reality, personhood, and systemic impact of evil celestial agencies, in Arnold, *Powers of Darkness*, 194–205.

Angelic or demonic activity might be at work behind the scenes, even where such activity is not explicitly recognized (cf. 2 Kings 6:16–17). With this in mind, we turn to OT depictions of celestial rulers.

Celestial Rulers of this World in the Old Testament

Daniel 10

Although evidence of demonic agencies is more explicit in the NT, the OT offers considerable evidence of these celestial rulers. Daniel 10 presents a particularly striking instance, in the context of a message of "great conflict" (v. 1). For weeks, Daniel fervently prayed for understanding, and although God heard Daniel's words "from the first day," the "prince of the kingdom of Persia" withstood God's angel for "twenty-one days." Thereafter, Michael "came to help" the angel who "had been left there with the kings of Persia" (vv. 2, 12–13; cf. vv. 20–21). This prince of Persia is widely understood as a celestial ruler who is behind the human ruler.[44] W. Sibley Towner comments, "The panoply of heavenly beings which is involved [in Dan. 10–12] bespeaks a cosmic struggle taking place in its own plane on a course parallel to the drama of human history."[45] Tremper Longman III adds that here "we have a clear case of spiritual conflict. On the one side stands God's powerful angelic army and on the other 'the prince of the Persian kingdom.'"[46] He writes further that Daniel 10 exposes "the spiritual realities behind the wars of Yahweh up to this point. In the description of the historical battles throughout most of the Old Testament, the concentration is on the earthly. Certainly the heavenly forces that have supported Israel have been revealed, but not [in most cases] the spiritual powers on the other side."[47]

On this reading, Daniel 10 depicts a cosmic conflict involving celestial beings wherein an angel of God is delayed for three weeks because the prince of Persia, apparently a celestial ruler behind and connected with the earthly ruler of Persia, withstood him. Here, writes Gleason Archer, we see that the "powers of evil apparently have the capacity to bring about hindrances and

44. As John J. Collins explains this widely held view, this prince "indicates the patron angel of Persia," consonant with the "widespread" ancient "notion that different nations were allotted to different gods or heavenly beings" and the ANE "concept of the divine council." J. Collins, *Daniel*, 374. So also Arnold, *Powers of Darkness*, 63; Page, *Powers of Evil*, 63. See the discussion of Deut. 32:8–9 later in this chapter.

45. Towner, *Daniel*, 147.

46. Longman, *Daniel*, 250.

47. Longman, *Daniel*, 256.

delays, even of the delivery of the answers to believers whose requests God is minded to answer" (cf. 1 Thess. 2:18).[48]

The nature of this conflict is addressed in chapter 4. For now, it is sufficient to note that Daniel 10 presents a *real* conflict between celestial rulers behind earthly nations and God's kingdom. As John E. Goldingay puts it, "Like other ancient Near Eastern writings, the OT assumes that the results of battles on earth reflect the involvement of heaven."[49] Longman adds that there is a "cosmic war that lies behind this human conflict," and such "spiritual warfare" is an "incredibly pervasive and significant biblical theme."[50]

Celestial Rulers and the Heavenly Council or "Assembly of the Gods"

Beyond Daniel 10, many other passages evince the reality of celestial agencies that exercise some ruling authority in this world, sometimes referred to as "gods of the nations." Beth Tanner notes that for ancient Israel "not only did other gods exist, but those gods were active in the world."[51] This does not, however, amount to polytheism. The OT term for "gods" (*elohim*) may signify merely celestial beings rather than the Supreme Being typically denoted in English by "God."[52] John Goldingay explains that in the OT, while idols are nothing, behind them are "so-called deities [that] do indeed exist, but they do not count as God, and they are subject to God's judgment"; yet these "supernatural centers of power" can "deliberately oppose Yhwh's purpose."[53]

According to Deuteronomy 32:8,

> When the Most High apportioned the nations,
>   when he divided humankind,
> he fixed the boundaries of the peoples
>   according to the number of the gods (NRSV)[54]

---

48. Archer, "Daniel," 124. So also Longman, *Daniel*, 249; Page, *Powers of Evil*, 64.

49. Goldingay, *Daniel*, 291.

50. Longman, *Daniel*, 254. See Longman's excursus on these issues in *Daniel*, 254–65; Longman and Reid, *God Is a Warrior*. Cf. Boyd, *God at War*.

51. Tanner, "Book Three of the Psalter: Psalms 73–89," 642.

52. Jeffrey H. Tigay explains, "Although *'elohim* and *'el(im)* literally mean 'god/gods,' they also refer to various types of supernatural beings and heavenly bodies that form God's retinue." Tigay, *Deuteronomy*, 514.

53. Goldingay, *Israel's Faith*, 43. Michael S. Heiser notes, "Common phrases in the Hebrew Bible which seem to deny the existence of other gods (e.g., Deut. 4:35, 39; 32:12, 39) actually appear in passages that affirm the existence of other gods (Deut. 4:19–20; 32:8–9, 17)" and tend to "express incomparability, not nonexistence of other gods (Isa. 43:10–12; cf. 47:8, 10)." Heiser, "Divine Council," 10. Cf. Block, *Gods of the Nations*.

54. Cf. Gen. 11; Deut. 4:19–20; 29:26. The MT of Deut. 32:8 reads "sons of Israel," but most scholars agree that the original most likely corresponds to the DSS "sons of God," which

Many scholars see this passage as setting forth a worldview wherein celestial beings ("gods") were allotted territory to rule on earth. Peter C. Craigie suggests that "the reference seems to be to the divine [or heavenly] council of the Lord," and "the poetry indicates that the number of nations is related to the number of these Sons of God."[55] Marvin E. Tate sees here "the assignment of the gods to each nation as patron deities" while God retained "ultimate hegemony over all the nations."[56]

Whether or not one adopts this reading of Deuteronomy 32:8, a host of other texts support the concept of celestial rulers with real authority behind earthly rulers.[57] Further, Deuteronomy 32 indicates that the "gods" or celestial rulers of the other nations were actually demons: "They sacrificed to demons who were not God, / To gods whom they have not known" (v. 17).[58] The gods of the nations, whom Israel is so frequently described as playing the harlot with throughout the OT, are described here explicitly as demons. In Derek

---

likely explains the LXX rendering "angels of God." So Tigay, *Deuteronomy*, 302; Craigie, *Deuteronomy*, 377; Christensen, *Deuteronomy 21:10–34:12*, 791; P. Miller, *Deuteronomy*, 228; Thompson, *Deuteronomy*, 326; Clements, "Deuteronomy," 2:529. Contra, e.g., Merrill, *Deuteronomy*, 413. For support of the reading "sons of God," see Heiser, "Deuteronomy 32:8"; Heiser, *Unseen Realm*, 114. Cf. Jub. 15:31.

55. Craigie, *Deuteronomy*, 379. Longman argues that this "refers to God's angelic creatures who make up his heavenly council as 'the sons of God.' There are angels, in other words, 'assigned' to different nation states." Longman, *Daniel*, 250. For Tigay, this refers to "when God was allotting nations to the divine beings." Tigay, *Deuteronomy*, 302. So also P. Miller, *Deuteronomy*, 228; Thompson, *Deuteronomy*, 326.

56. Tate, *Psalms 51–100*, 340. Similarly, Alexander Di Lella sees the "guardian angel" view of Dan. 10 as a vestige of the Deut. 32:8 view that "each city-state or nation or empire had a tutelary god who was in a particular way its protector." Hartman and Di Lella, *Daniel*, 283. Cf. Towner, *Daniel*, 172; Christensen, *Deuteronomy*, 796; Block, *Gods of the Nations*, 30–32.

57. The notion of deities assigned to geographic territories appears in other texts, such as Jephthah's message to the king of Ammon: "Do you not possess what Chemosh your god gives you to possess?" (Judg. 11:24; cf. Ezra 1:2–3; 1 Kings 20:23; cf. 20:28). Further, God "executed judgments on [Egypt's] gods" (Num. 33:4; cf. Exod. 12:12; 15:6, 11; 18:10–11; 23:32; Deut. 29:24–25; 1 Sam. 5:7; 6:5; 1 Kings 11:5, 33; 18:24; Jer. 5:19, 30–31; 46:25; 50:2; 51:44). Cf. also Rabshakeh's taunts: "Has any one of the gods of the nations delivered his land from the hand of the king of Assyria? Where are the gods of Hamath and Arpad? Where are the gods of Sepharvaim, Hena and Ivvah? . . . Who among all the gods of the lands have delivered their land from my hand?" (2 Kings 18:33–35; cf. 19:12–13; 2 Chron. 32:13–17; Isa. 36:18–20; 37:12). Many other passages refer to the gods of the nations (e.g., Exod. 12:12; Deut. 6:14; Josh. 24:15; Judg. 6:10; 10:6; 2 Kings 17:29–31; 1 Chron. 5:25; 2 Chron. 25:14–15, 20; 28:23; Jer. 34:12–13; Zeph. 2:11). Yet God is unequivocally superior (1 Chron. 16:25–26; 2 Chron. 2:5–6); there is "no one like [Yahweh] among the gods" (Ps. 86:8; cf. Pss. 77:13; 95:3; 96:4–5; 97:9; 135:5; 2 Chron. 6:14). See also Block, *Gods of the Nations*.

58. Cf. Lev. 17:7; Ps. 106:37; cf. 1 Cor. 10:20–21. The LXX translation of Ps. 96:5 (LXX 95:5) says, "All the gods of peoples are demons [*daimonia*]." There is also considerable evidence indicating that "Azazel" in the Day of Atonement ritual (Lev. 16:8–10) likely refers to a demon enemy of God. See Gane, *Cult and Character*, 247–51.

Kidner's view, such "'gods' are 'principalities and powers,' 'the world rulers of this present darkness' (cf. Eph. 6:12)."[59]

Many OT texts depict a heavenly council consisting of "gods" or celestial beings who are often described as possessing ruling authority relative to events on earth.[60] As E. T. Mullen Jr. explains, "The concept of an assembly of divine beings is found throughout the OT as an expression of Yahweh's power and authority. Yahweh is frequently depicted as enthroned over an assembly of divine beings who serve to dispense his decrees and messages," providing the background for the later "development of the angelic hierarchy."[61] While many of these beings are faithful servants of Yahweh, some (even within the heavenly council), are depicted as evil agencies who oppose God's kingdom (see, e.g., Ps. 82; cf. 1 Kings 22:19–23).[62]

Psalms includes numerous instances of this heavenly council. For instance, Psalm 29:1–2 proclaims, "Ascribe to the LORD, O heavenly beings [*bene 'elim*], / ascribe to the LORD glory and strength. / Ascribe to the LORD the glory of his name; / worship the LORD in holy splendor" (NRSV, cf. 97:7; 138:1). Further, Psalm 89 speaks of the praise of Yahweh's faithfulness "in the assembly of the holy ones" and maintains that no one "among the heavenly beings [*bibne 'elim*]" is "like the LORD, / a God feared in the council of the holy ones, / great and awesome above all that are around him" (Ps. 89:5–7 NRSV). This psalm not only emphatically differentiates Yahweh from such inferior "heavenly beings" but also includes one of many OT depictions of God as a divine warrior in conflict with pagan "gods" and cosmic forces such as the chaos sea monster Rahab (Ps. 89:9–10) and the great, multiheaded sea serpent or dragon Leviathan.[63]

59. Kidner, *Psalms 73–150*, 328.

60. E.g., 1 Kings 22:19–23; 2 Chron. 18:18–22; Job 1:6–12; 2:1–7; Pss. 29:1–2; 82; 89:5–8; Isa. 6:1–13; Zech. 3:1–7; Dan. 7:9–14; cf. Isa. 24:21–23; Jer. 23:18, 22; Ezek. 1–3; Dan. 4:13, 17; Amos 3:7–8.

61. Mullen, "Divine Assembly," 2:214. Mullen notes that some "idea of a council or assembly of the gods that met to determine the fates of the cosmos" was "common to the mythopoeic world of the ANE." This "council of the gods . . . constituted the major decision-making body in the divine world" (2:214). See also Mullen, *Divine Council*. However, the OT conception departs significantly from that of other ANE literature. John E. Hartley notes that whereas "several passages in the OT" appear "to assume that God governs the world through a council of the heavenly host . . . in the OT the complete dependence of these sons of God on God himself and their total submission to him is not questioned," in keeping with "monotheistic belief." Hartley, *Job*, 71n6.

62. Indeed Noll notes, "Heaven is populated by spiritual beings, whether they are loyal servants or not (Ps. 82)." Noll, "Angels," 46. Robert L. Alden comments, "Apparently God has a council or cabinet," but "not every one of them is good because 1 Kings 22:20–23 speaks of a 'spirit' willing to be a 'lying spirit in the mouths of all his [Ahab's] prophets.'" Alden, *Job*, 53.

63. Job 3:8; 41:1; Pss. 74:14; 104:26; Isa. 27:1; cf. Job 9:13; 26:12; Isa. 51:9; Rev. 12:3–9; 13:1–3. On the divine warrior motif, see Longman and Reid, *God Is a Warrior*. Such monsters

In a most striking heavenly council scene, God is depicted as judging "gods" (*'elohim*) from "his place in the divine [heavenly] council [*ba'adat-'el*]" (Ps. 82:1 NRSV; cf. 58:1; 89:5–8).[64] According to Tanner, this "psalm gives us a window on the assembly of the gods, a place where the gods are gathered to make decisions about the world."[65] Tate agrees that this "scene is pictured as that of a divine assembly" and adds that the "conceptual horizon" of the psalm "is that of the assignment of the gods to each nation as patron deities, who would be responsible for the welfare of each nation," as in Deuteronomy 32:8–9.[66] In this council, God chastises these "gods" for "judg[ing] unjustly" (Ps. 82:2 NRSV) and declares: "You are gods, / children of the Most High, all of you; / nevertheless, you shall die like mortals, / and fall like any prince" (vv. 6–7 NRSV; cf. Jer. 50:2; 51:44). Here, Tate believes "the great king [of the divine assembly] pronounces sentence on some of the gods who have failed in their duties."[67] Kraus adds, "Injustice on earth is attributed to those forces which carry on their activity between Yahweh and the world as lords and tutelary spirits of groups, peoples, and states."[68] As such, the temporary injustice is the result not of God's perfect rule (cf. Deut. 32:4) but of the unjust rule of the "gods," evincing their significant ruling authority. Thus God is called on: "Arise, O God, judge the earth! / For it is You who possesses all the nations" (Ps. 82:8; cf. Deut. 32:8).[69]

Similarly, Isaiah forecasts a day when "the LORD will punish the host of heaven on high, / And the kings of the earth on earth" (Isa. 24:21; cf. 2 Pet.

---

are closely associated with the nations that oppress Israel. At times, Rahab is another name for Egypt (e.g., Isa. 30:7), and Babylon is associated with a dragon (Jer. 51:34). Yet behind these and others stand the celestial "gods."

64. Some interpret this psalm as a reference to merely human judges, reading Christ's use of it in John 10:34 in this vein. However, nothing Jesus says in John 10:34 seems to demand reading "gods" as merely humans. Indeed, Christ's quotation appears to make more sense if Ps. 82 is taken as a reference to celestial beings. See Page, *Powers of Evil*, 57–58; Heiser, *Unseen Realm*, 68n3. Further, the internal data of Ps. 82 overwhelmingly support reading this as a reference to celestial beings ("gods"). The LXX supports this reading—rendering *ba'adat-'el* as *en synagōgē theōn*, "in an assembly/synagogue of gods"—and is favored by most commentators. So, e.g., Tate, *Psalms 51–100*, 334; Hossfeld and Zenger, *Psalms 2*, 331; Kraus, *Psalms 60–150*, 155; Tanner, "Book Three of the Psalter," 643; McCann, "Psalms," 4:1006.

65. Tanner, "Book Three of the Psalter," 641.

66. Tate, *Psalms 51–100*, 334, 340. Hossfeld and Zenger similarly see this as the "hierarchical assembly of the gods or the heavenly council," together with the idea of "the assignment of particular territories within the world to individual deities by the god-king." Hossfeld and Zenger, *Psalms 2*, 329. See also Noll, *Angels of Light*, 37.

67. Tate, *Psalms 51–100*, 334. Cf. Hossfeld and Zenger, *Psalms 2*, 334; McCann, "Psalms," 4:1006. Page adds that saying they will "'die like mere men' assumes that those addressed are not human." Page, *Powers of Evil*, 55.

68. Kraus, *Psalms 60–150*, 156.

69. James L. Mays writes that this is "a petition to God to take over as judge of the earth in place of the gods." Mays, *Psalms*, 268.

2:4). Whereas many other texts reference a loyal heavenly host, this passage refers to an explicitly rebellious "host," punished for their evil (cf. Job 4:18; 15:15). Punishment of this "host of heaven" makes sense only if they are morally responsible for evil and thus can neither refer to inanimate astronomical bodies or mere idols but rather to celestial beings behind the "kings of the earth on earth."[70] As Longman notes, "We must be careful not to speculate on the hints the Bible gives us, but that there are spiritual powers, good and bad, behind the various human institutions is a truth taught in the Old [and New] Testament."[71]

Although there is a tendency among post-Enlightenment readers to dismiss such references to "gods" as purely mythological, the OT and NT maintain that demons were behind the "gods" of the nations, usurping worship. There is much more to be said about these agencies and the heavenly council, with significant implications for events on earth and the problem of evil, discussed in chapter 4. For now, we turn to two more major instances, which feature the *satan* and shed further light on the heavenly council.

The Satan: An Old Testament Profile

The Heavenly Council Scene of Job 1–2

The book of Job includes one of the most illuminating instances of the heavenly council, which also sheds significant light on the cosmic conflict. After explaining that Job was a righteous man and describing his piety and prosperity (Job 1:1–5), the author of Job shifts from earth to a heavenly council scene: "The sons of God [*bene ha'elohim*] came to present themselves before the LORD, and [the *satan*] also came among them" (1:6; cf. 38:7). Scholars widely agree that the phrase "sons of God" here refers to "celestial beings" in the "council of the heavenly host," some of whom may come as "courtiers to give an accounting of their activities to God."[72] However, there is considerable disagreement among scholars about whether the character referred to as "the *satan*" (*hasatan*) corresponds to the Satan of the NT. This issue will be revisited after we've seen how Job 1–2 and Zechariah 3 depict "the *satan*."

---

70. For Joseph Blenkinsopp, this describes the punishment of the "celestial and terrestrial powers hostile to Yahweh's purposes," the "heavenly patrons to the nations of the world (e.g., 1 En. 90:22–25; Sir. 17:17; Dan. 10:13, 20–21; cf. Deut. 32:8–9)," the "malevolent celestial powers" in "league" with "the rulers of the nations." Blenkinsopp, *Isaiah 1–39*, 356–57.

71. Longman, *Daniel*, 250.

72. Hartley, *Job*, 71. See also Clines, *Job 1–20*, 17–18; Pope, *Job*, 9; Alden, *Job*, 53.

Before the heavenly council, God asks the *satan*, "From where do you come?"[73] The *satan* answers, "From roaming about on the earth and walking around on it" (Job 1:7). This identical question and answer appears in Job 2, suggesting they are procedural, perhaps indicating the *satan* attends the heavenly council as a representative or ruler of earth.[74] The focus then abruptly turns to an apparently prior and ongoing dispute between God and the *satan*. God asks, "Have you considered My servant Job? For there is no one like him on the earth, a blameless and upright man, fearing God and turning away from evil" (Job 1:8). Pope asks, "Why all the concern about Job's integrity?" He thinks "there is something of taunt and provocation in Yahweh's query. . . . Perhaps there is more involved than is made explicit."[75] Carol A. Newsom believes that "this is not a request for information. Narratively, Yahweh's challenging question suggests an ongoing rivalry with the satan."[76]

The *satan*'s response further suggests a broader point of contention between them. He alleges that Job does not "fear God for nothing" but does so only because God has blessed him and "made a hedge about him" and his belongings and would bitterly curse God if met with calamity (Job 1:9–11; cf. 2:5).[77] This not only attacks the sincerity of Job's loyalty but also amounts to an accusation against God, who previously declared that Job is "blameless" and "upright," both "fearing God and turning away from evil" (Job 1:8). The *satan* thus directly contradicts God's judgment of Job. Lindsay Wilson notes that this "is a questioning not just of Job's motives but also of God's rule. The accuser is saying to God that Job does not deserve all his blessings, and thus God is not ruling the world with justice."[78] Likewise, Frances Andersen comments, "God's character and Job's are both slighted."[79] Hamilton adds that this response is "patently slanderous."[80]

---

73. Victor P. Hamilton thinks this question might suggest the *satan* is "an intruder," while allowing the alternate view that he is "a legitimate member." Hamilton, "Satan," 5:986.

74. Carol A. Newsom comments that there "is a formal, almost ritual quality to the initial exchange between Yahweh and the satan." Newsom, "Job," 4:348. Further, some take *hithallek* in the *satan*'s reply as asserting "dominion or sovereignty over" the earth (cf. Ezek. 28:14). Klein, *Zechariah*, 100. Many others view the *satan* here as a rover or watcher of the heavenly court (cf. Dan. 4:13), perhaps reflective of the Persian "royal spy system" but more likely grounded in the much older ANE imagery of "the divine court scenes." So, e.g., Pope, *Job*, 9, 11.

75. Pope, *Job*, 11.

76. Newsom, "Job," 4:349. Newsom thinks the satan's charge "exposes" God "to dishonor" and that Yahweh here "defends his own honor." Newsom, "Job," 4:349.

77. Newsom believes this is "no wager but a challenge to a test." Newsom, "Job," 4:349. Cf. Andersen, *Job*, 89.

78. Wilson, *Job*, 34.

79. Andersen, *Job*, 89. Cf. Alden, *Job*, 55.

80. Hamilton, "Satan," 5:985. So also Day, *Adversary in Heaven*, 76.

God responds by allowing the *satan* to test his theory but only within limits, first granting the *satan* power over "all that [Job] has" but prohibiting personal harm (Job 1:12). Then in the second scene, God allows the *satan* to afflict Job personally (but the *satan* must spare Job's life) after the *satan* sadistically claims that although Job did not curse God after losing his children (2:3), Job would do so if physically afflicted himself (vv. 4–6). Whereas some consider God culpable for what happens to Job here (as discussed in chap. 4), Andersen believes God has "good reason" for what he allows here—"namely to disprove the Satan's slander" of God's character.[81] Although Satan brought numerous calamities against Job's household—including loss of wealth, the death of servants, and the death of his children (1:13–19)—and, later, afflicts intense suffering on Job personally (2:7), Job consistently refuses to curse God (1:20–22; 2:9), falsifying Satan's charges in this behind-the-scenes glimpse of the cosmic dispute between God and Satan.[82]

The Heavenly Council Scene of Zechariah 3

Besides Job 1–2, the heavenly council scene of Zechariah 3 provides the only other instances of "the *satan*" (*hasatan*). This passage depicts "Joshua the high priest standing before the angel of the LORD, and [the *satan*] standing at his right hand to accuse him" (Zech. 3:1; cf. Ps. 109:6–7).[83] Then, "the LORD said to [the *satan*], 'The LORD rebuke you, [the *satan*]! Indeed, the LORD who has chosen Jerusalem rebuke you! Is this not a brand plucked from the fire?'" (Zech. 3:2; cf. Jude 9). Here, the *satan* stands as an adversary against God, bringing an accusation against the high priest, which indirectly amounts to an accusation against God, who has chosen Jerusalem.

Yahweh, however, rejects the *satan*'s accusation, reiterating his election of Jerusalem. According to Carol Meyers and Eric Meyers, the term

---

81. Andersen, *Job*, 95. Conversely, Clines (as others) depicts God as guilty of wronging Job. Clines, *Job 1–20*, 25; cf. Newsom, "Job," 4:350.

82. Although the remainder of Job does not mention the *satan*, other hints of cosmic conflict appear, including Leviathan, other monsters, and Eliphaz's report: "A spirit passed by my face" and "I heard a voice:

'Can mankind be just before God?
Can a man be pure before his Maker?
He puts no trust even in His servants;
And against His angels He charges error.'" (Job 4:15–18; cf. 5:1; 15:15)

See Tonstad, *God of Sense*, 255–56.

83. According to Carol L. Meyers and Eric M. Meyers, the "technical language" of "*'md lpny*" ("standing before") itself "reveals" the vividly portrayed "Divine Council setting" as the "Heavenly Court over which Yahweh presides as chief judge." Meyers and Meyers, *Haggai, Zechariah 1–8*, 182. Citing similarities with Job 1–2, Ralph L. Smith concludes, "There can be no doubt that the scene is that of the heavenly council." Smith, *Micah–Malachi*, 199.

translated "rebuke" *(g'r,* "to scream, cry out") "denotes divine invective against those who stand in the way of Yahweh's plan."[84] Following this striking rebuke of the *satan,* Yahweh commands "those who were standing before him"—which likely refers to "the other members of the Divine Council or the other divine or angelic beings present in Yahweh's court"[85] (cf. Zech. 3:7)—to remove Joshua's "filthy garments" (v. 4). Thus Yahweh declares that Joshua's "iniquity" is removed (v. 4). Much more could be said about this scene. For now, notice the adversarial and accusatorial role of the *satan* against God within the heavenly council. Having surveyed the only two OT passages that include "the *satan,*" we can now revisit the questions regarding the *satan's* identity.

Profiling the Slandering Accuser

As mentioned, scholars do not agree regarding whether "the satan" *(hasatan)* of the OT corresponds to the enemy of God named "Satan" in the NT. Since the article *(ha)* is not typically used before proper names in Hebrew, many scholars believe that *hasatan* in Job 1–2 and Zechariah 3 does not depict the name of the agent but instead describes a person playing a divinely sanctioned prosecutorial role in God's heavenly court, rendering *hasatan* as "the adversary" or "the accuser." For example, Newsom believes that by the time Job was written, which she thinks is early postexilic period, "the expression 'the satan' had come to designate a particular divine being in the heavenly court, one whose specialized function was to seek out and accuse persons disloyal to God," citing Zechariah 3:1 as "the chief evidence for this."[86] On this view, *hasatan* is not adversarial to God but is God's servant in the heavenly council and thus cannot be the "archenemy" of God that appears in the NT. Accordingly, Newsom writes that "the hostile image of Satan" as the "opponent of God [that is] presumed by the New Testament

---

84. Meyers and Meyers, *Haggai, Zechariah 1–8,* 186. Cf. Gen. 37:10; Ruth 2:16. Yet they believe that "God's rebuke is not directed toward the function of the Accuser per se, but rather to the way in which he is carrying out his responsibilities."

85. Meyers and Meyers, *Haggai, Zechariah 1–8,* 188. Mark J. Boda likewise believes the standing ones "are attendants in the divine council (see Jer. 23:18) who participate in its deliberations and carry out its orders (1 Kings 22:19–23; Isa. 6, 40)." Boda, *Zechariah,* 248.

86. Newsom, "Job," 4:347. So, e.g., Pope, *Job,* 9; Meyers and Meyers, *Haggai, Zechariah 1–8,* 183; Boda, *Zechariah,* 229–30. However, Peggy L. Day notes, "No analogous office has been convincingly identified in the legal system of ancient Israel, nor do the divine councils of the surrounding cultures include a deity whose specific assignment is to be an accuser." Day and Breytenbach, "Satan," 728. While some argue that "professional informers/accusers existed in the early Persian period" and the *satan* is modeled after these, Day contends that the "evidence for this is inconclusive" (728).

(see, e.g., Mark 3:22–30; Luke 22:31; John 13:27; Rev. 20:1–10)" was a "later development."[87]

Before addressing these issues regarding the identity of *hasatan*, it will be helpful to briefly consider the root of *satan* in the OT. In Hebrew, *satan* generally refers to an accuser, often an adversary, enemy, or slanderer (noun), or one who opposes or accuses (verb), as in a legal context.[88] Job 1–2 and Zechariah 3 are the only two OT passages where *hasatan* (*satan* with the article) appears. However, the root of *satan* appears thirty-three times in twenty-eight OT verses (in noun and verb forms). Apart from the passages containing *hasatan*, however, only one other instance of the noun *satan* is frequently taken as a reference to a celestial adversary of God, 1 Chronicles 21:1: "Then Satan [*satan* without the article] stood up against Israel and moved David to number Israel."[89]

The identity of *satan* in 1 Chronicles 21 is disputed, but many scholars believe it depicts a personal name. For instance, *HALOT* interprets this "as a personal name," one that "clearly [identifies] a celestial figure who incited David to make a census."[90] Moisés Silva also believes that here *satan* "functions almost certainly as a proper name."[91] Meyers and Meyers believe this is "one of three cases in the Hebrew Bible in which this term occurs in reference to a figure in Yahweh's court," along with Zechariah 3 and Job 1–2.[92] They write that "the figure in this context is surely hostile to Yahweh's chosen one; and from a linguistic viewpoint, the lack of the definite article does not weaken the distinct image in Chronicles of a *śāṭān* figure."[93] Silva adds, "In all three books"—Job, Zechariah, and 1 Chronicles—the *satan* "appears as

---

87. Newsom, "Job," 4:347. Cf. Pope, *Job*, 9.

88. See Hamilton, "Satan," 5:985. Cf. *HALOT* 3:1317. Meyers and Meyers see in this root "a set of meanings that are derived from the hostility of one who is an opponent." Meyers and Meyers, *Haggai, Zechariah 1–8*, 183.

89. The infinitive construct (*lesitno*) in Zech. 3:1 is demonstrably of *hasatan*. Psalm 109:6 has sometimes been taken as referencing the devil but likely refers to a human accuser (in a legal context similar to Zech. 3); the same chapter uses *satan* of apparently human accusers in three other verses (Ps. 109:4, 20, 29). Two other instances refer to the "angel of the LORD" standing "as an adversary [*satan*]" against Balaam (Num. 22:22; cf. v. 32). Eleven other instances refer to human accusers or adversaries (1 Sam. 29:4; 2 Sam. 19:23 [ET 22]; 1 Kings 5:18 [ET 4]; 11:14, 23, 25; Pss. 38:21 [ET 20]; 71:13; 109:4, 20, 29).

90. *HALOT* 3:1317. According to Day, the "majority of scholars" believe *śāṭān* is a proper name, though Day does not hold this view. Day and Breytenbach, "Satan," 729–30.

91. "Σατάν, Σατανᾶς," *NIDNTTE* 4:265. So also Page, *Powers of Evil*, 24, 34; Arnold, *Powers of Darkness*, 62.

92. Meyers and Meyers, *Haggai, Zechariah 1–8*, 183. Hamilton similarly views this as the third "appearance of a malevolent celestial *śāṭān*," while recognizing it could be read otherwise. Hamilton, "Satan," 5:987.

93. Meyers and Meyers, *Haggai, Zechariah 1–8*, 183.

an enemy of God's people, whether enticing David to undertake the census of
the people, or seeking to bring Job's spiritual downfall, or accusing the high
priest Joshua. Moreover, at least in Job and Zechariah, Satan is clearly presented as some kind of heavenly being."[94] Whatever one concludes regarding
1 Chronicles 21, the instances of *hasatan* in Job 1–2 and Zechariah 3 portray
a figure who strikingly resembles the one whom the NT calls Satan. Notably,
the LXX consistently translates *hasatan* as *diabolos* with the article, which
always refers to the devil in the NT.[95]

The identity of *hasatan* does not hinge on whether *hasatan* is taken to
be a personal name or a description of an office or function in the heavenly
council or something else. It could be that a description of this agent came
to later be used as the name of that agent (perhaps by the time 1 Chron. 21
was written).[96] The use of the article, then, does not by itself indicate whether
hasatan should be identified with the person called Satan in the NT; it might
only indicate that at the time of writing, *satan* was not a proper name.

Further, even if one takes *hasatan* to be playing a prosecutorial role in the
heavenly council, we need not conclude that *hasatan* is doing so as a loyal servant of Yahweh. We've already seen that some of the "gods" (celestial rulers)
are themselves "judged" by Yahweh in the heavenly council for their evil (Ps.
82). Likewise, we've seen Isaiah's reference to a rebellious "host" in heaven
whom God punishes (Isa. 24:21; cf. Job 4:18; 15:15; 2 Pet. 2:4), and in 1 Kings
22:19–23 a "deceiving spirit" goes forth from the heavenly council, probably
one of the evil celestial rulers who first gets permission from the heavenly
council not unlike *hasatan* does in Job 1–2.[97] One should not assume, then,

94. "Σατάν, Σατανᾶς," *NIDNTTE* 4:265. The parallel in 2 Sam. 24:1 depicts Yahweh as the
agent who "incited David." Various views of why the Chronicler identifies *satan* instead as the
agent are possible. Some maintain that earlier OT literature emphasized divine causality, even
in instances of weak actualization. See Hamilton, "Satan," 5:987; Page, *Powers of Evil*, 35. This
view may dovetail with what Noll calls the "OT reticence to speak of evil angels and Satan in
particular," in keeping "with its 'apophatic angelology.'" Noll, "Angels," 46.

95. The only instances where *hasatan* is not translated by *diabolos* with the article is the
second instance in Zech. 3:2, rendered with the vocative, *diabole*, and one instance where it is
rendered by a pronoun (Job 1:8). Interestingly, the LXX uses *diabolos* to translate *satan* only in
Job 1–2; Zech. 3:1–2; 1 Chron. 21:1; and Ps. 108:6 LXX, without the article in the two instances
without the article in Hebrew (1 Chron. 21:1; Ps. 108:6 LXX). However, the infinitive *endiaballō*
and the feminine noun *diabolē* are used in some other instances.

96. Cf. Mordechai Cogan's view that "*śāṭān* developed the meaning 'prosecutor' (cf. Zech.
3:1–2; Job 1:6) and eventually became the name for the one who incites to sinful acts (cf. 1 Chron.
21:1)." Cogan, *1 Kings*, 330.

97. First Kings 22 might be read in various ways; space does not permit an adequate treatment here. For now, notice that some deliberation among council members (v. 20) precedes
the celestial being coming forward to deceive, who then offers his own plan (vv. 21–22; cf. Rev.
16:13–14). This pattern comports well with Joseph Blenkinsopp's description of "the deliberative

that the presence of a figure in the heavenly council entails that that figure is loyal to Yahweh (cf. Rev. 12:7–9).[98]

The text itself indicates the disposition of the *satan* as an opponent of Yahweh. In Job 1–2 the *satan* acts as a slanderous accuser of Job, contradicting Yahweh's claims about Job's righteousness and loyalty, which are later vindicated. The *satan* thereby indirectly alleges that God's judgment is unjust, revealing an antagonistic disposition toward Yahweh. As John E. Hartley comments, the *satan*'s "role in this scene deviates from" the explanation that he is a benign "prosecuting attorney of the heavenly council." Here "he acts as a troublemaker, a disturber of the kingdom" who displays a "contemptuous attitude."[99] Mark J. Boda likewise affirms that the *satan* "is not a benign opponent."[100] Andersen adds that the *satan* "is not God's minister of prosecution." Even "if he is still only the provoker of men, and not the opponent of God, we should not follow the commentators who see him here as simply another of God's loyal servants. His insolence shows a mind already twisted away from God" with "hostility" such that "there is evil here, but not dualism."[101] Whatever else is said, according to Wilson, the *satan*'s "insidious nature" may "be discerned by listening to the tone of his comments."[102]

Zechariah 3 also depicts the *satan* as opposing Yahweh's judgment in favor of Joshua the high priest, "standing at his right hand to accuse him" (v. 1). George L. Klein comments that the *satan* "opposes God in a malicious way, as verse 2 clearly indicates."[103] Not only is the *satan* depicted as adversarial to Yahweh's judgment,

---

nature of the council," according to which "Yahweh engages in discussion and solicits opinions but does not give orders (Isa. 6:8; 1 Kings 22:20–22; Job 1–2)." Blenkinsopp, *Isaiah 40–55*, 179. That Micaiah informed Ahab about the "deceiving spirit" suggests that God did not intend to actually deceive Ahab.

98. Robin Routledge notes, "Not all of the heavenly beings who have access to the divine council are necessarily Yahweh's loyal servants." Indeed, "the divine assembly in the Old Testament" may include "evil as well as good" celestial beings. Routledge, "'Evil Spirit from the Lord,'" 18–19.

99. Hartley, *Job*, 71, 71n8. Similarly, Robert Alter sees here "an element of jealousy" and "cynical mean-spiritedness." Alter, *Wisdom Books*, 12. Cf. Tonstad, *God of Sense*, 245–46. Page thinks it "obvious" that "the disasters heaped upon Job were Satan's [malicious] doing." Page, *Powers of Evil*, 28.

100. Boda, *Zechariah*, 230n29.

101. Andersen, *Job*, 87.

102. Wilson, *Job*, 32–33. After noting that some "scholars (e.g., Gibson, Newsom, Weiss, Clines, Seow) regard 'the satan' as an expression of the dark side of God himself," Wilson contends, "none of these scholars demonstrates from the text of the prologue that 'the satan' should be so understood" (32). Even Newsom recognizes that "Yahweh and the accuser take opposing views of the character of Job" such that the *satan* "subtly becomes God's adversary." Newsom, "Job," 4:348.

103. Klein, *Zechariah*, 136, 134. He thinks (without offering a compelling reason) nevertheless that "'Satan' in v. 1 probably is not Satan in the New Testament" (134).

however, but Yahweh's stern rebuke of the *satan* also indicates an adversarial relationship between the parties (cf. Jude 9). Newsom adds, "Yahweh rejects the accuser's indictment of the high priest and rebukes the accuser instead."[104]

According to Boda, both Job 1–2 and Zechariah 3 depict the *satan* "in an adversarial relationship, not only with the human they evaluate critically, but also with Yahweh."[105] While seeing a role of court accuser here "may be appropriate," Boda believes that "the tone of Yahweh's response to these two figures . . . suggests that this figure is not a normative character in its OT context."[106] Both cases, then, mirror the function of the devil in the NT as arch-slanderer. Indeed, adopting the view that the *satan* plays the role of a prosecutor (normative or not) fits precisely with the NT profile of Satan, the "accuser of our brethren" who "accuses them before our God day and night" (Rev. 12:10; cf. *antidikos* in 1 Pet. 5:8) and who "deceives the whole world" (Rev. 12:9) as "the father of lies" (John 8:44) and who even "disputed" (*diakrinō*) and "argued" with Michael over the body of Moses (Jude 9). In the NT, Satan plays a strikingly similar prosecutorial and adversarial role (e.g., as accuser) as the *satan* in Job 1–2 and Zechariah 3.

Further, as in NT depictions of Satan, the *satan* of Job possesses power to bring about calamity within specified (but dynamic) limits and demands permission to test or antagonize a servant of God. This function comports well with the NT depiction of Satan as the "ruler of this world" (John 12:31; 14:30; 16:11; cf. 2 Cor. 4:4), who "prowls around like a roaring lion, seeking someone to devour" (1 Pet. 5:8) and who "demanded *permission* to sift [Peter] like wheat" (Luke 22:31). In this regard, some scholars recognize that, as Day puts it, the *satan* "challenges God at a very profound level," but they do not identify him with the Satan of the NT because "he is nonetheless subject to God's power" and "is certainly not an independent, inimical force."[107] However, this view assumes that Satan in the NT is not "subject to God's power" and is an "independent" force, both of which are false. As Hartley explains, "While the Satan's role in this test [of Job] is much simpler than his ominous role as head of all evil powers that the later Judeo-Christian tradition ascribes to him, he reveals numerous characteristics which suggest that he is contiguous with the later Satan, God's primary antagonist."[108]

Job 1–2 and Zechariah 3 together depict the *satan* as (1) an accuser and slanderer of God's people and, consequently, an adversary against God; (2) one

104. Newsom, "Job," 4:348.
105. Boda, *Zechariah*, 230. Cf. Noll, *Angels of Light*, 103.
106. Boda, *Zechariah*, 230.
107. Day, "Satan," 728.
108. Hartley, *Job*, 71n8.

who sadistically tests Job (cf. 1 Chron. 21:1) and makes false claims about Job's loyalty; and (3) one who possesses power to bring about calamity in this world. This list strikingly corresponds to the previously discussed profile of Satan in the NT as (1) adversarial accuser and slanderer, (2) deceiver and tempter, and (3) usurping ruler of this world. The evidence together points toward the conclusion that the *satan* in Job 1–2 and Zechariah 3:1–2 corresponds to the creature later called Satan in the NT. As Boda puts it, "If these figures do not relate to the Satan figure of the New Testament, they function in a way that will be associated with that later figure and may provide insight into the original function of the one known later as Satan within Yahweh's divine court."[109]

Undoubtedly, there is significant development of the depiction of Satan in Scripture.[110] However, in my view, this development is not a late, evolving conception that contradicts an earlier one but is an instance of unfolding (progressive) revelation, analogous to the progressive revelation of the Trinity.[111] I thus agree with Wilson that it is likely that "we see here [in Job] the role of one who was later to become Satan as we know him."[112] The word *hasatan* might refer to a role (e.g., prosecutor) in the heavenly council, but it does not contradict the depiction of Satan in the NT, who plays a similar antagonistic role—permitted but not approved of by God within the context of an ongoing cosmic conflict. To be sure, this summary raises questions about why God would permit the enemy to function in this and other malevolent ways (addressed in chap. 4 of the present volume).

The view that the *satan* in Job 1–2 and Zechariah 3:1–2 corresponds to the creature later called Satan in the NT is significantly bolstered by a canonical approach. Recall that Revelation explicitly identifies the "serpent of old" of Genesis 3 as Satan himself (Rev. 12:9; 20:2), exposing the slanderous activity of this adversary from the very beginning of the canon to the end. Further, Revelation's depiction of Satan as the celestial dragon ruler behind earthly rulers and kingdoms who opposed God and his covenant people throughout the OT (Rev. 13) indicates that Satan was relentlessly active as God's enemy

---

109. Boda, *Zechariah*, 230. Cf. Page, *Powers of Evil*, 29.

110. For a brief introduction to the development of the concept of the devil in extra-canonical Second Temple literature, see Hamilton, "Satan," 5:987–88. Further, see the brief overview in D. Brown, *God of This Age*, 21–60; Russell, *Devil*, 174–220. Although the extra-canonical Second Temple literature displays a much more elaborate angelology and demonology than that found in the biblical canon (see, e.g., Stuckenbruck, *Myth of Rebellious Angels*), the core components of the reading offered in this chapter seem to be supported therein.

111. Noll suggests Satan's "full-fledged appearance in the Gospels" might be understood as "concomitant with the coming of the Son of God." Noll, "Angels," 47.

112. Wilson, *Job*, 32. Wilson cautions, however, against "reading later ideas of Satan or the devil back into this text" (32).

behind the scenes throughout the OT narratives. If this view is correct, although the NT develops a more detailed understanding of Satan and his minions, the main facets of a cosmic conflict are explicit in the OT. Even if one thinks the *satan* of the OT is not the same person as Satan in the NT, the OT data nevertheless exhibit a conflict between Yahweh and rebellious celestial beings in the heavenly council who oppose and accuse Yahweh of unjust judgment, thus shedding significant light on the nature of the conflict.

Retrieving the Supernatural Worldview of Christian Theism

The cosmic conflict framework faces two problems of plausibility: (1) the anti-supernaturalism of post-Enlightenment (modernist) thinking that has affected most in the West (though far less so others in the world) and (2) the theological conundrum of how to make sense of a conflict between the omnipotent creator God and mere creatures. The second of these problems is addressed in chapter 4. Here we briefly take up the first problem.

Particularly since the rise of modernism via the Enlightenment, the reality of supernatural agencies such as angels and demons has been widely questioned and often dismissed. As Rudolf Bultmann wrote in 1941, "Now that the forces and the laws of nature have been discovered, we can no longer believe in spirits whether good or evil."[113] Prior to modernism, however, the reality of a cosmic conflict was widely held by Christians through the ages. As Noll states, "Since Schleiermacher's time, angels have been seen as liturgical and aesthetic embellishments. In classical times, they were given a place in the dogmatic syllabus."[114]

Nearly all early Christians believed in supernatural agencies and took for granted that such agencies affect what occurs on earth. As Paul Gavrilyuk frames it, "The common core of patristic theodicy" included, among other things, the view that "God is not the author of evil" but that the "misuse of angelic and human free will is the cause of evil."[115] As Jeffrey Burton Russell explains in his excellent survey of early Christian views of Satan, "The devil has always been a central Christian doctrine, an integral element in Christian tradition."[116] Indeed,

---

113. Bultmann, *New Testament Mythology*, 4.

114. Noll, "Angels," 45.

115. Gavrilyuk, "An Overview of Patristic Theodicies," 6. Cf. Greg Boyd's argument that the "warfare worldview of the Bible was adopted and even expanded" in successive generations prior to Augustine. Boyd, *Satan and the Problem of Evil*, 39. Cf. Tonstad, "Theodicy," 169–202; Burns, *Christian Understandings of Evil*, 27–39, 45–58.

116. Russell, *Satan*, 226. In what many take as a description of the rule of faith, Irenaeus refers to "the angels who transgressed and became apostates." Irenaeus, *Against Heresies* 1.10.1

although "diabology" was "eclipsed in" the fourth and fifth centuries by the "debates on the Trinity and Christ," in both the "Greek East and Latin West," the core of early Christian diabology remained in place even through the tumult of the Reformation.[117] The "great change" came "with the Enlightenment."[118]

In Russell's view, "Theologians who exclude Satan in the interests of their own personal views run the risk of holding an incoherent view of Christianity."[119] He adds that "Scripture and tradition" both "clearly affirm the existence of the Devil" viewed as "a mighty person with intelligence and will whose energies are bent on the destruction of the cosmos and the misery of its creatures."[120] Thus "to deny the existence and central importance of the Devil in Christianity is to run counter to apostolic teaching and to the historical development of Christian doctrine."[121] Russell claims that "it makes little sense to call oneself a Christian while affirming a view contrary to scripture and tradition."[122] Russell is not alone in this assessment. Garrett DeWeese comments that rejecting the reality of "spiritual beings" entails that one "dismiss totally the worldview of both the Old and the New Testaments, and indeed of Jesus himself."[123] As Hans Urs von Balthasar puts it, the "stubborn persistence of this topic [of the devil and his minions] in Scripture and in the life of Jesus should cause us to pay greater attention to it."[124]

Not only does the Christian tradition strongly support a supernatural worldview, inclusive of spiritual beings, but as Keith Ferdinando explains, "Most peoples, for most of history, have believed in spirits, witchcraft and sorcery. The Ohio State University research project found that some 74 percent of 488 societies studied throughout the world had possession beliefs."[125] Ferdinando

---

(*ANF* 1:330). Similarly, Tertullian notes a baptismal formula wherein "we solemnly profess that we disown the devil, and his pomp, and his angels." Tertullian, *De Corona* 3 (*ANF* 3:94). A similar statement appears in many ancient baptismal formulas thereafter. See Gilmore and Caspari, "Renunciation of the Devil," 488–89. Noll, speaking of the Nicene Creed, which apparently draws on Col. 1:16 (itself widely understood as a very early christological hymn), adds, "Confession of 'things visible and invisible' seems indeed to be the dogmatic position of the historic catholic faith." Noll, "Angels," 47.

117. Russell, *Satan*, 187. "The main lines of the concept are clear: the Devil as created, fallen through his own free choice, the chief of evil forces in the cosmos, mortally wounded by Christ, and doomed to ruin" (220).

118. Russell, *Prince of Darkness*, 166.

119. Russell, *Satan*, 226.

120. Russell, *Mephistopheles*, 299, 301.

121. Russell, *Satan*, 225.

122. Russell, *Mephistopheles*, 299.

123. DeWeese, "Natural Evil," 63. Cf. Page, *Powers of Evil*, 180.

124. Balthasar, *Action*, 197–98.

125. Ferdinando, *Triumph of Christ*, 376. Reese adds, "Some conception of evil spirits or demons was held almost universally by the religions of the ancient world." Reese, "Demons,"

continues, "While truth is not established by majorities, the great consensus of most of humanity through time suggests that it may be modern scepticism which is idiosyncratic, and that the burden of proof should fall upon those who deny the reality of such phenomena."[126] Whether or not one goes as far as Ferdinando, one must note that he effectively highlights the danger of ethnocentrism when such supernatural worldviews are dismissed as "implausible."[127] Indeed, Kabiro wa Gatumu notes that "some scholars regard the Western church as having failed" to "give sufficient or serious attention to the topic of supernatural powers" because of "anti-supernaturalistic prejudice."[128]

As Alvin Plantinga puts it, many philosophers have claimed "that it is extremely implausible, in our enlightened day and age, to suppose that there is such a thing as Satan, let alone his cohorts. Plausibility, of course, is in the ear of the hearer, and even in our enlightened times there are plenty of people who think both that there are non-human free creatures and that they are responsible for some of the evil that the world contains."[129] From a modernistic, anti-supernaturalist perspective such a claim seems rather implausible indeed. However, from the vantage point of the Christian theism depicted in Scripture and most of the Christian tradition, the claim is eminently plausible, being deeply embedded in the very narrative of the Christ event.[130]

According to Ferdinando, the "skepticism of western academics" is an inheritance of the Enlightenment worldview no less than belief in spiritual realities is culturally conditioned and traditioned.[131] As such, Plantinga notes that "whether or not one finds the view in question plausible or implausible will of course depend on what else one believes: the theist already believes in the existence of at least one non-human person who is active in history: God. Accordingly the suggestion that there are other such persons . . . may not seem at all implausible to him."[132]

2:140. Cf. Boyd's survey of the "nearly universal intuition of cosmic conflict" across cultures. Boyd, *God at War*, 18.

126. Ferdinando, *Triumph of Christ*, 376.

127. In his extensive case for miracles, which documents numerous cross-cultural cases, Craig Keener decries the ethnocentrism of anti-supernaturalistic biases. Keener, *Miracles*, 1:222–23.

128. Wa Gatumu, *Pauline Concept of Supernatural Powers*, 52, 51. Cf. Moses, *Practices of Power*, 221–24.

129. Plantinga, "Self-Profile," 42.

130. As Brian Han Gregg notes, "The conflict between God and Satan is clearly a central feature of Jesus' teaching and ministry." Gregg, *What Does the Bible Say?*, 66. So also, Page, *Powers of Evil*, 135; Arnold, *Powers of Darkness*, 16.

131. Ferdinando, *Triumph of Christ*, 378.

132. Plantinga, "Self-Profile," 43. Anthony C. Thiselton adds, "Belief about supernatural interventions in the affairs of [humans] is not necessarily primitive or pre-scientific, as the Enlightenment view of myth would imply." Thiselton, *Two Horizons*, 289.

Just such a perspective is present in the work of theologian Thomas C. Oden, who contends that biblical reasoning is "incomplete if it lacks reference entirely to the demonic powers," particularly Satan, the "adversary, accuser, hater," and "calumniator." In his systematic theology, awash with citations from the Christian tradition, Oden affirms that the "Deceiver Satan is the primordial adversary to God," an "angelic being hostile to God, the chief of the fallen angels."[133] This "devil is not evil by created nature but by choice."[134] Further, Satan "is able temporarily to play the role of prince of this world (John 14:30)," though "his power is already being overcome and judged by the suffering Messiah (John 16:11)."[135]

C. S. Lewis likewise affirms a robust conception of the cosmic conflict in both his nonfiction and his fiction writings.[136] He affirms that "this universe is at war," though not "a war between independent powers" but a "rebellion, and . . . we are living in a part of the universe occupied by the rebel."[137] As such, "there is no neutral ground in the universe. Every square inch, every split second is claimed by God, and counterclaimed by Satan."[138] Whatever conclusions one arrives at relative to the viability of this view for today, in my view a canonical theology that seeks to derive its conceptual framework from the canon is obliged to incorporate a cosmic conflict framework, in keeping with Christian tradition throughout the ages.

Conclusion

We've seen that Scripture presents a robust cosmic conflict between God and his followers and the devil and his minions. We've seen, further, that this framework fits within and is eminently plausible, given the traditional framework of Christian theism, contra modernistic anti-supernaturalism. Now,

133. Oden, *Classic Christianity*, 831. Cf. T. F. Torrance's description of the "organized kingdom of evil and darkness" and "an utterly rebellious evil will or spirit which the Holy Scriptures call Satan." Torrance, *Christian Doctrine of God*, 227. Cf. Erickson, *Christian Theology*, 415–20.

134. Oden, *Classic Christianity*, 832.

135. Oden, *Classic Christianity*, 832. John G. Stackhouse Jr. adds, "Satan temporarily enjoys the status of the 'prince of *this* world,'" having "considerable influence over individuals, corporations, and structures throughout the world in this era." Stackhouse, *Can God Be Trusted?*, 39 (emphasis original).

136. Consider the prominence of the theme in Lewis's fictional works such as *The Screwtape Letters*, the Chronicles of Narnia series, and the Space Trilogy, inspired by John Milton's masterpiece, *Paradise Lost*.

137. Lewis, *Mere Christianity*, 45.

138. Lewis, "Christianity and Culture," 33.

however, we face a number of questions for this approach: What ramifications does it have for the problem of evil? Is such a view theologically compatible with a commitment to divine sovereignty? Does not a cosmic conflict theodicy push the problem back one step to why God created such agencies and why God has granted them, and continues to grant them, such freedom and power? The next chapter will take up the nature of this cosmic conflict toward addressing these and other issues and outlining how this framework fills the gaps in moving toward a theodicy of love.

4

The Nature of the Conflict
and Rules of Engagement

The previous chapter introduced the cosmic conflict framework by sur-
veying the biblical depiction of the conflict between God's kingdom of
light and the demonic realm of darkness. This framework raises significant
questions: How could there be any *real* conflict between the sovereign,
omnipotent God and anyone else? Could not God overpower anyone who
would oppose him?

Some worry that supposing a genuine conflict requires cosmic dualism,
the view that good and evil are eternal powers in perpetual conflict. Even if
dualism can be avoided, many wonder how a cosmic conflict could help to
address the problem of evil. In Jeffrey Burton Russell's view, "The idea of
the Devil ultimately does little to solve the problem of *why* there is evil in the
cosmos. At the center of the problem is the question of why God should freely
choose to create a cosmos in which the Devil and other evil beings produce
such immeasurable suffering. How can God, freely choosing this cosmos, not
be responsible for it? And if God is responsible, why do we need the idea of
the Devil?"[1] In order to address these and other crucial questions, we first need
to consider the nature of the conflict as depicted in Scripture. Then we will be
equipped to address the ramifications of the conflict for the problem of evil.

1. Russell, *Mephistopheles*, 300.

Considering the Nature of the Conflict

Scripture explicitly rules out cosmic dualism. As Colossians 1:16 explains, "For by Him [Christ] all things were created, both in the heavens and on earth, visible and invisible, whether thrones or dominions or rulers or authorities—all things have been created through Him and for Him." Yet Scripture frequently depicts God as a warrior involved in genuine conflict against real enemies, including celestial "rulers." How can this be? How could there be any conflict between the omnipotent God and finite creatures?

At the level of sheer power, no one could oppose an omnipotent being. Any conflict between the omnipotent God and others could not be one of *sheer power* but must be of a different kind. What, then, is the nature of the conflict? Scripture depicts the conflict as a dispute over God's moral character and government. Cosmic allegations have been raised before the heavenly council, claiming that God is not wholly good, loving, or just. This is, then, a largely epistemic conflict, which (insofar as God maintains his commitment to the epistemic freedom necessary for love) cannot be won by the mere exercise of power but is met by an extended demonstration of character in a cosmic courtroom drama.

Original Slander, Cosmic Allegations

The serpent of Genesis 3 brings forth the first of many slanderous allegations against God reported in Scripture. Genesis 3 introduces this "serpent" as "more crafty than any beast of the field which the Lord God had made" (v. 1). The term "crafty" (*'arum*) is ambiguous, perhaps evoking, via narrative tension, the uncertainty that Eve might have experienced regarding the character of this talking snake.[2] Notably, talking animals are not normal in the OT; besides this snake in Eden, the only other example is the story of Balaam's donkey, which stems from the action of a celestial being (the angel of the Lord).[3] As it turns out, the instance in Genesis 3 is also caused by a celestial being.[4]

The serpent's question draws Eve into a dangerous and ultimately tragic dialogue. Though God prohibited Adam and Eve from only one tree, the

---

2. Victor P. Hamilton comments, "*'ārûm* is an ambivalent term that may describe a desirable [cf. Prov. 14:8, "the wisdom of the sensible"] or undesirable characteristic [cf. Job 5:12, "the plotting of the shrewd"]." Hamilton, *Genesis 1–17*, 187.

3. See Tonstad, *God of Sense*, 94–95.

4. Gordon J. Wenham points to the seven-headed "serpent Leviathan, mentioned in Ugaritic mythology" (see *ANET*, 138) and "referred to in Isa 27:1 (cf. Job 26:13) as . . . evidence of the familiar association in biblical times of serpents and God's enemies." Wenham, *Genesis 1–15*, 73.

serpent "grossly exaggerates God's prohibition" in his "crafty" question: "Indeed, has God said, 'You shall not eat from any tree of the garden'?" (Gen. 3:1).[5] Eve responds that there is only one tree from which they may not eat, lest they die (vv. 2–3). The serpent then directly contradicts God, asserting, "You surely will not die! For God knows that in the day you eat from it your eyes will be opened, and you will be like God, knowing good and evil" (vv. 4–5).

If the serpent is believed, God is a liar who does not really want what is best for Eve. On the contrary, the serpent asserts, God is withholding something good from Eve (i.e., knowledge) in order to oppress her.[6] She should "be like God," but God is keeping her from becoming so. As Hamilton puts it, this is "a direct frontal attack" against God's character. There is a "mixture here of misquotation, denial, and slander fed to the woman by the snake."[7]

By this point in the narrative, the reader should be aware that evil is already present in the garden, both conceptually and actually. Conceptually, "evil" has already appeared in the name of "the tree of the knowledge of good and evil" (Gen. 2:9, 17). That evil exists and is *actually* present is apparent in that the serpent's accusations entail that someone must be lying. The continuing narrative reveals that the serpent is lying and slandering God's character. Evil is thus already present in Eden, actualized in the serpent, who acts as an enemy accuser of God.

From Eve's perspective, however, the serpent's assertion confronts her with an epistemic choice: believe God or entertain the serpent's insidious slander of God's character.[8] Either the serpent is a liar or God is. Whether or not Eve understands the choice in these terms, she chooses to disbelieve and distrust God and eat the fruit, as does Adam (Gen. 3:6), with enormously tragic consequences. At the outset of the canon, then, an epistemic conflict over the character of God is front and center.

Whereas numerous scholars (particularly since the Enlightenment) have questioned the traditional identification of this serpent with the devil, noting that Genesis does not make this identification, the wider canon explicitly identifies "the devil and Satan," the "great dragon," as the "serpent of old" (Rev.

5. Hamilton, *Genesis 1–17*, 188.

6. Eve already possessed knowledge of good; she lacked only the (experiential) knowledge of evil.

7. Hamilton, *Genesis 1–17*, 189. Kenneth A. Mathews adds that the "motivation for God's command is impugned by the serpent" and "the adversary argues the same case in Job (1:9–11; 2:4–5). God is not good and gracious; he is selfish and deceptive." Mathews, *Genesis 1–11:26*, 236. Cf. Sarna, *Genesis*, 25; Page, *Powers of Evil*, 13, 17–18.

8. As Donald E. Gowan notes, the very "setting of a limit shows that" Eve "does indeed have a choice and thus establishes" her "freedom." Gowan, *From Eden to Babel*, 42. Cf. Westermann, *Genesis 1–11*, 222; Sarna, *Genesis*, 21.

12:9).[9] This is a demonstrable allusion to Genesis 3. As Tremper Longman III explains, the "serpent, as later Scripture (Rev. 12:9) makes clear, was not an ordinary animal, but rather an incarnation of the evil one, Satan himself."[10] G. K. Beale notes, "Genesis 3 attributes to [the devil] the two functions of *slanderer* and *deceiver*" that are emphasized in Revelation 12:9 and elsewhere.[11] Kevin J. Vanhoozer adds, "Satan's verbal ploys are nothing short of an assault on the Creator and created order alike" via a campaign of "*disinformation.*"[12] "At its origin," Longman notes, "the spiritual nature of the conflict is clear" (cf. Gen. 3:15).[13]

Jesus appears to allude to Genesis 3 when he describes the devil as "a murderer from the beginning" and "a liar and the father of lies" (John 8:44; cf. 1 John 3:8).[14] Further, the serpent in Genesis 3 fits the profile of Satan elsewhere in Scripture. The serpent slanders God's character, deceives and tempts Eve, and leads God's creation into evil, mirroring the depiction of Satan throughout Scripture as the original (1) accuser and slanderer,[15] (2) deceiver and tempter of the whole world from the beginning,[16] and (3) usurping ruler of this world.[17]

Given this identification, we find the devil slandering God's character at the outset of Scripture, slyly alleging that God is not an all-benevolent ruler. This attack prompts humans to distrust God's character, leading to broken relationships with God and one another (Gen. 3:7–12) as humans are cut off from Eden and it is guarded by "cherubim and the flaming sword" (v. 24). Yet there is hope. Genesis 3:15, traditionally known as the "first gospel" (*protoevangelium*), presents what many have understood as a prophecy of the coming Messiah, namely, that the woman's seed will ultimately strike the serpent's head but not before being struck by the serpent.

9. Thinking that the serpent could not be the devil because he is not clearly identified as the devil in Genesis would be analogous to thinking that the character first identified simply as Strider the Ranger in *The Lord of the Rings* could not be Aragorn, the heir to the throne of Gondor, as he is later revealed to be.

10. Longman, *Daniel*, 256. This interpretation has been widely held in the Christian tradition. Thomas C. Oden explains, "Satan came in the form of a serpent in" Gen. 3. "By this means 'death entered the world' (Wis. 2:24)." Oden, *Classic Christianity*, 831.

11. Beale, *Revelation*, 656 (emphasis original).

12. Vanhoozer, *Faith Speaking Understanding*, 87 (emphasis original).

13. Longman, *Daniel*, 256.

14. Gerald L. Borchert comments, Jesus's "reference [in John 8:44] is obviously to the garden of Eden text where the deceit of the serpent/devil led to the 'death' of Adam and Eve (Gen. 3:1–4; cf. Wis. 2:24; Rom. 5:12)." Borchert, *John 1–11*, 305.

15. Rev. 12:10; cf. Job 1–2; Zech. 3:1–2; Jude 9.

16. Matt. 4:3; Rev. 12:9; cf. John 8:44; 1 John 3:8.

17. Luke 4:5–6; John 12:31; 14:30; 16:11. Many Christians have held that, as Vanhoozer puts it, "Adam and Eve failed to rule rightly in God's stead," and "consequently, the world is now under the dominion of the powers of darkness." Vanhoozer, *Faith Speaking Understanding*, 100.

It is appropriate, then, that the devil's temptation of Jesus in the wilderness (e.g., Matt. 4) mirrors the temptation of Eve. Jesus defeats the temptations of the arch-slanderer. Here again the conflict is a matter of epistemic decisions, not of sheer force. Further, the devil reveals his desire for worship by promising Jesus the world's kingdoms if only Jesus will "fall down and worship" him (Matt. 4:8–9; cf. 1 Cor. 10:20; Col. 2:18). In both instances, Satan aims his deceptions and temptations at tarnishing God's reputation, attempting to usurp the honor and worship due only to Yahweh. Here and elsewhere, the conflict is depicted as a battle of ideas, with at least two primary themes: (1) cosmic charges against God's character and (2) the enemy's desire to usurp God's worship as king.

The theme of cosmic allegations against God's character is bookended in the canon by Revelation, which is also deeply concerned with God's righteous character, worship, and an overarching cosmic conflict with the dragon and his angels (Rev. 12). As Beale describes it, "After the Fall, the serpent and his agents do on a worldwide scale what he began in the garden," which Beale characterizes as putting forth "claims" that "slander the character of God" such that Revelation 12:9 "calls him 'the one deceiving the whole earth,' and verse 10 refers to him as slanderer of God's people."[18] In Revelation 13 the sea beast, operating via the power and authority given him by the dragon (vv. 2, 5), "opened his mouth in blasphemies against God, to blaspheme His name and His tabernacle, *that is,* those who dwell in heaven" (v. 6).

From Genesis to Revelation, questions regarding God's character and government are raised in heaven and on earth. Since the enemy's slanderous allegations are epistemic in nature, they cannot be effectively answered by any display of power, however great. Indeed, no amount of power exercised by a king would prove to his subjects that he is not unjust. No show of executive power could clear the name of a president accused of corruption. A conflict over character cannot be settled by sheer power but requires demonstration.

Cosmic Lawsuit and Courtroom Drama

Throughout Scripture, creatures raise questions such as, Is God just? Does God love perfectly? Is evil God's fault? Why evil? Repeatedly, when things go wrong, people question God and his government. As the landowner's servants put it, "Sir, did you not sow good seed in your field? How then does it have tares?" (Matt. 13:27). Particularly in times of distress, God's people are prone to ask, What is God doing? Does he care for us? Is he still keeping

---

18. Beale, *Revelation*, 656.

the covenant? Why are these bad things happening to us? Why doesn't God punish the wicked? How can God be just, given the injustice in this world?[19]

One major theme of Scripture is God's defense and vindication of his name,[20] which is closely connected with his concern for justice. Scripture repeatedly depicts God as the cosmic judge involved in covenant lawsuits, bringing charges against the nations, their gods,[21] and sometimes his covenant people. In the majority of cases, observes Richard Davidson, "God defends/vindicates the cause of His covenant people," which also vindicates Yahweh himself in claiming such people as his own.[22] Davidson explains that such lawsuits and judgments are part of a larger covenant lawsuit and judgment theme in Scripture, a "cosmic divine lawsuit." Indeed, "such mini-lawsuits constitute a microcosm of the macrocosmic final 'assize,' the apocalyptic cosmic divine lawsuit described in such passages as Daniel 7 and throughout the book of Revelation." Further, such covenant lawsuits evince a significant pattern: "Before God executes judgment (either positively or negatively) toward an individual or a people, He first conducts legal proceedings, not for Him to know the facts, but to reveal in open court, as it were, that He is just and fair in all of His dealings."[23] In other words, God's very process of judgment provides evidence of God's fairness, contra the enemy's accusations.[24]

Noting the pervasive "covenant lawsuit motif" throughout Scripture, Vanhoozer comments that the "great theater of the world turns out to be a courtroom in which defendants and prosecutors plead their respective cases and witnesses give testimony."[25] In his view, "What is finally on trial in the covenantal courtroom drama of the Christ is the truth about the nature of

19. See the texts in chap. 1 of the present volume.

20. See, e.g., Gen. 18:24–25; Exod. 32:12–13; Num. 14:15–16; Pss. 31:3; 106:8; 109:21; Isa. 48:9–11; Ezek. 18:25; 20:9, 14, 22, 44.

21. Vanhoozer notes that the "trial motif is especially prominent in the contest between Elijah and the prophets of Baal (1 Kings 18)" and that the "identity of Yahweh is again at stake in Isaiah 40–55," wherein "'Yahweh and his witnesses are placed on one side and the gods of the nations and their supporters on the other.'" Vanhoozer, *Faith Speaking Understanding*, 106, quoting Trites, *New Testament Concept of Witness*, 44.

22. Davidson, "Divine Covenant Lawsuit Motif," 83.

23. Davidson, "Divine Covenant Lawsuit Motif," 83. Some dispute whether there is a distinct covenant lawsuit genre. Davidson makes a compelling case that "the divine covenant lawsuit is pervasive in Scripture, both as a discrete sub-genre and as a prominent motif throughout the various parts of both OT and NT," having "isolated at least 320 different references to a divine covenant lawsuit in the OT" alone (83). Apart from conclusions regarding literary form, the broader biblical pattern of disputes/lawsuits evinces at least a minimal covenant dispute/lawsuit motif.

24. Further, "the ultimate purpose of the divine covenant lawsuit directed toward Israel is to vindicate the juridical and moral correctness of Yahweh in the face of disasters that Israel experiences (see, e.g., Jer. 30:11; 46:28; Ezek. 5:13; Mic. 6:3–5). The covenant lawsuit is a statement of theodicy!" Davidson, "Divine Covenant Lawsuit," 69.

25. Vanhoozer, *Faith Speaking Understanding*, 104, 105.

God's reign and the identity of the king."[26] In short, "What is being tried is covenant faithfulness: the righteousness of God."[27]

Among the most striking instances of this motif is the "cosmic lawsuit" of Daniel 7, itself an apparent heavenly council or court scene.[28] In this vision, after a succession of kingdoms and kings signified by beasts and horns, a little horn arises with "eyes like the eyes of a man and a mouth uttering great boasts" or blasphemies (v. 8; cf. 11:36). The scene then shifts to a cosmic court, described by Daniel.

> I kept looking
> Until thrones were set up,
> And the Ancient of Days took His seat. . . .
> His throne was ablaze with flames. . . .
> Thousands upon thousands were attending Him,
> And myriads upon myriads were standing before Him;
> The court sat,
> And the books were opened. (Dan. 7:9–10)

After this judgment, Daniel writes, "I kept looking because of the sound of the boastful words which the horn was speaking; I kept looking until the beast was slain" (v. 11). He continues, "As for the rest of the beasts, their dominion was taken away, but an extension of life was granted to them for an appointed period of time" (v. 12). Thereafter, the Son of Man "was given" an "everlasting dominion," but first, time was given for the limited dominion of beasts and the process of judgment (v. 14).

The chapter later elaborates that this little horn opposes God and his people, having "eyes and a mouth uttering great boasts" (Dan. 7:20) and "waging war with the saints and overpowering them until the Ancient of Days came and judgment was passed in favor of the saints of the Highest One, and the time arrived when the saints took possession of the kingdom" (vv. 21–22).[29] Daniel continues, "He will speak out against the Most High and wear down the saints of the Highest One" who are "given into his hand for a time, times, and half a time" (v. 25). "But the court will sit for judgment,

26. Vanhoozer, *Faith Speaking Understanding*, 109.

27. Vanhoozer, *Faith Speaking Understanding*, 107. Vanhoozer describes the "informal testing" of Abraham and others by God as "a kind of covenant trial" that "belongs in the broad canonical sweep of the courtroom theodrama" (105).

28. Louis F. Hartman sees this as a depiction of the "celestial court" or "celestial tribunal," a picture of "the divine judge enthroned in the assembly of his angels." Hartman, *Daniel*, 217.

29. Cf. the little horn's activity, which "trampled" some "of the host" and "stars" and "even magnified *itself* to be equal with the Commander of the host" (Dan. 8:10–11; cf. 2 Thess. 2:4; Rev. 13:8, 12).

and his dominion will be taken away" (v. 26), and "the sovereignty, the dominion and the greatness of all the kingdoms under the whole heaven will be given to the people of the saints of the Highest One; His kingdom will be an everlasting kingdom, and all the dominions will serve and obey Him" (v. 27; cf. Rev. 20:4–6).[30]

A number of elements in this cosmic judgment scene warrant attention for our purposes. First, this little horn opposes God with "boastful words," indicating epistemic claims. Second, before judgment is executed, there are judgment proceedings before a heavenly council or court. Third, prior to "judgment" being "passed in favor of the saints," the saints are overpowered by the little horn for a specified time ("time, times, and half a time") during which the saints are "given into his hand." In other words, this little horn is granted power and authority for a specified time, evincing some "rules of engagement" (discussed later in this chapter).

This scene in Daniel 7 mirrors the scene in Job 1–2 in significant ways. In Job 1 the *satan* appears before the heavenly council as part of an apparently ongoing dispute with God. Whereas God declares Job is "blameless" and "upright" (v. 8), the *satan* claims Job is not sincere (vv. 9–11), which amounts to an accusation not only against Job but also against God's judgment (cf. Rev. 12:10). God responds to the *satan*'s charges before the heavenly council by agreeing to allow the *satan* to test his theory, within limits. However, despite numerous horrible afflictions by the *satan*, Job remains faithful (vv. 20–22; 2:9–10), falsifying the *satan*'s charges.

This scene shows that bad things happen to good people,[31] which falsifies the theology of retribution set forth by Job's friends.[32] The *satan*, not God, is the antagonist who instigates and wreaks havoc on Job (e.g., Job 1:12; 2:7). Readers are often troubled by God allowing the *satan* to harm Job and his family.[33] However, if we understand that the *satan* is bringing an implicit charge against God's judgment and protection of Job (Job 1:10) and that the heavenly council is more than merely decorative and has some real juridical function (cf. Dan. 4:17), it follows that God is not making these decisions unilaterally but is responding to the *satan*'s charges and requests before the heavenly council.[34] In doing so, God takes into account the other

---

30. "Behind the earthly struggle stands a cosmic struggle." Longman, *Daniel*, 188.

31. Cf. Eccles. 7:15; 8:14; Jer. 5:28; 12:1; Luke 13:1–5.

32. Scripture elsewhere falsifies the theology of retribution (e.g., Eccles. 3:16–17; 8:12, 14; 9:2; Matt. 5:45; Luke 13:1–5; John 9:1–3).

33. See, e.g., Newsom, "Job," 4:350; Clines, *Job 1–20*, 25.

34. As R. Dean Davis notes, "The [divine] council is consistently pictured as convening before divine actions are taken, suggesting that its chief function is executive/judicial decision-making." R. Davis, *Heavenly Court Judgment*, 109–10.

minds involved, toward the larger purpose of demonstration within the cosmic conflict (cf. 1 Cor. 4:9), for the flourishing of love and thus the best good of everyone in the universe.

Frances Andersen believes "the Lord did have a good reason" for this—"namely to disprove the Satan's slander" of God's character.[35] John Hartley notes that "the main function of this assembly here is to provide an open forum in which Yahweh permits the testing of Job. That is, the plan to test Job was not hatched in a secret meeting between Yahweh and the *satan*. Rather it was decided openly before the heavenly assembly. In this setting Yahweh's motivation, based on his complete confidence in Job, was fully known and thus it was above question."[36]

In Job, the *satan* possesses power to work evil in this world as its temporary ruler, but only within limits that are openly negotiated and modified before the heavenly council. At first, preexisting limits on the *satan*'s jurisdiction were in place, including a "hedge" around Job and his belongings. Then the parameters were twice modified before the heavenly council. These parameters, or "rules of engagement," are the product of negotiation within the context of a courtroom dispute and might, then, be thought of as *covenantal* rules of engagement, which are binding on both parties.[37] Insofar as God agrees before the heavenly council to extend the jurisdiction of the *satan*, God cannot (morally) prevent the *satan* from exercising power within that jurisdiction. Here, then, the *satan*'s restricted power as the temporary "ruler of this world" (John 12:31) functions within some dynamic "rules of engagement" that are known to both God and the *satan* (but that are not usually known to us). These rules of engagement are not unilaterally set by God but are subject to negotiation before the heavenly council. (Much more will be said about these covenantal rules of engagement later in this chapter.)

It is no coincidence that both Job 1–2 and Zechariah 3, the only OT passages containing *hasatan*, depict a dispute and judgment scene wherein God rebukes the enemy's allegations against God's people (and, indirectly, against God's judgment in favor of his people; cf. Jude 9). Indeed, according to Davidson, "Several studies contend that the entire book of Job may be

---

35. Andersen, *Job*, 95. Here, "if God is treating Job as righteous when he is not, then God is not acting fairly. Much is at stake." Wilson, *Job*, 32. Further, while Clines seems to think that God is guilty of wrongdoing here, he nevertheless comments, "We do not yet know, and the characters of the narrative do not yet know, whether Job's piety is disinterested or not; it is a question that we all, in company with the heavenly court, would like to hear settled." Clines, *Job 1–20*, 25.

36. Hartley, *Job*, 72. Cf. Wilson, *Job*, 34.

37. I use "covenantal" minimally here to indicate only some bilateral agreement.

regarded as a cosmic covenant lawsuit."[38] Here and elsewhere it is striking to notice the repeated legal context of the cosmic conflict wherein the devil is the accuser of the brethren (Rev. 12), an explicit legal opponent of God and his people before the heavenly council (1 Pet. 5:8; Jude 9). Indeed, in Beale's view, Job 1–2, Zechariah 3:1–2, and Jude 8–9 "are best understood" in the "context of Michael defending Israel in the heavenly courtroom against Satan's accusations."[39]

Many of the instances of cosmic conflict surveyed in chapter 3 exhibit this very context of cosmic judgment. As Michael Heiser observes, these include the judgment of the "gods" in the heavenly council in Psalm 82 for their "corrupt rule of the nations" (cf. Isa. 24:21–23).[40] Such judgment scenes make little sense if one mistakenly thinks they are for God's knowledge. Given God's omniscience (1 John 3:20), God could learn nothing from such judgment proceedings. Such judgments and the heavenly council itself must serve some broader function, which seems to include the open demonstration of God's government before celestial beings, countering the cosmic allegations against God's character.

Paul appears to understand his suffering in ministry as something like an exhibit in the cosmic trial proceedings. As he writes to the church in Corinth, "God has exhibited us apostles last of all, as men condemned to death; because we have become a spectacle to the world [*kosmos*], both to angels and to men" (1 Cor. 4:9; cf. 6:2–3). Paul's "witness" here is not merely for humans but functions as a "spectacle" or "theater" (*theatron*) for the "cosmos," including "angels."[41] This framework makes sense of Paul's later claim that "we will judge angels" (6:3).[42] Further, this concept of cosmic trial proceedings might suggest a broader framework for the repeated NT calls for Christians to be witnesses and testify, alongside other frequent imagery of legal court proceedings.

Richard Bauckham writes that in Revelation the "world is a kind of courtroom in which the issue of who is the true God is being decided. In this judicial contest Jesus and his followers bear witness to the truth."[43] Specifically,

---

38. Davidson, "Divine Covenant Lawsuit," 79.

39. Beale, *Revelation*, 661. This also corresponds to the devil's "role of a legal 'accuser' [in the heavenly court] in early Judaism (Jub. 1:20; 17:15–16; 18:9–12; 48:15–18; 1 En. 40:7; Test. Levi 5:6; Test. Dan 6:2)" (661).

40. Heiser, *Unseen Realm*, 27.

41. Gordon D. Fee observes that there is "a cosmic dimension to the spectacle: He is on display before the whole universe, as it were." Fee, *First Epistle to the Corinthians*, 175.

42. Fee comments that this "probably reflects an apocalyptic motif as to the judgment of fallen angels." Fee, *First Epistle to the Corinthians*, 234.

43. Bauckham, *Theology of the Book of Revelation*, 73.

"Jesus' and his followers' witness to the true God and his righteousness" is what exposes the enemy's program of deceit and slander.[44] This is situated within the broader context of "the cosmic conflict between good and evil."[45] Vanhoozer adds, "There will be satanic conflict until the end. Disciples do well to remember the nature of the conflict: will we side with those who respond to God's word rightly or with those who question, distort, and deny it?"[46] Here, "all human beings, like the heavens and earth, are called upon to be witnesses to the trial of truth at the heart of the gospel."[47]

This concept of a cosmic courtroom drama, particularly the heavenly council judgment scene of Daniel 7, relates in significant ways to the heavenly council or court scenes of Revelation.[48] David E. Aune identifies seven "heavenly court" or "heavenly throne-room scenes" in Revelation.[49] The longest of these is in Revelation 4–5, which according to Aune focuses on "God enthroned in his heavenly court surrounded by a variety of angelic beings or lesser deities (angels, archangels, seraphim, cherubim) who function as courtiers. All such descriptions of God enthroned in the midst of his heavenly court are based on the ancient conception of the divine council or assembly."[50]

In these heavenly council scenes, unlike many OT counterparts, no antagonist appears before the council. This absence is quite striking, given the prominence of the conflict between the kingdom of God and the kingdom of Satan throughout Revelation, which includes "a complex array of supernatural beings arranged in two competitive hierarchies, one headed by God and the other by Satan," who "plays a central role in the narratives as the chief antagonist."[51] Although the diabolical accuser of the brethren appears prominently throughout Revelation, he does not appear in the many heavenly court scenes. Some scholars believe that the evil celestial beings have finally been banished from the heavenly council or court, based on the victory of

---

44. Bauckham, *Theology of the Book of Revelation*, 72–73.

45. Bauckham, *Theology of the Book of Revelation*, 15.

46. Vanhoozer, *Faith Speaking Understanding*, 98.

47. Vanhoozer, *Faith Speaking Understanding*, 109. Cf. Deut. 4:26; 30:19; Isa. 43:10; Luke 24:48.

48. Beale sees "Dan. 7:9ff" as the "dominant background" in Rev. 4–5, which "repeats fourteen elements from Dan. 7:9ff in the same basic order." Beale, *Revelation*, 325, 314. Cf. also allusions to Ezek. 1–2.

49. Rev. 4:1–5:14; 7:9–17; 8:1–4; 11:15–18; 14:1–5; 15:2–8; 19:1–10. Aune, *Revelation 1–5:14*, xcvii. Aune also points to other "throne vision[s]" that are "judgment scenes," including Matt. 19:28–30; 25:31–36; Rev. 20:4–6, 11–15; cf. Dan. 7:9–12 (277).

50. Aune, *Revelation 1–5:14*, 277. Beale likewise notes that here "John catches a glimpse of Yahweh's heavenly council." Beale, *Revelation*, 319.

51. Aune, *Revelation 1–5:14*, lxxxvii.

Christ at the cross (see the discussion in chap. 5 of the present volume). This view is based, in part, on Revelation 12's depiction of the "war in heaven," wherein the "dragon and his angels waged war," but "there was no longer a place found for them in heaven. And the great dragon was thrown down . . . to the earth, and his angels were thrown down with him" (vv. 7–9).

Noting that "to cast out" can denote "excommunication (cf. John 9:34–35) and 'judicial punishment,'"[52] Ranko Stefanović explains that "this 'casting down' of Satan from heaven suggests his excommunication from the heavenly council."[53] This appears to be what Revelation 12:10 describes: "The accuser of our brethren has been thrown down, he who accuses them before our God day and night" (cf. Luke 10:18). As Beale explains, the "'place' the devil lost was his hitherto privileged place of accusation, formerly granted him by God as a privilege."[54] Based on the description of Satan here and in Job 1–2 and Zechariah 3, "it can be concluded that God permitted the devil to 'accuse' his people of sin. The OT texts portray Satan accusing saints of unfaithfulness, with the implication that they did not deserve God's salvation and gracious blessings (Zech. 3:1–5, 9; cf. Numbers Rabbah 18.21). Implicit also in the accusations was the charge that God's own character was corrupt."[55]

Because of Christ's victory via the cross, the "accuser of our brethren has been thrown down" (Rev. 12:10; cf. Luke 10:18; John 12:31). According to Revelation 12:10–12, as Beale reads it, "Christ's 'authority' (resulting from the resurrection) and 'blood' have conquered the serpent and cast him from heaven."[56] More specifically, the "death and resurrection of Christ have banished the devil from this privilege formerly granted him by God because Christ's death" has paid the "penalty" of sin and vindicated God's character (cf. Rom. 3:25–26).[57] Further, Beale comments, the "emphasis on Satan's accusatorial role in 12:10 reveals that the angelic battle of verses 7–9 was figurative for a courtroom battle between two opposing lawyers, with one losing the argument and being disbarred for employing illegal tactics." In his view, the "legal defeat of Satan is part of the essence of the inaugurated kingdom that has 'now come about,'" even though the "actual

---

52. Cf. Matt. 3:10; 13:41–42; John 15:6; Rev. 2:10.

53. Stefanović, *Revelation of Jesus Christ*, 387.

54. Beale, *Revelation*, 656. So also Löfstedt, "Ruler of This World," 65.

55. Beale, *Revelation*, 659.

56. Beale, *Revelation*, 657.

57. Beale, *Revelation*, 659. Steven Grabiner suggests that "Christ has revealed enough about God's character to dispel Satan's lies so that his access to the heavenly council is closed," though "Satan does not cease his accusations (12.10) or his attempts at war (12.13)." Grabiner, *Revelation's Hymns*, 67.

execution of the devil and his hordes comes at the consummation of history" (see chap. 5).[58]

This triumph of Christ corresponds to the heavenly court scene of Revelation 4–5, wherein the resurrected Christ appears as the only one "worthy" to open the book and break its seals. Adela Yarbro Collins explains that in light of Revelation as a whole, "it is clear that the problem facing the heavenly council is the rebellion of Satan which is paralleled by rebellion on earth. . . . The tears of the prophet" when at first no one was found to open the book (Rev. 5:4) "emphasize the quandary of the heavenly council" and "express the desire of the faithful to have this situation rectified."[59] Then one of the elders calms the prophet by telling him that the "Lion that is from the tribe of Judah, the Root of David, has overcome so as to open the book and its seven seals" (Rev. 5:5). Beale explains, "Christ was wrongfully accused and executed by Satan's earthly pawns. But his resurrection vindicated him in the law court of heaven and enabled him to take away the devil's right and power as heavenly prosecutor (cf. 1:18)."[60] Accordingly, Paul depicts Christ's triumph at the cross as the ultimate demonstration of God's character: "God displayed [Christ] publicly" in order "to demonstrate His righteousness . . . for the demonstration . . . of His righteousness at the present time, so that He would be just and the justifier of the one who has faith in Jesus" (Rom. 3:25–26; cf. 5:8).

As Vanhoozer suggests, the NT "testimony to Jesus Christ" is best viewed against "the backdrop of covenant lawsuit and trial."[61] The NT testifies that Christ is "God's vindicated (i.e., resurrected) truth claim"; he is "God's covenant faithfulness, both its promise and judgment," the "righteousness of God."[62] Whereas the devil is a corrupt, prosecuting attorney, Christ is the "Amen, the faithful and true Witness" (Rev. 3:14), the just and righteous advocate (1 John 2:1), and the perfect judge (John 5:22).[63] Although Christ

---

58. Beale, *Revelation*, 661. Further, he believes, "Jesus' defeat of the nations in fulfillment of Psalm 2 is indicated in heaven by Michael's defeat of the heavenly representatives of those nations in fulfillment of Daniel 2" (655).

59. A. Collins, *Apocalypse*, 39. Tonstad adds, "The premise [that] compasses the main body of Revelation (4.1–22.5)" is the cosmic conflict over the character of God's government, which "underlies the actions in the heavenly council" and impacts "what happens on earth." Tonstad, *Saving God's Reputation*, 118.

60. Beale, *Revelation*, 664.

61. Vanhoozer, *Faith Speaking Understanding*, 105.

62. Vanhoozer, *Faith Speaking Understanding*, 108.

63. Here, "several commentators have noted" that "*the whole of John's Gospel is structured as a courtroom drama.*" Vanhoozer, *Faith Speaking Understanding*, 107 (emphasis original). See Köstenberger, *Theology of John's Gospel and Letters*, 436–56; Lincoln, *Truth on Trial*.

defeated Satan at the cross, the enemy and his forces are not yet rooted out and destroyed. Even though they may have forfeited admission to the heavenly council, evil celestial beings remain forces to be reckoned with as the "rulers" and "powers" of "darkness" (Eph. 6:12).

The Righteousness of God and Special Privileges of God's Portion

Not only does Revelation 4–5 highlight Christ's cosmic victory that shuts the mouth of the accuser, but the last two heavenly court scenes Aune identifies also offer verdicts in favor of God's righteousness. In Revelation 15:3–4, the victorious saints sing,

> Great and marvelous are Your works,
> O Lord God, the Almighty;
> Righteous and true are Your ways,
> King of the nations!
> Who will not fear, O Lord, and glorify Your name?
> For you alone are holy;
> For all the nations will come and worship before You,
> For Your righteous acts have been revealed.[64]

Likewise, in Revelation 19:1–2, John hears "something like a loud voice of a great multitude in heaven, saying, 'Hallelujah! Salvation and glory and power belong to our God; because His judgments are true and righteous.'"

These visions of Revelation stand as (eschatological) testimony to God's righteousness, and a case can be made that the entire canon of Scripture functions as a covenant witness document, recording God's faithfulness.[65] Although many creatures raise profound questions about God's character, the testimony affirmed consistently throughout Scripture is that God is always and only upright, righteous, faithful, and just: "The LORD is righteous in all His ways / And kind in all His deeds" (Ps. 145:17); "there is no unrighteousness in Him" (Ps. 92:15); "He will do no injustice" (Zeph. 3:5); "God is Light, and in Him there is no darkness at all" (1 John 1:5); and "God cannot be tempted by evil" (James 1:13; cf. Hab. 1:13).[66]

---

64. Cf. Ps. 86:8–9.
65. See the discussion in Peckham, *Canonical Theology*, 21–28.
66. See, further, 2 Chron. 5:13; Pss. 7:7–11; 9:7–8; 18:30; 25:8; 33:4–5; 34:8; 67:4; 89:5, 14; 96:10; 106:1; 119:137–38; 129:4; 145:9; Isa. 26:7; 49:7; Jer. 9:24; Lam. 3:23; Rom. 2:5–6; 1 Cor. 1:9; 2 Cor. 9:9; 2 Thess. 3:3; James 1:17. On those texts some mistakenly take to attribute moral evil to God (e.g., Isa. 45:7), see the discussion in chap. 2 of this book regarding how *ra'a'* can refer to calamity or judgment without any connotation of moral evil.

Among many other passages proclaiming the righteousness of God, despite the injustice in this world, Deuteronomy 32 stands out, presenting nothing short of a basic outline of a theodicy in the form of a divine covenant lawsuit. In this Song of Moses, the author writes,

> I proclaim the name of the LORD;
> Ascribe greatness to our God!
> The Rock! His work is perfect,
> For all His ways are just;
> A God of faithfulness without injustice,
> Righteous and upright is He. (Deut. 32:3–4)

Embedded in this lawsuit that defends and vindicates God's character is the understanding that the "gods" were allotted territory to rule the nations (Deut. 32:8).[67] Whereas the nations were allotted to celestial rulers (the "gods"), this arrangement afforded God the jurisdiction to elect and raise up a people from out of the nations as "the LORD's portion"—that is, "his people; / Jacob is the allotment of His inheritance" (Deut. 32:9; cf. Gen. 12; Deut. 10–11). In Jeffrey H. Tigay's view, Deuteronomy 32:9 "implies that [God] assigned the other nations to those divine beings, and states explicitly that He kept Israel for Himself."[68] God thus took "from among the Gentiles a people for His name" (Acts 15:14; cf. v. 17) and the "LORD alone guided him, / And there was no foreign god with him" (Deut. 32:12; cf. 4:19–20; 10:17).

God reserves special rulership and jurisdiction over his covenant people, not only for their sake but also so that through the "seed" of Abraham "all the nations of the earth shall be blessed" (Gen. 22:18; cf. 12:1–3; Acts 15:17). Whereas the nations were given over to the "gods," apparently as a consequence of their rebellion against God's rule at Babel (Gen. 11),[69] God reserved the right to raise up, sustain, and protect one people through whom he might reclaim all the nations of the world (cf. Gen. 12). The so-called scandal of particularity (Israel's election), on this view, provides the avenue for the scandal of the cross to bring redemption to all peoples (see, e.g., Matt. 28:19; Rev. 7:9; 14:6).

Given God's covenant with Israel, it is not hard to see why Israel's exclusive love and fidelity to God over against the "gods" of the nations would be

---

67. Cf. Gen. 10–11; Deut. 4:19–20.

68. Tigay, *Deuteronomy*, 302. Michael S. Heiser adds, "Israel, as Yahweh's inheritance, was holy ground. Similarly, the territory of other nations, according to Yahweh's decree, belonged to other gods." Heiser, "Deuteronomy 32:8–9," 2.

69. See Tigay, *Deuteronomy*, 302.

such a focal point of the OT (cf. Deut. 32:16–17, 21, 37–39), which includes abundant, urgent warnings against spiritual adultery (e.g., Jer. 3).[70] Under God's rule within a unique covenant relationship (Amos 3:2), Israel was God's special conduit of the plan of redemption for all nations and was afforded special privileges and promised blessings that were explicitly contingent on covenant faithfulness. These covenantal privileges include God's repeated strong actions to prosper them, including miraculous protection and sustenance on many occasions. However, these special privileges were contingent on their relationship with God (cf. Deut. 8); unfaithfulness to the covenant would separate the people from God, forfeit divine blessings, and bring appropriate judgments and curses as specified in the covenant (Deut. 32:20).[71] Accordingly, the surrounding nations (under demonic rule: vv. 8, 17) repeatedly attempted to seduce God's people into worship of their "gods" (often succeeding: e.g., Num. 25:1–3), which would separate them from the special covenant relationship and protection of Yahweh. While God was attempting to reclaim the world through Israel, the demons were attempting to pry Israel away from God, leaving God without an inheritance and allotment from which he could advance his plan to reclaim and redeem the world.

Events on earth thus relate to a celestial conflict over rulership of this world wherein evil celestial beings have significant power and jurisdiction. Although God is sovereign, throughout Scripture God consistently allows some shared governance, particularly evidenced in the heavenly council. For example, regarding the judgment against Nebuchadnezzar, Daniel 4:17 states,

> This sentence is by the decree of the angelic watchers,
> And the decision is a command of the holy ones,
> In order that the living may know
> That the Most High is ruler over the realm of mankind,
> And bestows it on whom He wishes,
> And sets over it the lowliest of men.[72]

70. See Peckham, *Concept of Divine Love*, 290–300, 451–56.

71. See John H. Walton's concept of "covenant jeopardy," according to which failure to meet covenant responsibilities may lead to forfeiting the benefits of covenant relationship (cf. Lev. 26:14–30; Deut. 28:15–68; 1 Kings 9:6–9). Walton, *Covenant*, 113. Walton traces Israel's history of covenant jeopardy from the childbearing difficulties of some matriarchs to slavery in Egypt and beyond. At nearly every turn dangers jeopardize Israel's special privileges.

72. Cf. 1 Kings 22:19–23; Dan. 1–2; 4:13, 23; Matt. 4:14; and the "watchers" in Zech. 1:10, "whom the LORD has sent to patrol the earth." According to George L. Klein, these "watchers" appear to possess significant jurisdiction, carrying out "authoritative patrol of the whole earth" (cf. Job 1:7; 2:2; Zech. 1:7–17; 4:8, 11). Klein, *Zechariah*, 97. On the extra-canonical development of the "watchers" traditions (e.g., 1 En. 1–36), see Harkins, Baunch, and Endres, *Watchers in Jewish and Christian Traditions*.

According to John E. Goldingay, "This heavenly cabinet discusses and makes decisions about earthly events more broadly (see, e.g., 1 Kings 22:19–22; Ps. 82; Isa. 6; Dan. 7:9–14), and its members are then involved in the implementing of these decisions."[73]

Now that we've seen that the cosmic dispute is primarily an epistemic conflict over God's character, God's mode of operation makes sense. Since God's very character and government has been challenged, it makes sense that he would operate in a transparent way that involves celestial beings, allowing them and others to see that God is wholly fair and just and loving. Doing so involves parameters, or "rules of engagement," in which the allegations can be settled and defeated once and for all.

The Rules of Engagement

We've seen so far that the cosmic conflict is primarily a dispute over God's character, prompted by demonic allegations against God's justice and rule. Insofar as God maintains his commitment to epistemic freedom, the use of force can do nothing to counter such allegations, so another strategy is required to meet the allegations. Thus in the case of Job, God allows such allegations to have a hearing before the heavenly council and to be put on display so that creatures can make their own decisions. Toward answering such cosmic allegations, God allows Satan parameters within which he might make his case.

In order for a finite being to be able to make such a case against the omnipotent God, there must be consistent parameters within which that finite being is allowed to operate. The finite being must be granted some jurisdiction that the omnipotent being covenants not to override. This is just what we see in Job 1–2. Satan is initially restricted and later brings requests to the heavenly council to have more license to demonstrate his charges. This evinces not only that Satan works within limits that are known to him and to God but that these "rules of engagement" can be modified by agreement before the heavenly council. Insofar as God covenants to act or refrain from acting in a certain way, he is morally bound to do so. Given such covenantal "rules of engagement," then, God's action is (morally) restricted.[74]

---

73. Goldingay, *Israel's Faith*, 45.
74. Such rules of engagement function similarly to what Michael Bergmann and Daniel Howard-Snyder call "omnipotence-constraining connections," which might exist between outweighing "goods and the permission of" evil. Bergmann and Howard-Snyder, "Reply to Rowe," 138.

To understand this line of thought further, suppose that love requires free will of the kind suggested in chapter 2 of this book, which includes epistemic freedom to trust or distrust God. In his response to demonic allegations against his character, then, God could not immediately bring about a state of affairs wherein everyone *freely* recognizes his perfect goodness and love. Demonic allegations call for rules of engagement that provide the parameters in which the allegations could be proven true or false via demonstration. Accordingly, God covenants to allow the devil a specified jurisdiction, including agreed on parameters within which to work, which I am calling covenantal rules of engagement. The description of these rules of engagement as covenantal means they are part of a bilateral agreement between parties that effectively limits the action of both and that neither party can unilaterally change.

This framework allows us to make sense of the many passages in Scripture where God's action appears to be restricted and, conversely, where the power and authority or jurisdiction of the kingdom of darkness appears to be quite robust. Alongside the case of Job, Daniel 10 presents a striking instance of such rules of engagement. Therein an angel of God is delayed for three weeks because the prince of Persia—apparently a celestial ruler behind the earthly ruler of Persia—withstood him (vv. 12–13; cf. 10:20–21).[75] As Longman puts it, "Though the divine realm heard and began responding immediately to Daniel's prayers three weeks earlier, there was a delay because of a conflict, an obstacle in the form of the 'prince of the Persian kingdom' (v. 13)."[76]

Longman asks, "What power could resist God for twenty-one days, as the 'prince of the Persian kingdom' apparently had done?"[77] Being all-powerful, God possesses the sheer power to respond to Daniel immediately. Yet the Bible presents a real conflict here between the forces of goodness and darkness, which continues even after this episode (cf. 10:20–11:1). In order for such a conflict to transpire, God must not be exercising all of his power, and

---

75. In the majority view of scholars, the "'prince of the Persian kingdom' is a supernatural being who fights on behalf of that human kingdom." Longman, *Daniel*, 250. While downplaying its contemporary significance, W. Sibley Towner notes that "the parallelism of the verse alone suggests that this prince is a peer of and counterpart to the angel Michael, who is the prince of Israel (cf. v. 21)." Towner, *Daniel*, 153. Alexander Di Lella believes this prince of Persia is "the tutelary spirit or guardian angel of the Persian kingdom, as the rabbis and most Christian commentators have rightly acknowledged." Hartman and Di Lella, *Daniel*, 282. So, among many others, Goldingay, *Daniel*, 292; J. Collins, *Daniel*, 374; Smith-Christopher, "Daniel," 7:137; S. Miller, *Daniel*, 285. Even if this "prince" is taken to be the human ruler (as in Calvin's view), an angel of God is nevertheless delayed three weeks.

76. Longman, *Daniel*, 249. Cf. S. Miller, *Daniel*, 284.

77. Longman, *Daniel*, 249.

the enemy must be afforded some genuine freedom, power, and jurisdiction that is not removed capriciously but is governed by some rules of engagement known to both parties (the details of which are not revealed to us). This jurisdiction includes the authority to exercise power within specified limits, entailing corresponding limitations regarding God's intervention.

There are many other indications of these rules of engagement sprinkled throughout Scripture, notably including

1. the devil's claim while tempting Jesus, "I will give you all this [world's] domain and its glory; for it has been handed over to me, and I give it to whomever I wish" (Luke 4:6; cf. Matt. 12:24; John 12:31; 14:30; 16:11);
2. the explicitly arranged nature of Jesus's temptation, including the statement, "When the devil had finished every temptation, he left Him until an opportune time" (Luke 4:13; cf. Gen. 3);
3. the demons' response to encountering Jesus, revealing time parameters: "What business do we have with each other, Son of God? Have You come to torment us before the time?" (Matt. 8:29);
4. the statement that the devil knows "he has only a short time" (Rev. 12:12);
5. Jesus's statement to Peter, "Satan has demanded permission to sift you like wheat" (Luke 22:31);[78]
6. the fact that Jesus "could do no miracle [in Nazareth] except that He laid His hands on a few sick people and healed them" (Mark 6:5) alongside indications that casting out of demons is tethered in at least some cases to prayer (9:29) and the extent of faith (Matt. 17:20); and
7. Paul's explanation that "Satan hindered" him and his traveling companions from going to the Thessalonians as desired (1 Thess. 2:18; cf. Rev. 2:10).

These instances indicate significant jurisdiction possessed by the enemy within specific limits.

Indeed, according to Revelation, this significant jurisdiction of the enemy has been at work behind the scenes throughout earth's history. Not only does the dragon (Satan) war against God (Rev. 12:7–9) and his servants (vv. 1–6), but he is also depicted as the worship-usurping ruler behind the earthly

---

78. Brian Han Gregg notes that the verb *exaiteō* ("demand") "includes the idea that the one making the request has a right to do so" and notes further the "fascinating" implication that here "both God and Satan seem compelled to operate within certain constraints." Gregg, *What Does the Bible Say?*, 64.

kingdoms that persecute God's people throughout the ages.[79] The dragon "gave . . . his power," "his throne," and "great authority" to the sea beast (13:2; cf. 13:5; 17:13–14), and the "whole earth . . . worshiped the dragon because he gave his authority to the beast; and they worshiped the beast" (vv. 3–4). This sea beast is given a

> mouth speaking arrogant words and blasphemies, and authority to act for forty-two months was given to him. And he opened his mouth in blasphemies against God, to blaspheme His name and His tabernacle, that is, those who dwell in heaven. It was also given to him to make war with the saints and to overcome them, and authority over every tribe and people and tongue and nation was given to him [cf. Deut. 32:8]. All who dwell on the earth will worship him, everyone whose name has not been written from the foundation of the world in the book of life of the Lamb who has been slain. (vv. 5–8; cf. 13:1, 12)

Notably, this sea beast is a composite beast, made up of characteristics of the four beasts of Daniel 7 ("like a leopard," with feet like a "bear," "the mouth of a lion," and ten horns; Rev. 13:1–2; cf. Dan. 7:4–8).[80] Daniel 7:17 explains these four "great beasts" are "four kings, who will arise from the earth." The sea beast appears to encapsulate these kings (or kingdoms) that persecute God's people and fight against God's kingdom, with the dragon ruler standing behind them all. As Beale notes, the "dragon in Revelation 12 was seen as the ultimate force behind the earthly kingdoms of the world."[81] Further, Beale comments, "The affirmation that the kingdoms of Persia, Greece, and Rome had heavenly counterparts suggests that they were all puppets of an evil heavenly force (cf. Dan. 10:20)." Even as "Satanic evil expressed itself through the kingdoms of Assyria, Egypt, Babylon, Persia, Greece, Sodom, and Rome," this "system of evil will continue so to manifest itself in yet future kingdoms of the world."[82]

---

79. Beale notes the "mosaic of OT imagery" used of "this monster" in v. 3 is "all imagery of evil kingdoms who persecute God's people." Beale, *Revelation*, 632. While the dragon here refers at least partly to first-century Rome, it also "stands for the devil himself as the representative head of all evil kingdoms, as Rev. 12:9 and 20:2, 10 make explicit. The devil is the force behind the wicked kingdoms who persecute God's people" (634).

80. Beale notes that Rev. 13:1–2 is "a creative reworking of Daniel 7:1–7," with the "seven heads" best understood "as a composite of the heads of the four beasts in Daniel 7." Beale, *Revelation*, 683.

81. Beale, *Revelation*, 683. This beast—like the dragon—is "transtemporal," since "the OT uses *the same sea monster image* to represent successive evil kingdoms spanning hundreds of years" (686, emphasis original).

82. Beale, *Revelation*, 686. Cf. "the man of lawlessness" and "son of destruction, who opposes and exalts himself above every so-called god or object of worship, so that he takes his seat in the temple of God, displaying himself as being God" (2 Thess. 2:3–4; cf. vv. 6–9).

Here Satan (the dragon) gives power and ruling authority over the nations to a beast (representing the earthly kingdoms that persecute God's people), which is exercised to usurp God's worship, blaspheme God's name, and war against God's holy ones, or saints, for a period of time. Insofar as Satan possesses jurisdiction over earthly kingdoms, God's jurisdiction is correspondingly limited. There are also corresponding limitations on Satan and his minions, including temporal limits. Satan "knows that his time is short" (Rev. 12:12 NRSV). As Vanhoozer puts it, "The world is now under the dominion of the powers of darkness," and it therefore "resists and rejects God's authoritative rule."[83]

Ramifications of the Rules of Engagement

As we've seen, Scripture depicts a cosmic conflict between God and Satan over God's character wherein Satan and his minions possess significant jurisdiction according to covenantal rules of engagement. We now address how such an understanding of the cosmic conflict sheds light on the problem of evil. As noted previously, there is wide agreement that the free will defense is successful against the logical problem of evil. Yet, many thinkers believe it is insufficient relative to the evidential problem of evil. Put simply, these thinkers believe the amount of evil in the world renders it improbable that an omnibenevolent and omnipotent God exists. On this view, such a God should be able to grant free will and yet significantly reduce (if not eliminate) the horrendous evils in this world. Some even suggest that there could not possibly be a morally sufficient reason for God to refrain from preventing horrendous evils insofar as God possesses the raw power to prevent those evils.

The approach offered in this book responds that God *is* doing everything that he (morally) can do to mitigate or eliminate evil within the context of some (covenantal) rules of the cosmic conflict. As seen above, biblical evidence indicates that there are rules of engagement in the cosmic conflict such that both parties know the limits within which they might operate toward settling this conflict. Further, these rules of engagement appear to be both dynamic and covenantal. Recall that by "covenantal," I mean they exist as part of a bilateral agreement between parties that effectively limits the action of both

---

83. Vanhoozer, *Faith Speaking Understanding*, 100. David Bentley Hart adds that the world is under the "mutinous authority of angelic and demonic 'powers'" and that the NT does not endorse "*total* and *direct* divine sovereignty in all the eventualities of the fallen world." Hart, *Doors of the Sea*, 65–66 (emphasis original).

and that neither party can unilaterally change.[84] God does not set these rules of engagement unilaterally or arbitrarily, but they are the product of negotiation and thereby far from ideal.

Insofar as God agrees to rules of engagement, his future action is (morally) limited. Because God never lies (Titus 1:2) or breaks his promises (Heb. 6:18), any agreement that God enters into is effectively binding on God's future action. Whereas God remains omnipotent (with no *ontological* reduction of his power), there may be things that God cannot *morally* do that he otherwise might want to do. Perhaps one example of this occurs in Mark where Jesus "could do no miracle [in Nazareth] except that He laid His hands on a few sick people and healed them. And He wondered at their unbelief" (6:5–6; cf. 9:23–24, 28–29).

This instance not only appears to reveal the existence of some limitations on divine activity; it also indicates that such limits might be related somehow to human belief, such as when Jesus told the disciples they could not drive out a demon "because of the littleness of [their] faith" (Matt. 17:20; cf. Mark 9:23–24)—or prayer, such as when Jesus replies to his disciples' question about why they could not cast out a demon, "This kind cannot come out by anything but prayer" (Mark 9:28–29; cf. Mark 11:22–24). Although these and other texts do not explain precisely how faith and prayer relate to miracles, the textual data depict an explicit correlation, indicating impediments on what God can (morally) do that are yet dynamic, seemingly tethered to prayer and faith and perhaps other factors. As such, prayer may grant God jurisdiction to act in ways that otherwise would not be available within the rules of engagement. Since other factors are involved, it might be that in some situations those other factors are such that no matter how much people pray in good faith, the outcome regarding a specific event would not change (cf. Matt. 26:39; Luke 22:32).

Here and elsewhere it appears there are "rules" that might prevent God from doing or preventing what he otherwise would choose to do or prevent. If this is correct, there are real limitations on and impediments against God's action. These include at least those entailed by (1) the consistent granting of consequential free will to creatures and (2) the covenantal rules of engagement. Such limitations and impediments on divine action have significant implications for God's (moral) ability to reduce or (immediately) eliminate evil.

Whereas we might at times be tempted to think God should have taken some action, from our limited human perspective we cannot perceive or calculate the numerous factors at work in any given situation. It may be that some courses of action that we might think God should take are not available to

---

84. This agreement is not, however, symmetrical as if between equals. Satan lacks the power to unilaterally change the agreement, and God is morally restricted from doing so.

him because of the rules of engagement; others might impinge on the extent of consequential free will that has been covenantally (and thus irrevocably) granted to creatures; and still others, if taken by God, would result in a (perhaps far) worse outcome than the course that God has chosen in his perfect wisdom, which accounts for all factors and available options. Put briefly, in any instance where God does not intervene to prevent some horrendous evil, to do so might have (1) been against the rules, (2) impinged on creaturely free will in a way that would undercut the love relationship, or (3) resulted in greater evil or less flourishing of love.

We might wonder why God would enter into a covenantal arrangement that would grant Satan such jurisdiction in the first place, even if only temporarily. As suggested in part earlier in this chapter, it may be that the kind and extent of free will necessary for the maximal flourishing of love—coupled with the enemy's slanderous allegations against God's character and government—required a context in which a demonstration could take place, apart from which the conflict could not be settled without severely damaging the flourishing of love (cf. Matt. 13:29).

Since the cosmic war is not one of sheer force but one of character—a challenge to God's moral government and thus a battle for hearts and minds— there must be known limits or rules within which the enemy can operate (cf. Job 1–2; Dan. 10). Further, if Satan is to set forth a real, demonstrative counterclaim, he must possess *some* jurisdiction to do so. This jurisdiction is seemingly connected (at least partially) to the decisions of other creatures who might refuse to "give the devil an opportunity" (Eph. 4:27) or who might "resist the devil," causing him to "flee" (James 4:7; cf. 1 Pet. 5:8–9; 2 Tim. 2:26). This jurisdiction was presumably triggered or greatly increased by humanity's fall, providing the context for Satan to manifest his government as temporary "ruler of this world" and concomitantly to lay forth his charges against God's government of love. Insofar as this covenantal arrangement is itself morally justified as the best (or only) available avenue to settle the cosmic dispute, the great good of ensuring that love flourishes throughout the universe for eternity serves as the morally sufficient reason for God's allowance of evil, without affirming that any such evil itself is justifiable or necessary for such flourishing.

Although we are not in a position to make confident judgments relative to God's decisions, we might note a significant biblical principle here: God always does what is best, given the avenues available to him.[85] However we

---

85. Cf. Gen. 18:25; Deut. 32:4; 1 Sam. 3:18; Ps. 145:17; Dan. 4:37; Hab. 1:13; Rom. 3:25–26; Rev. 15:3.

understand the rules of engagement, we might maintain that whenever God does or refrains from doing something in a way that *prima facie* seems less than optimally good, it follows from this principle that either it was not in God's purview to do otherwise or doing otherwise would have been worse.

Given the nature of a cosmic dispute over God's character that, if left unresolved, would severely harm (if not ultimately destroy) the divine-creature love relationship and with it all other kinds of love in this world, it follows that an omnibenevolent God should do something to answer allegations against his character. Since such allegations cannot be effectively answered by sheer force, the avenues available to God involve some kind of demonstration by both parties in the dispute. We are hardly in a position to judge what parameters such a demonstration would require or even what would count as a sufficient demonstration. If it is God's goal that this demonstration not only answer the devil's charges but also inoculate the universe from evil forevermore (Rev. 21:3; cf. Nah. 1:9), then only one who is omniscient could perfectly calculate just what is sufficient to this end.

The Charge Revisited

Above we discussed the charge that there could not be a morally sufficient reason for God to refrain from preventing horrendous evils insofar as God possesses the raw power to do so. Responsive to this charge, this chapter has suggested a rules-of-engagement model, which entails temporary but significant moral limitations on divine action. Within this framework, love provides the morally sufficient reason for God's allowance of evil. However, this conclusion does not amount to a justification of any evils. Evil remains evil. God does not want or need evil to accomplish his purpose. The freedom requisite for love requires only the possibility of evil, not its necessity.

Creatures have departed from God's ideal will, thereby actualizing evil. Insofar as God respects the consequential freedom of creatures necessary for love, the avenues available to God to restore the universe to perfect harmony are limited by the free decisions of creatures (including celestial beings) and further limited by covenantal rules of engagement. This approach sheds significant light on an issue raised earlier regarding the basic free will defense. It seems that God could eliminate many evils without impinging on creaturely free will. Relative to any recent terrorist event, for instance, it would seem that God could have somehow alerted the authorities with sufficient information to prevent an imminent attack without impinging on free will. Scripture depicts God doing just this kind of thing (e.g., 2 Kings 6:8–9), indicating that such revelations by themselves do not injure the kind of free will God grants according to Scripture.

However, if covenantal rules of engagement grant significant jurisdiction to the enemy and correspondingly (morally) restrict God's action, it might simply be against the rules of engagement (as they pertain to a given case) for God to supernaturally reveal a specific imminent danger or to otherwise intervene. It may be that in some cases the rules permit God to intervene by alerting someone in a way sufficient to prevent evil, while in other similar cases, the rules at that time and place might not permit God to do so.[86] This possibility is relevant to the problem of selective intervention—that is, the question of why God strongly intervenes in one situation but does not do so in another similar situation. Although many defenses and theodicies fail to address this issue, the biblical narratives themselves evoke the question. For instance, Herod is able to put James to death, but Peter is freed from prison by an angel (Acts 12:1–11). And, as discussed, Jesus's miracle-working is inhibited in some places (Mark 6:5).

Since we are not privy to the rules of engagement, which are themselves dynamic and connected to numerous factors (including, but not limited to, prayer and faith), we are not in a position to know when a given event falls within the enemy's jurisdiction such that God's intervention is restricted. Accordingly, we need not assert that there is something good (instrumentally or otherwise) about each evil that God does not prevent. It might be that God greatly desires to prevent that evil but morally cannot do so, given the wider parameters of the rules of engagement or without leading to some worse result (cf. Matt. 26:39).

The rules of engagement might also offer a response to the claim that an omnipotent God ought to prevent any evil (or at least any horrendous evil) that he could (ontologically) prevent. For example, Thomas Oord has argued that, because God is love, God cannot coerce and thus (on his definition of coercion) cannot (ontologically) prevent the evils in this world.[87] Oord differentiates this from other accounts of free will theism, which he criticizes, claiming that God would be evil if he chose not to prevent horrendous evils that he could prevent.[88] In my view, a rules-of-engagement model possesses all the salient advantages of Oord's position but does so without any of what I consider its significant disadvantages.[89] By positing that God is morally restricted by

---

86. Israel's special privileges as God's allotted "portion" might have included more miracle-working jurisdiction among them, which could be diminished by their unfaithfulness.

87. Oord, *Uncontrolling Love of God*, 183–84.

88. Oord, *Uncontrolling Love of God*, 135.

89. See also chap. 6 in the present volume.

rules of engagement, this model can coherently maintain that there are a great many evils that God wishes to prevent but cannot prevent without breaking his word and thus contradicting the consistent claims of Scripture that God "cannot lie" (Titus 1:2; cf. 2 Tim. 2:13; James 1:13) and that if God makes a promise, he will keep it (Heb. 6:17–18). God himself proclaims,

> I will not break off My lovingkindness from him,
> Nor deal falsely in My faithfulness.
> My covenant I will not violate,
> Nor will I alter the utterance of My lips. (Ps. 89:33–34; cf. Jer. 31:35–
>   37; 33:20–21)

It follows that divine promises morally limit God's future action without diminishing his omnipotence. Unless one makes the self-defeating argument (relative to theodicy) that God *ought* to break his promise, God is morally constrained insofar as he has committed to covenantal rules of engagement. He is thus justified in not exercising his raw power to prevent any evil that would require him to break the rules of engagement.

This rules-of-engagement model thus expands and clarifies the conception of divine self-limitation that Oord and others have criticized. If God unilaterally limits his own action, it stands to reason that God could and should unilaterally remove such limits to prevent horrendous evils. However, it is crucial to recognize that the rules of engagement operative in this model are not unilateral or arbitrary divine self-limitations but are the product of mutual (albeit asymmetrical) agreement involving other parties, including the heavenly council. The rules are thus covenantal and consequently not subject to change by only one party. Since God always keeps his word, God is morally bound to act or refrain from acting in some way insofar as God covenants to do so. It is not up to him alone (morally speaking) to simply modify those covenantal parameters.

This allows the proponent of a cosmic conflict theodicy of love to coherently affirm that God is ontologically capable of intervening to eliminate evil but that in some instances God cannot exercise his power to do so without breaking his promises and thus acting immorally. So there may be many situations wherein God morally cannot prevent some horrendous evil while retaining the ontological ability to overcome evil in the end.

This model holds significant advantages over Oord's model (as well as any finitist model), particularly with respect to accounting for the biblical data and maintaining a robust conception of divine omnipotence and sovereignty. If love is, by nature, incapable of the kinds of things Oord claims it is, it would create significant problems relative to Scripture's depictions of God doing things such as providing manna from heaven (Exod. 16:35) and raising people from the dead (e.g., 1 Kings 17:17–24). If God actually intervenes in the ways attributed to him in Scripture, it follows that God is ontologically capable of intervening in these ways and that such interventions are not incompatible with God's love. If so, one cannot coherently claim that God cannot prevent hunger because he is ontologically incapable of intervening in a way that would prevent hunger. In order to coherently claim that God is simply ontologically incapable of intervening in such situations, one must reject the biblical depiction of God's intervention in such situations.

The same applies not only to the examples above but also to many other instances of strong divine interventions and miracles recorded in Scripture, each of which would prevent some of the evils we see around us. Contra the finitist approach, this rules-of-engagement approach maintains that God has intervened in such ways in the past and thus possesses the ontological ability to do so in the future (especially eschatologically) but in some instances may be temporarily restricted from doing so by the covenantal rules of engagement.

Similarly, this approach provides an avenue of response to the "bad parent" argument, which claims that an all-loving God would do at least as much as any good parents would do to prevent evils from befalling their children. Indeed, as J. L. Schellenberg argues, any good parents would at least make their presence known to their child who cries out for them.[90] Perhaps God desperately wants to do so, but it is against the rules for him to do so in some situations. While writing this book, I came down with a very bad case of the flu and thus temporarily quarantined myself from my then five-year-old son to prevent him from catching it. I could not be with him and play with him the way I wanted to. However, it was for his best good that I be temporarily removed from him in order to protect him. In analogous fashion, perhaps God is sometimes restricted from even making his presence known or acting in ways he otherwise would.

A rules-of-engagement model, understood within a broader theodicy of love, offers a morally sufficient rationale and framework for understanding why God might not prevent horrendous evils while upholding divine omnipotence, omniscience, and a robust conception of divine providence and special divine action. It thus avoids finitism while possessing the salient advantages that finitist proposals offer. On this view, God maintains the sheer power sufficient to prevent any and all evils and possesses the power to finally eradicate evil in the future; for the time being, however, there are some evils

90. Schellenberg, "Divine Hiddenness Justifies Atheism," 62.

that God cannot (morally) prevent. In any case where God does not intervene to prevent some horrendous evil, to do so might have (1) been against the rules, (2) impinged on creaturely free will, or (3) resulted in greater evil or less flourishing of love.

What about Evil in Nature?

This cosmic conflict framework might be helpful relative to moral evil, but we still have not dealt with so-called natural evil. Natural evil is often defined as evil that does not result from the free decisions of creatures. However, I am not convinced that *any* evil is merely "natural" or springs from nature as it was created by God or from the (primordial) laws of nature in and of themselves.[91] Yet while there might not be merely "natural evil" (so defined), there is much evil in nature.

Within this cosmic conflict framework, evil in nature is a by-product of the entrance of moral evil and the subsequent subjection of the earth. As Paul writes to the church in Rome, "The creation was subjected to futility, not willingly, but because of Him who subjected it, in hope that the creation itself also will be set free" in the future (Rom. 8:20–21). In the meantime, "the whole creation groans and suffers the pains of childbirth together until now" (v. 22).[92] Although evil in nature is often not immediately caused by the free decisions of creatures, on this view evil in nature is at least distantly caused by the misuse of creaturely freedom.[93]

Whatever might be said about *why* such effects on nature resulted from the entrance of moral evil, the biblical narrative indicates that this planet was not always the way it is now (Gen. 3:14–19) and was not originally intended by God to be the way it is now; "evil," including in nature, stems initially from

91. Plantinga suggests that both moral and natural evil might be "cases of what we might call broadly moral evil—evil resulting from the free actions of personal beings, whether human or not." Plantinga, *God, Freedom, and Evil*, 59.

92. On the traditional view, evil in nature is a by-product of humanity's fall. As Michael Murray notes, "For almost every major Christian thinker reflecting on evil, the Fall has played a central role in explaining both the origin and persistence of evil in the universe." Murray, *Nature Red in Tooth and Claw*, 74. Hart adds, "It is a patristic notion" that "in the fall of man, all of material existence was made subject to the dominion of death." Hart, *Doors of the Sea*, 63. Others have suggested that evil in nature might stem from the prior fall of Satan and his cohorts, who perhaps brought evil to earth (including in nature) before humankind. Gavin Ortlund contends that this view "does not deviate from the principle embedded in the more traditional Christian view—that evil corrupts nature—but simply applies this principle to an earlier phase of the history of evil." Ortlund, "Fall of Angels," 115.

93. However, people often suffer the results of evils that were neither immediately nor distantly caused by them.

creaturely misuse of freedom.[94] Put simply, this view holds that the "evil" that appears in nature *now* does not result merely from nature taking its original course as created and intended by God. Rather, nature itself has been thrown out of equilibrium by creaturely decisions to disobey God and thus depart from God's ideal will.

Even if this model provides a general account of natural evil, the question still remains of why God allows purportedly natural evils such as hurricanes, famines, pestilences, and cancer and other diseases. If these are (at least in some cases) only distantly caused by misused freedom, why might they not be mitigated or eliminated? Scripture indicates that at least some calamities in nature are directly caused by supernatural agents (e.g., Job 1:16, 18–19; Luke 13:16). The Gospels do not shy away from associating illnesses with the demonic realm. In many cases where Jesus heals a malady, the healings are connected to the casting out of demons. As Garrett DeWeese notes, the "Gospels abound with accounts of physical effects caused directly by demonic activity: dumbness (Matt. 9:32–33); blindness (Matt. 12:22–23); epileptic seizures (Matt. 17:14–18); supernatural strength (Mark 5:1–10); physical deformity (Luke 13:10–13)."[95]

As least some calamities in nature, then, are not (properly speaking) "natural" evils. However, supposing that some other evils in nature are not caused directly by supernatural agents, it might be that there are some laws, orderings, or processes of nature that God has ordained or covenanted not to break (cf. Jer. 31:35–37; 33:20–26). If so, many evils in nature that occur might not be (morally) preventable by God given the rules of engagement. Here, some of the operations that we think of as natural laws or processes might be (1) those laws primordially ordained by God as requisite to the maximal flourishing of love and thus unchangeable, given his constant commitment to love; or (2) other ramifications or rules (or forces) that might have been introduced as the result of evil according to the parameters of the cosmic conflict, or rules of engagement, which thus cannot be contravened by God without breaking his promises.[96]

Given a rules-of-engagement model, it may well be that the laws, order, or processes of nature have been modified or their results manipulated or

---

94. The post-fall curses (Gen. 3:14–19) indicate that the world is not as it would have been apart from the fall. Murray notes that Genesis appears to "signal that the wrongdoing of the initial human pair carried in its wake consequences not only for them and their progeny, but also for their environment." Murray, *Nature Red in Tooth and Claw*, 74–75. Cf. Gen. 5:29; Isa. 24:4–6.

95. DeWeese, "Natural Evil," 63.

96. On consequential freedom, the necessary relationship of cause and effect, and sufficient nomic regularity, see chap. 2 of the present volume.

otherwise negatively impacted by the activity of Satan and his minions within the parameters of Satan's rulership in this world, as suggested by Plantinga and many others.[97] Plantinga quotes Dom Bruno Well to clarify that "this does not mean that, for instance, an earthquake or a thunderstorm is due directly to satanic action. It is because of purely natural causes, but these causes are what they now are owing to the deep-set disorder in the heart of nature resulting from" the "action of fallen spirits," which "have power over the universe and over this planet in particular," such that "'an enemy came and sowed tares'" (Matt. 13:25).[98] Along these lines, citing the connection between demonic activity and "physical effects on earth" that appears frequently throughout Scripture, DeWeese suggests that events in the cosmic conflict "introduced the initial perturbations into the dynamical situations which God had created in equilibrium. And continued activity of the demonic horde could, over the history of the world, continue to perturb chaos systems as part of their on-going campaign against the establishment of the kingdom of God."[99]

Greg Boyd similarly argues that "there is no such thing as 'natural' evil. Nature in its present state," he believes, "is not as the Creator created it to be. . . . Nature exhibits diabolical features that are not the result of human wills." Instead, these features are "the direct or indirect result of the influence of diabolical forces," including on natural processes and the laws of nature.[100] As Richard Rice explains this view, "God has enemies, and these enemies have great power." He continues, "Their interference with the processes of nature has transformed the world from the perfect home God intends it to be into an ominous and threatening environment, marked by pain, disease and death."[101]

Thus the processes of nature may well have changed, with some additional regulations introduced as part of the covenantal agreement relative to the jurisdiction allotted to Satan. The way things work in nature now may be a

97. See, e.g., Plantinga, "Supralapsarianism or 'O Felix Culpa,'" 15–17. Cf. the cosmic conflict perspective of Lewis in *Problem of Pain*. See further discussion of this kind of pre-human fall approach in Boyd, *Satan and the Problem of Evil*, 242–318; DeWeese, "Natural Evil"; Ortlund, "Fall of Angels"; Lloyd, "Are Animals Fallen?," 158–60; Page, *Powers of Evil*, 268; Balthasar, *Action*, 197–99. Cf. Pannenberg, *Systematic Theology*, 2:274; Torrance, *Divine and Contingent Order*, 123. Creegan, *Animal Suffering*, 93, 143–51.

98. Plantinga, "Supralapsarianism or 'O Felix Culpa,'" 16n22.

99. DeWeese, "Natural Evil," 63.

100. Boyd, *Satan and the Problem of Evil*, 247. He maintains that "Satan and other spiritual beings rebelled against God in the primordial past and now abuse their God-given authority over aspects of the creation. The one who 'holds the power of death—that is, the devil' (Heb. 2:14) exercises a pervasive structural, diabolical influence to the point that the entire creation is in 'bondage to decay' (Rom. 8:21)," which makes "perfect sense" of "the pain-ridden, bloodthirsty, sinister and hostile character of nature" (302).

101. Rice, *Suffering and the Search for Meaning*, 78.

combination of both God's primordial laws and orderings *and* additional rules introduced after evil originated, as part of the covenantal rules of engagement.[102] In short, a cosmic conflict framework may maintain that God has ordained or permitted nature to operate the way it does because such operations of nature and the cause-effect relationship are those that are the best available to God to further the maximal flourishing of love, consisting perhaps of a combination of primordially (and thus maximally) good laws and orderings, the results of the free will decisions of others to disobey, and *maybe* some additional covenantal rules of engagement. God may wish to prevent all kinds of so-called natural evils. For example, God may wish to rescue the deer that burns to death in the forest fire (cf. William Rowe's famous case) and may wish to mitigate or eliminate the vast amount of animal suffering in this world.[103] However, it might be against the rules of engagement for God to do so—that is, doing so might affect the jurisdiction of the temporary ruler of this world. If so, it is not that God desires this state of affairs but that, as Jesus states, "an enemy has done this" (Matt. 13:28).

Numerous other factors may be at work of which we know nothing. We know far less than we would like and thus lack adequate data to provide conclusive answers in this regard. However, given a cosmic conflict perspective, evil in nature might be broadly accounted for by the same or a similar mechanism that has been used previously to address evil generally. Some of the evil in nature might be directly caused by the free choices of human or celestial creatures, and the other evils in nature might be the indirect product of the consequences of moral evil, in accordance with the rules of engagement.

Although it raises many additional issues and cases for further inquiry, so-called natural evil stands as part of the broader problem regarding why God does not mitigate or prevent evils. If the rules are such that the order of causes and effects in this world are bound up in the rules of engagement, limiting the extent of divine intervention, it is no more difficult to see why

102. This view has some consonance with the claim there is some necessity relationship between law-like or nomic regularity and some great goods, yet without claiming that *all* evil in nature is explainable by such necessity relationships. See the discussion in chap. 6 of this book.

103. For an excellent discussion of prominent approaches to the problem of animal suffering, see Murray, *Nature Red in Tooth and Claw*. While Murray himself questions the plausibility of this and prefers other approaches, he allows that an appeal to a fall of Satan and his cohorts "has some support in Christian revelation and the history of Christian thought" and is a "defensible" avenue (106). Further, he raises the question of whether Satan or demons "have exercised control over which natural laws obtain in our physical cosmos" and other factors. He writes that, if one "believe[s] in the existence of powerful and yet fallen disembodied angelic beings, it is hard to be confident that the answers to these questions is no. Furthermore, even the nontheist who merely lacks evidence for the existence of such beings is not in a position to reject such a position outright" (104).

God might allow a tree to fall on a house than why he might allow a person to fire a gun. In both cases, for God to intervene might be against the rules, contravene creaturely free will, or result in greater evil or less flourishing of love.

Conclusion

This chapter has addressed the nature of the cosmic conflict and its ramifications for the problem of evil. We have seen that Scripture depicts a cosmic dispute between God and Satan over God's character, primarily of an epistemic nature that cannot be settled by sheer power, wherein both parties know the (dynamic, covenantal) limits within which they can operate to settle this conflict—what I have called rules of engagement. Within this conflict, Satan and his minions are temporarily granted significant jurisdiction in this world, according to covenantal rules of engagement, which correspondingly limit (morally) the exercise of God's power to eliminate or mitigate evil that (temporarily) falls within the enemy's jurisdiction.

Whereas God maintains the sheer power sufficient to prevent all evils, there are some evils that God cannot (morally) prevent because of his commitment to the rules of engagement. This understanding provides a rationale for why God *might* not prevent horrendous evils, while upholding divine omnipotence, divine omniscience, and a robust conception of God's providence. Whereas God does everything he (morally) can to eliminate evil, in some cases doing so would be against the rules, affect creaturely free will, or result in greater evil or less flourishing of love. Even granting the broad contours of this model, we may still wonder whether God has done everything he could for this world and on what basis we should have confidence that God is wholly good, righteous, and loving and will finally eradicate evil. The next chapter takes up these issues.

5

Evil Defeated but Not Yet Destroyed

The previous chapters outlined a cosmic conflict framework for a theodicy of love wherein God grants creatures the kind and extent of free will necessary for love relationship and, further, acts within covenantal parameters, or rules of engagement, within the context of a cosmic dispute over his character that cannot be settled by sheer power. Given this framework, while God remains omnipotent, there are some evils that God cannot (morally) prevent because of his covenantal commitments. Whereas God does everything he (morally) can to eliminate evil, in some cases eliminating evil directly would be against the rules of engagement, affect creaturely free will, or result in greater evil or less flourishing of love. In this chapter we expand this model by addressing a number of questions that remain: Has God indeed done everything he (morally) could do to eliminate, or at least mitigate, evil in this world? Why should we have confidence that God is wholly good and loving and will finally put an end to evil? What is taking so long for God to bring justice? How long must the horrendous evils in this world be endured? To respond to these questions we will focus especially on the demonstration of God's character of love and the defeat of evil at the cross—a prerequisite to the final eschatological destruction of evil.

The Defeat of the Evil Powers by the Suffering God of the Cross

According to 1 John 3:8, "The Son of God appeared for this purpose, to destroy the works of the devil."[1] As the book of Hebrews states, he "partook"

---

1. G. K. Beale notes, "That Christ's coming was intended to nullify Satan's purposes is also affirmed in Matt. 12:28–29; John 12:31; 16:11; Acts 10:38; 2 Cor. 4:4–6; Eph. 6:10–18; 1 John 3:8; 4:4; 5:19." Beale, *Revelation*, 657.

of "flesh and blood" so "that through death He might render powerless him who had the power of death, that is, the devil" (Heb. 2:14). Here, the "power of death" is defeated by the life and death of the perfect Lamb of God, who, as Revelation states, is alone "worthy" to open the scroll before the heavenly court and "to receive power and riches and wisdom and might and honor and glory and blessing" (Rev. 5:12; cf. vv. 5, 9). Through the work of Christ, the "power" of evil is defeated by that which initially appears as weakness but which is a manifestation of the greatest strength—the endurance of unfathomable suffering for the sake of love (cf. John 15:13; Heb. 12:2).

If the cosmic conflict involves a courtroom drama regarding God's character, it could not be settled prematurely by the exercise of divine power but first requires a public demonstration of God's justice and character to defeat the enemy's slanderous allegations. This demonstration has been set forth ultimately and definitively in Christ. As Paul states, "God displayed [Christ] publicly as a propitiation [*hilastērion*[2]] in His blood through faith. This was to demonstrate His righteousness, because in the forbearance of God He passed over the sins previously committed; for the demonstration, I say, of His righteousness at the present time, so that He would be just and the justifier of the one who has faith in Jesus" (Rom. 3:25–26; cf. 3:3–6, 21–22).[3] Twice, Romans 3:25–26 emphasizes the purpose of the *demonstration* of God's righteousness. As F. F. Bruce puts it, "In the self-offering of Christ, God's righteousness is vindicated and the believing sinner justified."[4] This demonstration of God's righteousness was at the same time a demonstration of his character of love: "But God demonstrates His own love toward us, in that while we were yet sinners, Christ died for us" (Rom. 5:8).

The conflict over God's character and moral government is thus proleptically resolved by the voluntarily suffering Son of God on the cross.[5]

2. There is considerable debate over the meaning of *hilastērion*. It is used in Heb. 9:5 in reference to the "mercy seat" in the most holy place, and, as Douglas J. Moo notes, it probably should be taken similarly here, depicting Christ as the "antitype" to this "'place of atonement,' and, derivatively, to the ritual of atonement itself." Moo, *Romans*, 232.

3. What Paul means here by "his righteousness" is disputed. Moo explains that there are "two general approaches": The "first takes 'righteousness' *(dikaiosynē)* to designate what we might call an aspect of God's character" (e.g., justice, impartiality, fairness, or congruence of his actions with his own character). The "second interpretation understands 'righteousness' here to be God's saving, covenant faithfulness." Most scholars today favor the second view, but Moo believes that "there are sound reasons for adopting the first," more traditional, view. Moo, *Romans*, 237, 238. Either interpretation complements Scripture's broader emphasis on God's righteous, promise-keeping character.

4. Bruce, *Romans*, 114. He adds, "Although the problem in theodicy may not be as obvious to the modern mind as it was to Paul's, yet to pass over wrong is as much an act of injustice on the part of a judge as to condemn the innocent" (113).

5. In Derek R. Brown's view, Paul "considered Satan to be in one sense proleptically defeated by the death, resurrection, and vindication of Jesus," while "in another sense engaged in serious

Whereas Romans 3 depicts God "as defendant in a lawsuit," as James D. G. Dunn notes, Christ's ministry effectively defeats the devil's allegations in the heavenly council by providing the ultimate demonstration of God's righteousness and love, decisively refuting the enemy's slander.[6] Christ's mission was, in large part, one of epistemic revelation of God's kingdom of truth and justice (contra the enemy's kingdom of slander), which is made clear in Christ's stated purpose: "For this I have been born, and for this I have come into the world, to testify to the truth" (John 18:37; cf. 8:44–45). As Vanhoozer sees it, the "cross is the climax of the courtroom drama where God judges the covenantal unfaithfulness of humankind and displays his own covenant faithfulness, his love and his justice."[7] Indeed, Vanhoozer explains, "Jesus' death on the cross is the victory of God not merely over Israel's covenant rebellion but over the cosmic powers of sin, Satan, and death."[8] The false "accuser" and "slanderer," who was given limited jurisdiction to bring accusations in the heavenly court, is ultimately "thrown down" (Rev. 12:9; cf. Luke 10:18), first via the cross event, by which he is legally defeated in the heavenly court and then eschatologically when his usurping kingdom and limited dominion are finally removed altogether (Rev. 20:2–3, 10; cf. Matt. 25:41).

First, the cross event brings judgment against the devil and his supporters, ushering in the kingdom of God. As Revelation 12:10–11 puts it, "Now the salvation, the power, and the kingdom of our God and the authority of His Christ have come, for the accuser of our brethren has been thrown down, he who accuses them before our God day and night. And they overcame him because of the blood of the Lamb and because of the word of their testimony" (cf. 1:5; 1 John 2:1). This is a decidedly legal victory in the cosmic courtroom drama. As Beale observes, "In line with Zechariah 3, Christ's death and resurrection decisively refute the devil's accusations against believers (Rev. 12:10–12)," which are also accusations against the justice of God's judgment in their favor (cf. Jude 8).[9]

---

opposition to God's people until the end of the present age when he will be destroyed once and for all." D. Brown, *God of This Age*, 196.

6. Dunn, *Romans 9–16*, 134. Romans 3:4 states, "Let God be found true though every man be found a liar, as it is written, 'That You may be justified in Your words, / And prevail when You are judged.'" Here, as Dunn explains, Paul "is confident" that "God's covenant purpose" and "faithfulness to Israel" will "be vindicated in the final judgment." Further, the "vision of the whole of human history as a trial between the truth of God and the claims of man [and others, given a *cosmic* lawsuit] is impressive" (134).

7. Vanhoozer, *Drama of Doctrine*, 52.

8. Vanhoozer, *Drama of Doctrine*, 55.

9. Beale, *Revelation*, 660.

Further, Beale maintains, "Christ's death and resurrection have resulted in Satan's excommunication from heaven."[10] Beale sees this "understanding of Satan's fall from heaven" as "comparable to that of Luke 10:18" wherein Jesus said, "I was watching Satan fall from heaven like lightning."[11] Beale adds, "Luke 10:17, 19–20 explains this statement as meaning that the disciples have begun to have power over Satan by being able to cast out demons. . . . Their power over demons is an initial indication of the devil's defeat."[12]

As Jesus states, just before referencing the cross, "Now judgment is upon this world; now the ruler of this world will be cast out" (John 12:31). Christ's victory via the cross amounts to the condemnation of the devil and his slanderous charges. Leon Morris explains, "Just as the cross represents the judgment of this world, so it represents the defeat of Satan."[13] Although the cross "looked like the triumph of evil," in actuality "Satan was defeated in what appeared outwardly to be the very moment of his triumph."[14] In this way, Christ "gave Himself for our sins so that He might rescue us from this present evil age" (Gal. 1:4) and accomplish nothing short of cosmic reconciliation (Col. 1:20; cf. 2:14–15).[15]

Accordingly, "the ruler of this world has been judged" (John 16:11). Morris explains, "The work of judgment refers to the defeat of Satan," so "this defeat is not an arbitrary feat of power, but a judgment."[16] As Beale puts it, "Christ was wrongfully accused and executed by Satan's earthly pawns. But his resurrection vindicated him in the law court of heaven and enabled him to take away the devil's right and power as heavenly prosecutor (cf. 1:18)."[17] The triumph over the devil and his slander, by the ultimate demonstration of God's righteousness and love in the Christ event, unleashed God's kingdom by (legally) disarming the evil celestial powers.[18] As Colossians 2:15 states, "When He had disarmed the rulers and authorities, He made a public display of them, having triumphed over them through Him" (cf. 1 Cor. 2:6–8; 1 Pet.

10. Beale, *Revelation*, 658.

11. Beale, *Revelation*, 660. I. Howard Marshall adds, "Behind this picture [in Rev. 12:7–10] lies the myth of the fall of Lucifer from heaven (Isa. 14:12; cf. the allusion to this myth in Luke 10:15)." Marshall, *Gospel of Luke*, 428.

12. Beale, *Revelation*, 660.

13. Morris, *John*, 531. Cf. Beale, *Revelation*, 660.

14. Morris, *John*, 531.

15. F. F. Bruce comments, "The redemption that is in Christ Jesus is a cosmic redemption." Bruce, *Colossians, Philemon, Ephesians*, 112.

16. Morris, *John*, 620.

17. Beale, *Revelation*, 664.

18. Beale writes, "Christ's redemptive work on earth unleashes the effect in heaven of Michael's victory" and the "defeat of the devil and his hosts." Beale, *Revelation*, 652.

3:22).[19] Ephesians 1:19–21 adds that by "the working of the strength of His might" God "raised Him [Christ] from the dead and seated Him at His right hand in the heavenly places, far above all rule and authority and power and dominion, and every name that is named, not only in this age but also in the one to come." As 1 Peter 3:22 states, Christ is thus "at the right hand of God, having gone into heaven, after angels and authorities and powers had been subjected to him."

A distinct two-part process comes into view here, consisting of the legal defeat of Satan and his allegations and, only thereafter, the execution of judgment wherein Satan's dominion will be utterly eradicated. Beale explains that the "legal defeat of Satan is part of the essence of the inaugurated kingdom that has 'now come about.' The actual execution of the devil and his hordes," however, "comes at the consummation of history (Rev. 18; 19:20–21; 20:10–15)."[20] This two-part process may be in view when Christ appears to portray Satan as a "strong man" who must first be bound in order for Christ to "plunder his house" (Matt. 12:29).[21] Since Christ is infinitely stronger than this strong man and could immediately overpower him (Luke 11:22), the statement that Satan must first be "bound" makes little sense if the binding is thought of in terms of sheer force. However, it makes sense if understood in light of the NT pattern wherein Christ's ministry defeats the devil's slander, removing his legal standing as accuser and casting him out of the heavenly court.

Hebrews 2:14 explains that "through death [Christ] might render powerless him who had the power of death, that is, the devil" (cf. 1 John 3:8), which apparently legally and morally enables the one who is immeasurably "stronger" than the strong man to "overpower" and finally defeat him (Luke 11:22; cf. Rev. 5:5, 9–13). In other words, before Christ exercises his power to eradicate evil, he first "binds" Satan and removes his jurisdiction by a manifestation of God's character that effectively defeats the enemy's slander. By temporarily subjecting himself to the enemy's power, the suffering God of the cross

19. Although some interpret this imagery otherwise, Douglas J. Moo affirms the majority view that these "rulers and authorities" are "spiritual powers" and that via the cross, God "has won a victory over the rebellious powers." Moo, *Letters*, 212.

20. Beale, *Revelation*, 662.

21. R. T. France comments, "Jesus destroys Satan's kingdom not from within (as the Pharisees alleged: see vv. 25–26) but by direct assault on the strong man." France, *Matthew*, 213. France notes that the "'binding of Satan' was a feature in Jewish apocalyptic hope (Testament of Levi 18:21; cf. 1 Enoch 54:3–5; 69:27–28) and became also part of Christian eschatology (Rev. 20:1–3)." France, *Matthew*, 213. Further, the "figure" here "may be drawn from Isaiah 49:24–26," which itself includes God's promise regarding a dispute: "I will contend [*rib*] with the one who contends with you" (Isa. 49:25). France, *Matthew*, 213. Cf. Isa. 49:24–26; Mark 3:27; Luke 11:21–22; Rev. 20:2.

provides the grounds to finally remove the devil's power. F. F. Bruce states, "Jesus broke the devil's grip on his people when in death he became the death of death."[22] Christ "invaded the strong man's fortress, disarmed him, bound him fast, and robbed him of his spoil (Luke 11:21f)."[23] Beale adds, "Through his death Jesus nullified the devil's power to put others to death (Heb. 2:14) and took this power for himself (Rev. 1:18)."[24] And Stephen Noll explains, "Salvation in the Bible is not merely salvation *from* an enemy, nor is God's victory merely a display of overwhelming power. God's victory is always the vindication of his righteousness, and salvation is always directed toward the establishment of his kingdom."[25] Further, "by receiving unjustly the curse of the law in his flesh, Christ 'disarmed' the accusations of the principalities in open court (Gal 3:13; Rom 8:3–4)."[26]

Timing matters a great deal here. As Christ portrays in the parable of the wheat and tares, if evil were uprooted prematurely, there would be horrible collateral damage (Matt. 13:29–30). The harvest is thus delayed until "when the crop permits" (Mark 4:29; cf. 2 Pet. 3:9).[27] Accordingly, Christ teaches that the kingdom of heaven is like a mustard seed; it does not immediately come in full force but grows and expands (Mark 4:30–32).[28] Since Satan must first be (legally) defeated (via demonstration) before his kingdom can be eradicated, the execution of judgment is delayed until the appointed time.[29] Christ receives his kingdom only after judgment is conducted before the heavenly court (Dan. 7:13–14; cf. Rev. 5). As Hebrews 10:12–13 explains, Christ, "having offered one sacrifice for sins for all time, sat down at the right hand of God, waiting from that time onward until his enemies be made a footstool for his feet" (cf. 1:13; Ps. 110:1–2).

By his ministry, Christ unmasks, judges and condemns, and then dethrones the usurping ruler of this world, reclaiming the kingdom that was temporarily given over to the enemy—"the rulers of this age, who are passing away" (1 Cor.

---

22. Bruce, *Hebrews*, 86.

23. Bruce, *Hebrews*, 85. Clinton E. Arnold similarly notes that through the cross and resurrection, "Satan and his hosts were dealt the fatal blow that spelled their final doom. The 'strong man' was defeated." Arnold, *Powers of Darkness*, 79–80. N. T. Wright adds, "*Something has happened to dethrone the satan and to enthrone Jesus in its place. The story the gospels think they are telling is the story of how that had happened.*" Wright, *Day the Revolution Began*, 207 (emphasis original).

24. Beale, *Revelation*, 659.

25. Noll, *Angels of Light*, 157.

26. Noll, *Angels of Light*, 140.

27. Joel Marcus notes that this delay "invokes the apocalyptic concept of the eschatological measure: certain things must happen before the end can come." Marcus, *Mark 1–8*, 322.

28. See also Luke 13:18–21, 32–33; Rev. 11:15–17; cf. Dan. 2.

29. Matt. 8:29; cf. Ps. 75:2; 1 Cor. 4:5; Jude 9.

2:6; cf. Heb. 2:5). Ultimately, Christ will abolish "all rule and all authority and power" and "put all His enemies under His feet" (1 Cor. 15:24–25). Though defeated, Satan is not yet destroyed. The kingdom of God is already and not yet. While Satan has been condemned in heaven, he has not yet been finally judged in the hearts and minds of all creatures (cf. John 16:8–11). Accordingly, as Adela Yarbro Collins puts it, the devil is "defeated in heaven, but he [still] reigns on earth."[30] The final destruction of Satan and eradication of all evil awaits the eschaton. In the meantime, Satan possesses temporary power (*dynamis*; 2 Thess. 2:9) and jurisdiction or authority (*exousia*; cf. Acts 26:18), but he knows "that he has only a short time" (Rev. 12:12). As Paul proclaims, the "God of peace will soon crush Satan under your feet" (Rom. 16:20). As such, according to G. E. Ladd, "Those who meet satanic evil on earth" can be assured "that it is really a defeated power, however contrary it might seem to human experience."[31]

What More Could He Do?

We now return to the question of whether God has done everything he (morally) could do to eliminate or mitigate evil in this world. Isaiah 5 raises and addresses a similar question in a song about the relationship between God and his people, symbolized by a vineyard owner and his vineyard. The vineyard owner makes every preparation for his vineyard, locating it on "a fertile hill," clearing its stones, planting the "choicest vine," and building a watchtower (Isa. 5:1–2). Though the vineyard should have brought forth good grapes, it brought forth rotten stink-fruit, raising the question, Was this the vineyard owner's fault? (cf. Matt. 13:27).

In Isaiah 5:3–4 God says, "Judge, please, between Me and My vineyard. / What more could have been done to My vineyard / That I have not done in it?" (NKJV). Amazingly, God instructs his people to render a judgment regarding his care of his vineyard. What more could God have done? The implication of preceding verses and of the question itself is that God has done everything that he could do. Culpability for the failure of the vineyard lies elsewhere.[32]

The question of what more God could have done is decisively answered by Jesus's use of this passage in Matthew 21. Jesus quotes Isaiah 5 regarding all that the landowner did for his vineyard and then adds that the owner "rented

30. A. Collins, *Apocalypse*, 141.

31. Ladd, *Commentary on the Revelation of John*, 171.

32. Although this passage is about Judah's failure, the principle that God does all he can applies more broadly to God's providence throughout this world (cf. Ps. 145:9–17; Rom. 8:32).

it out to vine-growers and went on a journey" (Matt. 21:33). When he sent his servants (the prophets) to collect the produce, those renting his vineyard beat and killed them (vv. 34–36; cf. 11:12). Finally, he sent his beloved son (Christ), saying, "They will respect my son" (21:37). But the renters murdered his son, attempting to "seize his inheritance" (vv. 38–39)—that is, God repeatedly sent his prophets, but they were killed for their testimony as God's witnesses (within the cosmic lawsuit). Finally, "God so loved the world, that He gave" his beloved Son (John 3:16)—Jesus, the ultimate "faithful and true Witness" (Rev. 3:14; cf. 1:5)—who willingly submitted to death, "even death on a cross" (Phil. 2:8). The Second Person of the Trinity willingly laid down his life for us, demonstrating his surpassing love (Rom. 5:8; cf. John 10:17–18). There is no greater love than this (John 15:13). What more could he do?

If there was any preferable way to ensure the unending bliss of love relationship, would he not have chosen it, if only to spare himself the suffering (cf. Matt. 26:39; Mark 14:35)? What more could he do than give himself to die for us, so that he might justify us without in any way compromising his justice and love (Rom. 3:26)? The cross demonstrates that God is love and testifies that God has done everything that could be done to mitigate and eliminate evil without destroying the context for the unending flourishing of love. Although the cross is the ultimate manifestation of God's love in history, it is not alone; the entire canon testifies to God's love. God has suffered more than any other. God has voluntarily taken on his shoulders and suffered all the evil of this world.[33] As Nicholas Wolterstorff states, "God's love for his world is a rejoicing and suffering love."[34] Although creatures suffer immensely because of evil, God himself suffers most of all.

The conflict over God's character that could not be settled by the exercise of divine power is met by the voluntarily suffering God of the cross, who remains omnipotent and sovereign and assures us that "the sufferings of this present time are not worthy to be compared with the glory that is to be revealed to us" (Rom. 8:18)—that "eternal weight of glory far beyond all comparison" (2 Cor. 4:17). As John Stott argues, the God who is love subjects himself to suffering, making himself "vulnerable to pain," without thereby diminishing his omnipotence or sovereignty.[35] Stott thus asks, "In the real world of pain, how could one worship a God who was immune to it?"[36]

---

33. Cf. Isa. 53:4–6; 63:9; Matt. 8:17. On the claim that God suffers when we suffer, see Peckham, *Love of God*, 147–89.

34. Wolterstorff, "Suffering Love," 136.

35. Stott, *Cross of Christ*, 323.

36. Stott, *Cross of Christ*, 326. Jürgen Moltmann goes further, arguing that a God incapable of suffering is "a loveless being." Moltmann, *Crucified God*, 222.

Although a God who *only* suffers along with us would not be effective to finally deliver us from our sufferings, particularly eschatologically, Dietrich Bonhoeffer's words ring true: "Only the suffering God can help."[37] Only one who knows the suffering of this world could be in a position to make the rightful judgment that "the sufferings of this present time are not worthy to be compared with the glory" to come (Rom. 8:18). Jesus Christ the righteous (1 John 2:1) has experienced the suffering of this world; he not only can "sympathize with our weaknesses" (Heb. 4:15), but he also has borne the sufferings of the entire world and been deeply wounded and grieved by all evil.[38] As Alvin Plantinga puts it, "God does not stand idly by, coolly observing the suffering of his creatures. He enters into and shares our suffering."[39] Indeed, he "was prepared to accept this suffering in order to overcome sin, and death, and the evils that afflict our world, and to confer on us a life more glorious than we can imagine."[40] This God of love has shown himself to be eminently worthy and trustworthy.

The suffering God of the cross teaches us that we can trust that God has done and will do everything he can for us. As Paul states, "He who did not spare His own Son, but delivered Him over for us all, how will He not also with Him freely give us all things?" (Rom. 8:32). Because of what God has done and is doing (v. 34), no one can successfully "bring a charge against God's elect," and nothing can separate believers from God's love, not even "angels" or "principalities" and "powers" of darkness (vv. 33, 38–39). God need not have suffered for us, but he chose to endure suffering because of his great love for us. God's voluntary condescension to suffer with and for us temporarily appears as weakness but culminates in God's final victory over evil. By willingly suffering on the cross, Christ demonstrated that he considered *this* world, despite evil, to be worth the cost to himself (Rom. 8:18; Heb. 12:2). In doing so, he also demonstrated God's righteousness (Rom. 3:25–26) and love (5:8) and proved that he always keeps his promises (15:8). What more could he do?

---

37. Bonhoeffer, *Letters and Papers from Prison*, 479.
38. Here I think of the stirring conclusion of G. K. Chesterton's novel, *The Man Who Was Thursday*. The main character, Sunday, symbolic of God, notes that via suffering, "the real lie of Satan may be flung back in the face of this blasphemer," and "by tears and torture we may earn the right to say to this man [Satan], 'You lie!'" The main protagonist, Syme, asks Sunday, "Have you ever suffered?" Everything goes dark and Syme hears, "Can ye drink of the cup that I drink of?" (278–79; cf. Mark 10:38).
39. Plantinga, "Self-Profile," 36. Further, "God's capacity for suffering" is "proportional to his greatness" (36). John G. Stackhouse Jr. adds, God *"knows what it is to suffer"* and "suffers along with us." Stackhouse, *Can God Be Trusted*, 115 (emphasis original).
40. Plantinga, "Self-Profile," 36.

The Cross as Proleptic Theodicy

The questions surrounding theodicy will be finally answered eschatologically. In the meantime, looking to the cross provides grounds to trust that God has done everything he could for our best good. In short, God perfectly knows and wants what is best for everyone, and in light of the God of the cross, we can trust him even while many questions remain. As Henri Blocher states, "From the cross there will spring light sufficient to illuminate even the darkest night."[41]

Although we may fail to understand precisely why particular evils occur, in light of the ultimate display of God's love in Christ we can have confidence in God's goodness and justice.[42] We might, then, humbly approach the mystery of accounting for specific evils along the lines of something like skeptical theism, which, simply put, doubts the present ability of humans to make sufficiently knowledgeable judgments regarding why God has acted or refrained from acting as he has.[43] Something like this appears to be voiced in Scripture, particularly in Job.[44]

On the one hand, the book of Job includes something like what some philosophers call noseeum arguments.[45] These arguments claim: I cannot see x; therefore there is no x. Relative to the evidential problem of evil, such arguments go something like this: as far as we can see, there is no morally sufficient reason for an omnipotent God to permit the (particular) kinds and amount of evil in this world. Therefore, there is no morally sufficient reason for God to permit the evil in this world.

In this regard, Plantinga argues that Job "suspects that God doesn't have a good reason" for the suffering that befalls him because Job "can't imagine what that reason might be. In reply, God does not tell him what the reason is; instead, he attacks Job's unthinking assumption that if he, Job, can't imagine what reason God might have, then probably God doesn't have a reason at all." God does this by "pointing out how limited Job's knowledge is." Although Job "can't see what God's reason might be," writes Plantinga, it "doesn't follow that probably God doesn't have a reason."[46]

---

41. Blocher, *Evil and the Cross*, 18.

42. As Plantinga states, while "we don't know why God permits evil; we do know" that God "was prepared to suffer on our behalf." Plantinga, "Self-Profile," 36.

43. See the section on skeptical theism in McBrayer and Howard-Snyder, *Blackwell Companion to the Problem of Evil*, 377–506.

44. E.g., Job 38:1–4; 42:1–3; cf. Isa. 55:8–9.

45. See Wykstra, "Rowe's Noseeum Arguments from Evil," 126–50.

46. Plantinga, *Warranted Christian Belief*, 497.

God's response to Job—reminding Job how little he knows—should effectively remind us of the same. Interrupting Elihu's speech, God "answered Job out of the whirlwind":

> Who is this that darkens counsel
> By words without knowledge? . . .
> Where were you when I laid the foundation of the earth?
> Tell Me, if you have understanding. . . .
> Have the gates of death been revealed to you,
> Or have you seen the gates of deep darkness?
> Have you understood the expanse of the earth?
> Tell Me, if you know all this. (Job 38:1, 4, 17–18; cf. 11:7; 38:33)

Job knows little of the unfathomably insidious darkness against which he rails and appears to know nothing of the cosmic dispute in which he is embroiled. Put simply, Job does not know the whole story. Neither do we. Who are we, then, to think we know better than God what he should have done?

God asks Job,

> Will the faultfinder contend with the Almighty?
> Let him who reproves God answer it. . . .
>
> Will you really annul My judgment?
> Will you condemn Me that you may be justified? (Job 40:2, 8)

God alone is perfectly wise and good and possesses the perspective necessary to judge comprehensively and righteously. Further, God emphasizes, he alone possesses the power to judge and defeat evil:

> Can you draw out Leviathan with a fishhook?
> Or press down his tongue with a cord?[47] . . .
> Will he [Leviathan] make a covenant with you?
> Will you take him for a servant forever? . . .
> No one is so fierce that he dares to arouse him [Leviathan];
> Who then is he that can stand before Me? (Job 41:1, 4, 10)

God's response to Job—as well as the fact that Job's friends were so confident but wrong about what was happening—should evoke the recognition that we are not in a position to know everything necessary to evaluate God's action

---

47. While some take this as a poetic reference to a crocodile, Marvin H. Pope notes that the "supernatural character of Leviathan is abundantly clear" when compared with the ANE data regarding this cosmic sea monster. Pope, *Job*, 331. See chap. 3 of the present volume.

or inaction in specific instances. Job 38:2 sums this up well: "Why do you talk so much / when you know so little?" (CEV). With Job we might respond, "I have declared that which I did not understand, / Things too wonderful for me, which I did not know" (42:3; cf. 40:3–5).

The call for epistemic humility is not unique to Job. Isaiah 55:8–9 adds,

> "My thoughts are not your thoughts,
> Nor are your ways My ways," declares the LORD.
> "For as the heavens are higher than the earth,
> So are My ways higher than your ways
> and My thoughts than your thoughts."

Likewise, Romans 11:33 states, "Oh the depth of the riches both of the wisdom and knowledge of God! How unsearchable are His judgments and unfathomable His ways!" As Peter van Inwagen puts it, "If anyone insists that he has good reason to believe that nothing of any great value depends on the world's being" as it is, then "we must ask him why he thinks he is in a position to know things of that sort. We might remind him of the counsel of epistemic humility that was spoken to Job out of the whirlwind."[48] Just because we do not see any good reason for God to permit this or that evil, it does not follow that God has no good reasons.[49]

This recognition need not commit one to an extreme form of skeptical theism that refrains from saying anything else about the problem of evil. This cosmic conflict theodicy of love provides a biblical framework for approaching the problem of evil. However, this framework does not answer why God allowed any specific evil occurrence (short of divine revelation). We might surmise that if God allowed something, then to do otherwise would be against the rules of engagement, contravene the creaturely free will necessary for the flourishing of love, or result in greater evil or less flourishing of love. Short of divine revelation we do not know which one (or more) of these apply to a given situation. It is futile—and may even be harmful—to speculate.

---

48. Van Inwagen, "Problem of Evil," 219. Cf. Eleonore Stump's illustration of Martians "whose sole knowledge of human[s]" comes from recordings of a "city hospital." Seeing limbs amputated, organs extracted, and people sometimes dying, the Martians might "be filled with horror and moral indignation at the doctors." Stump, *Wandering in the Darkness*, 17.

49. Consider Wykstra's "Condition of Reasonable Epistemic Access" (CORNEA), which "says that we can argue from 'we see no X' to 'there is no X' only when X has 'reasonable seeability'—that is, is the sort of thing which, if it exists, we can reasonably expect to see in the situation." Wykstra uses an illustration of "tiny flies," or "noseeums," which "are so small you 'no see 'um.'" That one does not see noseeums does not render it probable that there are no noseeums. Wykstra, "Rowe's Noseeum Arguments," 126.

We should remember this warning against speculation, especially when attempting to comfort someone suffering. However well-meaning they were, Job's friends added to Job's sufferings by their attempts to make sense of precisely what was happening to him.[50] Laura W. Ekstrom comments, "There is little worse than suffering a tremendous loss and, while struggling to cope with it, rather than being embraced humanely and assisted in a tangible way, being told by others that the horrible thing that has happened is 'a part of God's plan' or 'is for your own good' or that 'everything happens for a reason'"; attempts to explain suffering "are often the last thing a suffering person needs to hear" in the midst of their distress.[51] Nicholas Wolterstorff adds, "But please: Don't say it's not really so bad. Because it is. Death is awful, demonic." If you say "it's not so bad," then "you do not sit with me in my grief but place yourself off in the distance away from me. Over there, you are of no help."[52]

Job's friends did not know what they were talking about. When we face individual instances of evil, we also do not know what we are talking about (short of divine revelation). We thus might remain silent relative to explanation and reserve our voices to grieve with those who grieve (as in the book of Lamentations). Such an approach does not amount to simply throwing up our hands and saying nothing in the face of evil. This cosmic conflict theodicy of love has the advantage of expositing a framework that can (broadly) account for why God might refrain from preventing even horrendous evils without justifying those evils themselves or attempting to provide the specific reasons why God acts or refrains from acting as he does. In short, this theodicy of love maintains that this world is not supposed to be this way. We can confidently claim that, either directly or indirectly, "An enemy has done this!" (Matt. 13:28).

Job offers at least two approaches to the problem of evil. First, Job 1–2 pulls back the curtain and reveals the cosmic conflict framework. Second, Job emphasizes that even with this framework many questions remain, and we should recognize how little we know, not expecting to have an answer for everything. As Plantinga states, "If God is good and powerful as the theist believes, then he will indeed have a good reason for permitting evil; but why suppose the theist must be in a position to figure out what it is?"[53] He adds, "Perhaps God has a good reason, but that reason is too complicated for us

---

50. At first, however, Job's friends sympathized and sat with him silently for seven days (Job 2:11, 13).

51. Ekstrom, "Christian Theodicy," 266.

52. Wolterstorff, *Lament for a Son*, 34.

53. Plantinga, "Reply to the Basingers," 28.

to understand. Or perhaps He has not revealed it for some other reason."[54]
Stephen Davis acknowledges that, given what Christianity "says about God's
transcendence and our cognitive limits, we would expect that there will be
evils that we cannot explain (but God can) and goods so great that we cannot
comprehend them (although God can)."[55]

Greg Ganssle and Yena Lee provide a helpful illustration: "A five-year-old
may consider her pediatrician evil as he gives her a shot each time she sees
him. No matter how much she thinks, no justifying reason appears for the
sharp metal prod in her arm. But her mother, who has the wisdom of decades, knows the reason for the pain. If the difference in knowledge from a
few decades supplies a justifying reason unimaginable to the five-year-old, the
difference between finite and infinite knowledge may also supply a justifying
reason unimaginable to those with limited understanding."[56] Thus "given the
gulf between God's knowledge and our knowledge, it seems unreasonable to
expect that we could know the God-justifying reason for every case of evil,
even if such a reason were to exist."[57]

Even though we do not know God's specific rationale in each instance, we
can have confidence that God would prevent any evil that either (1) he could
prevent without breaking his promises (relative to free will and the rules of
engagement) or (2) he could prevent without leading to more deleterious
results. Scripture affirms that all God's "ways are just" and that he is a "God
of faithfulness and without injustice, / Righteous and upright is He" (Deut.
32:4). I take the evidence of Scripture to affirm that God always does what is
most preferable and loving, given the options available to him (cf. 1 Sam. 3:18).

The rules of engagement or other factors might prevent God from doing
what he otherwise would—that is, there may be some "omnipotence-
constraining" factors at work, of which we know little or nothing.[58] As Michael Bergmann and Daniel Howard-Snyder argue, "If we are in the dark
about what goods there are and what omnipotence-constraining connections
there are between such goods and the permissions of such evils," then we are
not in a position to make a valid judgment.[59]

We only "see in a mirror dimly" and "know in part" (1 Cor. 13:12). We are
not in a position to see enough of the factors involved, and we lack the cognitive

---

54. Plantinga, *God, Freedom, and Evil*, 10.
55. S. Davis, "Free Will and Evil," 88.
56. Ganssle and Lee, "Evidential Problems of Evil," 18–19.
57. Ganssle and Lee, "Evidential Problems of Evil," 15.
58. The rules of engagement are a bit like a spiderweb, which is invisible from some angles
but visible from others.
59. Bergmann and Howard-Snyder, "Reply to Rowe," 138.

ability and moral standing to "judge" divine actions (cf. 4:5). Whereas some may think they could conceive of a better way that God should have governed the world, no one is aware of all the factors. Given the butterfly effect, we have no idea how things would turn out if history took a different course. As William Hasker puts it, it is "wholly inappropriate" to think as if God is "sitting nervously in the dock hoping that we, his attorneys, will be able to get him off from the charges." Rather, "God is the holy and righteous One, the One before whom we ourselves will be judged, not someone subject to our judgment." As such, "God does not need a theodicy, but we do—at least, some of us do."[60]

We should, then, continually recognize two points. First, just because we do not see the sufficient reasons why God may permit evils or appears to be hidden, it does not follow that there are no sufficient reasons. Absence of evidence is not evidence of absence. Second, though we only "know in part" (1 Cor. 13:12), we can look to the cross as the ultimate manifestation of God's love, which offers sufficient reason to trust that God does everything that can be done for everyone's best good. If there had been a preferable way available to him, he would have chosen it (cf. Matt. 26:39).

The Eschatological Destruction of Evil

The final answer to evil is eschatological. Ultimately, God provides a historical solution to the problem of evil, amounting to universal recognition of God's justice and the eradication of evil. While the cross is the capstone event that ensures the settling of the cosmic conflict over God's character, the final settling of the matter in the minds of all creatures is eschatological.

The settling of this cosmic dispute follows a distinctive pattern: a process of trial and judgment and, only thereafter, the execution of judgment. As discussed earlier, the cosmic dispute is first settled epistemically by a cosmic judgment, and then God exercises his power to execute judgment (Dan. 7; Rev. 20). This "demonstration then execution" pattern is bound up with the nature of the conflict as a cosmic dispute over God's character.

Eventually, "the glory of the LORD will be revealed, / And all flesh will see it together" (Isa. 40:5).[61] Indeed, God declares,

> I have sworn by Myself,
> The word has gone forth from My mouth in righteousness

60. Hasker, *Triumph of God over Evil*, 120.
61. Notably, the following chapters of Isaiah emphasize a *rib* controversy, including what many have called the "trial of the gods." See, e.g., Hanson, *Isaiah 40–66*, 88.

> And will not turn back,
> That to Me every knee will bow, every tongue will swear allegiance.
> They will say of Me, "Only in the LORD are righteousness and
>   strength."
> Men will come to Him,
> And all who were angry at Him will be put to shame.[62] (Isa. 45:23–24;
>   cf. Jer. 23:20; 30:24)

Paul likewise affirms that "we will all stand before the judgment seat of God" and that "it is written, 'As I live, says the LORD, every knee shall bow to Me, / And every tongue shall give praise to God'" (Rom. 14:10–11).[63] As Dunn comments, Paul uses Isaiah 45 here "in its original sense," over against the gods of the nations, "all who would contest the supreme and final authority of the one God will in the end-time judgment bow and acknowledge that there is no other God than Yahweh, 'a righteous God and a Savior' (Isa 45:21)."[64]

Finally, the victorious servants of God will proclaim,

> Righteous and true are Your ways,
> King of the nations! . . .
> All the nations will come and worship before You,
> For Your righteous acts have been revealed. (Rev. 15:3–4; cf. 19:1–2;
>   Deut. 32:4; Ps. 86:8–9)[65]

Beale notes that "God's 'righteous and true ways' in 15:3 are parallel with 'great and marvelous works,' showing that God's sovereign acts are not demonstrations of raw power but moral expressions of his just character."[66]

In the end, there will be sufficient revelation to vindicate God once and for all in a way recognized by everyone. As Stephen Davis states, in the eschaton "it will be evident that God chose the best course and that the favorable balance of good over evil that will then exist was obtainable by God in no other way or in no morally preferable way."[67] Eventually the injustice of this life

---

62. John N. Oswalt notes that God's "absolute faithfulness to his promises" and "the utter reliability of all that he has said," in "contrast to the failure of the gods to keep their promises, will bring all the world to the Lord's feet." Oswalt, *Isaiah*, 225.

63. Cf. Isa. 45:23; 1 Cor. 4:5; Phil. 2:9–11.

64. Dunn, *Romans 9–16*, 809.

65. David E. Aune notes of v. 3, "This is an allusion to Deut 32:4 (a song of Moses)," perhaps "combined with Psalm 145:17." Aune, *Revelation 6–16*, 874. So also Beale, *Revelation*, 793–94. God's victory over the beast here parallels the declarations, "There is no one like You among the gods" and "All nations whom You have made shall come and worship before You, O Lord, / And they shall glorify Your name" (Ps. 86:8–9).

66. Beale, *Revelation*, 795.

67. S. Davis, "Free Will and Evil," 75.

will be overturned (cf. Prov. 11:17–21). As the psalmist writes, "Weeping may last for the night, / But a shout of joy comes in the morning" (Ps. 30:5). Or as it is written in Isaiah 60:2,

> Darkness will cover the earth
> And deep darkness the peoples;
> But the LORD will rise upon you
> And His glory will appear upon you.

Providing the ultimate answer to the question of Malachi 2:17 ("Where is the God of justice?"), God's "Servant" will faithfully "bring forth justice to the nations" and will establish "justice in the earth" (Isa. 42:1, 4).[68] Although the forces of the enemy "will wage war against the Lamb," as in the vision of Revelation, ultimately "the Lamb will overcome them, because He is Lord of lords and King of kings, and those who are with Him are the called and chosen and faithful" (Rev. 17:14; cf. 16:13–16).[69]

In the end, God accomplishes two primary things. First, he manifests his character over against evil such that the universe will be forevermore inoculated against it. Second, once the matter of his character has been settled, God exercises his power to destroy evil. God will finally eradicate pain and evil forevermore. Evil will never arise again. The universe will be eternally secure. As is written in Isaiah 25:8–9,

> He will swallow up death for all time,
> And the Lord GOD will wipe away tears from all faces,
> And He will remove the reproach of His people from all the earth;
> For the LORD has spoken.
> And it will be said in that day,
> "Behold, this is our God for whom we have waited." (cf. Isa. 51:8–11)

Indeed, according to Revelation 21:4, "He will wipe away every tear from their eyes; and there will no longer be any death; there will no longer be any mourning, or crying, or pain; the first things have passed away."

The problem of evil is thus finally and decisively answered by divine action. The cries for justice from the souls under the altar (Rev. 6:9) and

---

68. Cf. Isa. 16:5; Jer. 23:5–6; 33:14–17.
69. Here the poem in Lewis's *The Lion, the Witch, and the Wardrobe* (74–75) comes to mind:
Wrong will be right, when Aslan comes in sight,
At the sound of his roar, sorrows will be no more,
When he bares his teeth, winter meets its death
And when he shakes his mane, we shall have spring again.

all others will be answered by God's eschatological victory over death and suffering.[70] As Paul writes to the Corinthians, "Then will come about the saying that is written, 'Death is swallowed up in victory. O death, where is your victory? O death, where is your sting?'" (1 Cor. 15:54–55; cf. 1 Thess. 4:16–17).[71]

When the cosmic conflict is finally ended, all will clearly see that God has done only and always what is best. All will understand that God is love; all his commands have always been and always will be out of love, for the ultimate happiness of all.[72] So God's name will finally be vindicated (cf. Phil. 2:10). Then God will make an utter end of evil, suffering, and death and will "wipe away every tear" (Rev. 21:4). Finally, Christ's dominion will be all in all. "His dominion is an everlasting dominion / Which will not pass away; / And His kingdom is one / Which will not be destroyed" (Dan. 7:14).[73] In the meantime, Paul assures us that it will all be worth it: "The sufferings of this present time are not worthy to be compared with the glory that is to be revealed" (Rom. 8:18). The solution to the problem of evil, the ultimate theodicy, will be fully understood in the world to come. Until then, the suffering God of the cross demonstrates that God is righteous and that God is love. We can trust that

70. Cf. 1 Cor. 15:26, 54–55; Rev. 20:13–14.

71. Although I cannot adequately make the case for the following view here, I believe Scripture teaches that the wicked will finally be destroyed rather than suffer eternal conscious torment. On this view, death, the "last enemy," will be "abolished" (1 Cor. 15:26). Even "Hades" will finally be thrown into the lake of fire (Rev. 20:14). There "will no longer be any death; there will no longer be any mourning, or crying, or pain" anywhere in the universe, for "the first things have passed away" (Rev. 21:4). In my view, although God has no pleasure in the death of anyone (Ezek. 18:32), is longsuffering so that as many as possible might be saved (2 Pet. 3:9), and "does not afflict willingly" (Lam. 3:33), the final destruction of those who finally and intractably reject God's love is the most loving thing God can do for them, since misery is the inevitable and unavoidable result of estrangement from God. Whereas some think that a God of love should not destroy anyone, it seems that it would be worse to allow beings to waste away and wallow in suffering than to end their suffering sooner. As Claus Westermann states, "To say no to God—and this is what freedom allows—is ultimately to say no to life; for life comes from God." Westermann, *Genesis 1–11*, 222. On the case for conditionalism, see Fudge, *Fire That Consumes*. See further Stott's brief summary of his tentative case for conditionalism in Edwards and Stott, *Evangelical Essentials*, 312–20. See also Stackhouse, "Terminal Punishment." Further, see the essays by Wenham, Ellis, Thiselton, Swinburne, and others who reject everlasting torment in Date, Stump, and Anderson, *Rethinking Hell*.

72. Regarding those who seemingly had no opportunity to accept salvation, I believe that, whereas salvation comes only through Jesus (Acts 4:12), God holds each person accountable for their response to the light available to them (see, e.g., Acts 17:30; cf. Luke 12:47–48; John 9:40–41). I understand texts like John 1:9 (Christ "enlightens every [hu]man," cf. John 12:32) to mean that some divine light has shone on every person so that none will be condemned because of (nonresistant) ignorance (cf. John 3:18); all will be judged based on their response to the light available to them. On why I reject universalism, see Peckham, *Love of God*, 204–9.

73. Cf. Ps. 45:6–7; Dan. 2; Mark 14:62; Luke 1:32–33; Rev. 5:11–13.

God's "work is perfect, / For all his ways are just; / A God of faithfulness and without injustice, / Righteous and upright is He" (Deut. 32:4).

Conclusion

This chapter focused on the defeat of evil at the cross and the final eschatological destruction of evil. Although creatures suffer immensely because of evil, God suffers most of all and has done everything he (morally) could for this world (cf. Isa. 5:1–7; Matt. 21:33–40). God provides the ultimate demonstration of his love and justice by Christ's voluntarily giving himself for us on the cross (Rom. 3:25–26; 5:8). The suffering God of the cross is the conclusive demonstration of God's justice and character of unselfish love, which evokes confidence in God's goodness even as many questions remain unanswered as we await the final eschatological solution to and eradication of evil.

6

Evaluating the Theodicy of Love

The previous chapters have developed what I call a theodicy of love. In this final chapter, we assess how this theodicy of love stacks up against potential objections and other approaches. We begin with a brief summary of the theodicy of love before turning to an evaluation of this theodicy in light of questions and objections that might be raised. Finally, we consider some advantages of this approach in dialogue with some of the most prominent defenses and theodicies.

The Theodicy of Love Model in Outline

This theodicy of love begins with the premise that love must be freely given and freely received. A genuine love relationship between God and creatures is possible only if God consistently grants creatures the freedom to will otherwise than God desires, which entails epistemic and consequential freedom. Accordingly, a genuine love relationship requires the possibility that creatures might reject God's ideal will and, consequently, the possibility of evil.

Whereas God's (ideal) desires are sometimes unfulfilled because creatures sometimes exercise their consequential freedom otherwise than God desires, God remains sovereign and omnipotent and will finally accomplish his overarching purpose (his remedial will), the certainty of which is established via (complex) divine foreknowledge, without compromising creaturely freedom. Meanwhile, evil occurs because creatures have willed otherwise than God ideally desires.

However, there appear to be evils that God could prevent without under-mining the kind of free will necessary for love. Accordingly, this theodicy of love goes beyond two-dimensional conceptions of providence, which account only for the agency of God and earthly creatures. It does so by espousing a three-dimensional conception, which also accounts for the agency of celestial beings such as angels and demons. A cosmic conflict wherein the devil and his minions oppose God's moral government of love is robustly supported in both Scripture and the Christian tradition. Whereas neither the devil nor any other creatures could oppose the omnipotent God at the level of sheer power, this cosmic conflict is primarily of an epistemic nature, revolving around the devil's slanderous allegations that God is not fully good, just, and loving. Such an epistemic conflict cannot be settled by sheer power but requires a cosmic demonstration.

Within this conflict, Satan and his cohorts are temporarily granted signifi-cant jurisdiction over the earth, limited according to jointly negotiated and thus covenantal rules of engagement, which correspondingly limit (morally) the exercise of God's power to eliminate or mitigate the evils that (temporar-ily) fall within the enemy's jurisdiction. Whereas God maintains the sheer power to prevent all evils and ideally desires that no evil occur, there are some evils that God cannot (morally) prevent because of his commitment to the flourishing of love and the covenantal rules of engagement. This model pro-vides a framework for understanding why God sometimes does not prevent horrendous evils, while upholding divine omnipotence, omniscience, and a robust conception of God's providence. Whereas God does everything he (morally) can to prevent or eliminate evil, in some cases doing so would con-travene the covenantal rules of engagement, subvert the creaturely free will necessary for love, or otherwise result in greater evil or less flourishing of love.

Although creatures suffer immensely because of evil, the voluntarily suf-fering God of the cross suffers most of all, providing the conclusive dem-onstration of his utter love and justice by Christ's subjection of himself to death on a cross. In so doing, God demonstrates that he considers *this* world to be worth the cost to himself. While this God suffers, he nevertheless main-tains the power to eliminate evil and, once the epistemic conflict is settled, will exercise his power to eliminate evil once and for all, ushering in an eternity of pure bliss. This theodicy thus posits love—within the context and constraints of a cosmic conflict—as the morally sufficient reason for God to permit evil in this world. Some might question whether this cosmic conflict approach is viable, coherent, and successful relative to various issues. In what follows, I briefly respond to what I consider to be the most pressing questions relative to the viability and effectiveness of this approach.

Is This Model Viable?

Some object that a cosmic conflict model is not plausible. As discussed in chapter 3, however, plausibility is largely subjective. Whereas some claim there is not sufficient evidence for the existence of the demonic realm, others contend that there is evil in this world that cannot be adequately accounted for without understanding it as demonic. Even John Hick—who denies the reality of demons and rejects what he calls the "official Christian myth" of the "great cosmic drama"—nevertheless characterizes evil in this world as "the depths of demonic malice and cruelty that each generation has experienced," such as the Holocaust.[1] He writes, "In the demonic, evil as a necessary element in a soul-making universe seems to have got out of hand and to have broken loose from God's control."[2]

As Michael Murray puts it, "Something about our world seems more deeply and radically askew—something that can only be explained by a corruption which has eroded the integrity and thwarted the flourishing of the natural order on a cosmic scale."[3] Jeffrey Burton Russell adds, "The depth and intensity" of the radical evil in this world "exceeds and transcends what could be expected in an individual human," and "despite a generally shared worldview that is powerfully and dogmatically materialistic, a great many people still experience what they take to be the Devil."[4]

Although Western academic thought is dominated by anti-supernaturalism, the majority of the world believes in supernatural agencies. As we have seen, the cosmic conflict is well supported in Scripture and Christian tradition and has been believed by the vast majority of Christians through the ages. Although many recent Christian approaches to the problem of evil make little or no reference to the demonic realm, Russell maintains that "the devil has always been a central Christian doctrine."[5] Thus, he concludes, "no theodicy that does not take the Devil fully into consideration is likely to be persuasive."[6]

---

1. Hick, *Evil and the God of Love*, 283; Hick, "An Irenaean Theodicy," 49. Conversely, Stephen T. Davis contends that Hick's theodicy does not meet Hick's own standard definition for theodicy, which must be "consistent with the data" of "the religious tradition on which it is based." S. Davis, "Critique of Irenaean Theodicy," 60. Hick himself notes that his own theodicy might be considered implausible because any theodicy that "requires an eschatology will thereby be rendered implausible in the minds of many people today." Hick, "Irenaean Theodicy," 51.

2. Hick, *Evil and the God of Love*, 325. Hick's views changed drastically throughout his career, but in earlier writings, he clarified that he did "not intend to deny the existence of energies and structures of evil transcending individual human minds" (19).

3. Murray, *Nature Red in Tooth and Claw*, 74.

4. Russell, *Satan*, 225, 221. Cf. Wright, *Evil and the Justice of God*, 37.

5. Russell, *Satan*, 226.

6. Russell, *Devil*, 288.

Further, as we observed earlier, Alvin Plantinga reasons that it is "less than clear that Western academia has much to say by way of evidence against the idea. That beings [such as Satan and his cohorts] should be involved in the history of our world seems to me (as to, e.g., C. S. Lewis and many others) not at all unlikely, in particular not unlikely with respect to Christian theism." He continues, "It isn't nearly as improbable with respect to 'what we now know' as most philosophers seem to assume."[7]

Does the Idea of the Devil Help to Address the Problem of Evil?

On this cosmic conflict framework, evil arose in the universe via the free decision of a previously flawless creature to rebel against God. But as Hick argues, an "unqualifiedly good creature" could not commit evil, since, if certain creatures sin, "we can only infer that they were not flawless."[8] However, while the decision of any flawless creature to do evil would be utterly nonsensical, I do not see why we should accept Hick's assertion that it is impossible, particularly if love requires consequential freedom. Although some contend that a being in paradise would lack sufficient motivation to do evil, Murray notes that "there is nothing about satisfaction concerning one's current condition that entails that one would not find another condition," such as "equality with God," to "be even more enriching or satisfying."[9]

We are nevertheless left with this question: If God created the devil knowing the havoc he would wreak, is not God to blame for all that the devil causes? Russell contends, "The idea of the Devil ultimately does little to solve the problem of *why* there is evil in the cosmos. At the center of the problem is the question of why God should freely choose to create a cosmos in which the Devil and other evil beings produce such immeasurable suffering."[10] However, given the indeterministic freedom of creatures, it is not simply up to God to "create" or actualize just any world that he pleases.[11] When inclined to suppose God should have done otherwise, we might recall that we do not know whether any preferable avenues were available to God, given his commitments to love, freedom, and promise-keeping. It might be that, all things considered, any world that God could have actualized without the devil would have been

---

7. Plantinga, "Supralapsarianism or 'O Felix Culpa,'" 16. Cf. Lewis, *Problem of Pain*.

8. Hick, *Evil and the Love of God*, 68–69.

9. Murray, *Nature Red in Tooth and Claw*, 86. See also Plantinga, *Warranted Christian Belief*, 212–13.

10. Russell, *Mephistopheles*, 303.

11. Contra what Plantinga calls "Leibniz' Lapse," the supposition that, given omnipotence, God "could have created any possible world he pleased." Plantinga, *God, Freedom, and Evil*, 44.

less preferable than this one, particularly considering the infinite future bliss of the eschaton, beyond the temporary evil in this world (cf. Rom. 8:18).

In my view, it would have been better if no creature ever sinned. However, given consequential freedom, it was not up to God whether and to what extent anyone would sin in any given possible world. Whereas some possible worlds may be better than this one, there may not be any preferable worlds that God could actualize. For all we know, it might even be that had God chosen to not create the devil solely because the devil would exercise his freedom against God's desires, then the kind of creaturely freedom necessary for the flourishing of love would be compromised. This would not restrict God from making decisions that have ramifications regarding who exists, but it might be that God cannot (morally or without contravening love) exclude certain creatures' existence for the sole purpose of denying their ability to depart from God's ideal will.

In addition, it might be that God actualized this world not because of an evaluation that it was better than any other actualizable world. Perhaps it is not. Perhaps there is no *best* actualizable world.[12] As William Hasker notes, different worlds might contain competing values that are "incommensurable in the sense that there is no common measure, no fixed 'ratio' as it were, by which they can be measured against one another" to compare their overall value.[13] If so, perhaps God chose to actualize *this* world because of the unique value of this world.[14] Perhaps any world God could actualize without the devil would not include us or myriad other creatures, and perhaps God chose to create this world because he wanted to actualize the incommensurable value of an endless love relationship with the very creatures in this world. If so, this scenario would indicate an even deeper aspect of election than is usually recognized—an indeterministic understanding of the riches of God's grace in that God "chose us in Him before the foundation of the world" (Eph. 1:4). Perhaps similar to the way a mother chooses to endure the pain of childbirth for the joy of her child, God considered this world to be worth the cost in order to give us the joys of eternal life, which may comport with Paul's imagery of the "pains of childbirth" of "the whole creation" (Rom. 8:22).

12. Cf. Robert M. Adams's argument against Leibniz's claim that this must be the best possible world because "God cannot fail to produce the best." R. Adams, "Must God Create the Best?," 24.

13. Hasker, *Triumph of God*, 79. Consider the incommensurable value of a loving relationship with one's child.

14. Whereas God is the ultimate source of value and needs nothing, I have elsewhere argued that God's love is evaluative such that creatures can bring him value "similar to the way that a human father is pleased when his son brings him" a gift that is "otherwise worthless." Peckham, *Love of God*, 142.

Admittedly, I do not know which, if any, of these potential reasons why God actualized this world is true. Nevertheless, insofar as God is justified in granting creatures consequential freedom, it does not follow that God is culpable for the actions of the free creatures that he creates. Whereas some portray middle knowledge as the means by which God might micromanage every occurrence by simply actualizing the situation wherein a given agent will freely do just what God wants, things are not nearly so simple. All situations and events are inseparably connected to antecedent conditions and events and have massive implications for all subsequent situations and events. Given such an order, God might not be able to actualize a given situation without having to actualize unacceptably undesirable antecedent conditions or future events. Consequently, even in cases where God could actualize a situation such that Edmund freely does precisely what God wants, the cost of actualizing such a situation might be too great, with ramifications for what Peter and Susan and Lucy freely do as well. We should keep in mind the interconnectedness of past causes and present effects such that any situation or event that God might wish to actualize is connected to a great many antecedent conditions or events and has considerable implications for all future situations and events. As Stephen Davis puts it, "John Jones Jr. could not exist, could not be John Jones Jr., without being the son of John Jones Sr."[15]

Nevertheless, Richard Rice contends that "the idea that God foresees future free decisions makes the problem of suffering particularly vexing because it gives God the perfect way to prevent it."[16] However, even if God lacked foreknowledge of free decisions and possessed only exhaustive knowledge of the past and present, given omnipotence (absent other constraints), he would be able to prevent every instance of evil a millisecond before it occurs. Indeed, it appears that many instances of evil could be prevented simply by God warning of danger. Consider, for example, a plane crash caused by a mechanical failure resulting from a mechanic's error. The failure could be anticipated by anyone who had full knowledge of the aircraft's condition. If there were a justifiable reason why God does not warn of such dangers or prevent evils just before they would occur, then that justifiable reason would apply whether or not God possesses foreknowledge.

---

15. S. Davis, "Free Will and Evil," 87. Davis continues, "Why then did God create people whom God foreknew would be damned? Because that was the price of creating people who would be saved." In my view, God grants each person a genuine opportunity to accept and enjoy the exceedingly outweighing value of God's eternal love (cf. John 3:16). One might surmise that God could immediately actualize the eschaton and implant memories of the past in our minds, but such a proposal would involve deception.

16. Rice, *Suffering and the Search for Meaning*, 91.

Many who deny foreknowledge, however, contend that God cannot eliminate evil in such ways for other reasons, such as his commitment to the parameters necessary for love.[17] If such commitments count as sufficient moral
reasons for God to not prevent evil a millisecond before it occurs, it seems
they would likewise be sufficient for God to not prevent that evil, even if he
foreknew it would occur.[18]

Thus, why, despite foreknowledge, God created the devil or did not prevent
Satan's evil actions is not more problematic than why God allows the kind and
amount of evil in this world. In short, to do otherwise might have (1) been
against God's character or moral commitments, (2) led to more deleterious
results or less flourishing of love, or (3) been less preferable in some other way.
The supposition of the devil, then, does not introduce additional conceptual
problems by itself, but it does greatly illuminate the impediments God faces
regarding immediately bringing about his ultimate purpose. Specifically, the
enemy ruler of this world possesses temporary jurisdiction because there is
no preferable avenue available to God to settle the cosmic courtroom dispute
over his character raised by this arch-slanderer.[19] Accordingly, it seems appropriate to echo Christ's indictment of the devil: "An enemy has done this"
(Matt. 13:28; cf. 13:37, 39).

Is This Approach Dualistic?

Miguel A. De La Torre and Albert Hernández worry that to "suggest that
there exists another being that rivals God," powerful "enough to challenge
the might and love of God, makes Satan into another God" and compromises
"radical monotheism."[20] This raises the question of whether a cosmic conflict
approach amounts to eternal cosmic dualism. This theodicy of love explicitly
denies cosmic dualism and unequivocally upholds divine omnipotence. Satan
and his cohorts are creatures, not eternal beings (cf. John 1:1–3; Col. 1:16;
1 John 4:4). Not only do these creatures have a beginning, but their temporarily granted power and "reign" will also come to an end (cf. Matt. 25:41; Rev.
20:10). As C. S. Lewis puts it, "Christianity agrees . . . that this universe is at
war. But it does not think that this is a war between independent powers"; it

17. E.g., "God does not prevent us from hurting each other" because "God always acts in
ways that take into account the decisions of God's creatures." Rice, *Suffering and the Search
for Meaning*, 99.

18. Some maintain that the salient difference is that foreknowledge could be used to prevent
the very existence of any evildoer. See Rice, *Suffering and the Search for Meaning*, 91. On this
issue, see the earlier discussion in this section relative to the devil's existence.

19. See John 12:31; 14:30; 16:11.

20. De La Torre and Hernández, *Quest for the Historical Satan*, 212.

is rather "a civil war, a rebellion." Thus Lewis concludes, "We are living in a part of the universe occupied by the rebel. Enemy-occupied territory—that is what this world is."[21]

As I have argued above, the cosmic conflict is not one of sheer power but is a primarily epistemic conflict over allegations against God's character that cannot be settled by force. That God is omnipotent does not entail that God exercises all of his power. God remains omnipotent even as he consistently grants genuine power to free creatures within limits because doing otherwise would undercut the requisite context for the flourishing of a love relationship. Ultimately, God will exercise his power to finally destroy evil, but he will not do so until the epistemic conflict over character has been settled. In the meantime, the devil and his cohorts possess significant jurisdiction according to covenantal rules of engagement.

Nevertheless, one might suppose that a cosmic conflict gives the devil too much credit. However, culpability for evil does not amount to credit; just the opposite. God has temporarily granted the devil a limited jurisdiction within rules of engagement in order to effectively refute the devil's slanderous charges against God's government, resulting in Satan's condemnation. Just as a ruler would remain sovereign while granting a limited jurisdiction to a tax collector to collect taxes, God remains sovereign even as he temporarily allows the enemy limited jurisdiction, in order to settle the cosmic dispute and forever inoculate the universe from evil.

Alternatively, one might worry that such a perspective encourages unhealthy preoccupation with the devil and may support the demonization of those with whom one disagrees. With regard to the latter, one need only consider history to see that demonization of opponents requires no belief in the devil's existence. Further, understanding that this cosmic conflict is primarily an epistemic dispute—and recalling that we are not privy to much of the relevant data—should engender deep humility among Christ-followers. Because there is so much humans do not know, Christians should "not go on passing judgment before the time, but wait until the Lord comes who will . . . bring to light the things hidden in the darkness" (1 Cor. 4:5).

With regard to unhealthy preoccupation with the devil, some do have an unhealthy interest in the demonic realm, but this theodicy of love encourages quite the opposite. I have tried to restrict this framework to elements that are discernible, demonstrable, and defensible from Scripture, while treading softly regarding matters requiring speculation, particularly the intricacies of the rules of engagement or the demonic realm itself. Rather than focusing

---

21. Lewis, *Mere Christianity*, 45–46.

on these things that do not appear to be revealed, understanding the cosmic conflict should only elevate one's affection for God and desire to "dwell," as Paul admonishes, on "whatever is true, whatever is honorable, whatever is right, whatever is pure, whatever is lovely, whatever is of good repute," and whatever is "excellent and . . . worthy of praise" (Phil. 4:8). Although Scripture sets forth a robust depiction of the cosmic conflict, it focuses primarily on the God of love's character and plan of redemption. We should do likewise.

Is It Coherent for God to Restrict His Own Action?

One might ask whether God really could or should agree to any rule that restricts his own action.[22] Why would God agree to any rules that would morally require him to allow the evil in this world? Even if God does so, should God respect such commitments? Why does God not simply revoke such commitments whenever doing so would prevent horrendous evil? One might think, anthropomorphically, that if a human ruler puts forth a decree but later recognizes that it leads to some horrendous evil, that ruler ought to simply revoke the decree.

For divine providence, however, things are quite a bit more complicated. First, in this model the rules of engagement are not unilateral decrees but are covenantal; that is, they are the product of negotiated agreement, which entails duties of treaty relationship. One might contend that a ruler should breach any treaty that would harm the ruler's people. However, this seems to overlook the ramifications of unilaterally breaking a treaty. If a nation possesses vastly superior military power, that does not justify a nation in unilaterally breaking a treaty with a weaker nation. Such action would rightfully be viewed as disgraceful and immoral. There are countless differences between merely human treaties and any covenantal relationship that includes God. However, if it is disgraceful and immoral for a stronger party to unilaterally break a treaty or contract with a weaker party, it would be even more so for God to break an agreement or promise, if it is even possible.[23] It seems that God

---

22. J. L. Mackie called this the "paradox of Sovereignty." Mackie, "Evil and Omnipotence," in Adams and Adams, *Problem of Evil*, 35.

23. It is beyond this book's scope to sufficiently address the debate over whether God *could* do anything "evil," such as breaking a promise. This is bound up with numerous other issues, including debates over the Euthyphro dilemma, divine command theory, and moral praiseworthiness. See the excellent treatment of such issues in Baggett and Walls, *Good God*. The traditional view that goodness is grounded in God's essential nature such that God is incapable of doing evil is compatible with this theodicy of love *as is* the view that God *could* do evil but never *would* do so. Whereas some argue that if love *requires* libertarian freedom relative to good and evil, then God could not love unless he *could* do evil, the traditional view might be coherently maintained via a sourcehood conception of libertarian freedom. Here, God would remain the

would be morally required to respect any covenant to which he has agreed. God "cannot lie" (Titus 1:2), always keeps his promises (Heb. 6:17–18), and always "remains faithful," for "He cannot deny Himself" (2 Tim. 2:13; cf. Rom. 3:3–4; James 1:13).

Further, God would have foreknown all the ramifications of any agreement. Even if unforeseen ramifications could justify a human ruler in breaking a treaty, there would be no unforeseen ramifications for God. One might instead be tempted to criticize God for entering into any such agreement in the first place. It is often supposed that a morally sufficient reason for God permitting an evil requires that some good results that sufficiently outweighs the evil (the outweighing condition) and that God could not achieve in any preferable way (the necessity or only-way condition).[24] If so, God would be justified in agreeing to the rules of engagement, despite the evil they permit, insofar as doing so achieves a sufficiently outweighing value that God could not achieve in any preferable way.

As argued in chapter 2, whether the outweighing condition is met depends on whether love is a sufficiently outweighing value. Whether the necessity condition is met depends on (1) whether the kind of free will necessary for love requires the necessary possibility of evil, and (2) whether agreeing to the rules of engagement that further restrict divine intervention was the most preferable way to settle the cosmic dispute and thus achieve the outweighing good of the everlasting flourishing of love.[25] Here, the rules of engagement need not themselves be necessary as long as God's agreeing to them was the

---

ultimate source of his free actions even if he could not do evil because, as the uncreated, perfect being, God would have nothing external to him cause his essential goodness. This could not be so for creatures, conversely, because God is the external source of their nature and if bound by that nature, they could not be the ultimate source of their moral decisions. On the debate over divine freedom relative to evil, see Timpe, *Free Will in Philosophical Theology*, 103–18; Yandell, "Divine Necessity and Divine Goodness," 313–34; Manis, "Could God Do Something Evil?," 209–23; Reichenbach, *Evil and a Good God*, 139–53.

24. See, e.g., Murray, *Nature Red in Tooth and Claw*, 14. Relative to suffering, Eleonore Stump frames the outweighing condition as requiring that an outweighing benefit accrues *to the sufferer*. Stump, *Wandering in the Darkness*, 455. She maintains, however, that this benefit need not be restricted to "this-worldly elements" (463). Further, given "libertarian free will," a "sufferer might choose not to exercise the power mediated by suffering" and thus not enjoy the benefit (457). If the benefit of an eternal love relationship with God is made available to all and could not be achieved *by God* in any preferable way, God would be justified even if some reject that eternal, inexhaustibly outweighing good (cf. Rom. 3:3–4). Further, it might be that beholding the ultimate manifestation of God's perfect love and righteousness, finally recognized by all (cf. Rom. 14:11; Isa. 45:23–24), constitutes an exceedingly great good, even for those who finally reject a loving relationship with God.

25. By intervention, here and elsewhere, I mean only some action that prevents what would otherwise have occurred.

most preferable way available to God to settle the conflict without damaging love. This theodicy of love suggests this was indeed the case because of the questions raised by the devil's slanderous allegations before the heavenly court (cf. 1 Cor. 4:9). Had there been a preferable way, God would have chosen it, particularly considering the incalculable cost to himself, at the cross and otherwise (cf. Matt. 26:39; Heb. 12:2).

Could God Directly Reveal His Goodness to Settle the Conflict?

One might wonder why God couldn't settle the conflict by simply explaining or otherwise directly revealing that he is entirely just. But given a cosmic rebellion wherein the devil alleges that God is not just, it is not hard to see why a mere explanation by God would be insufficient to settle the conflict, particularly for those who may doubt whether God is trustworthy. Perhaps nothing short of a cosmic demonstration could finally defeat such allegations and, with them, evil itself. If epistemic freedom is necessary for love, God's simply overwhelming the epistemic faculties of creatures such that everyone would immediately recognize his justice would undercut love relationship.

Richard Rice worries that the supposition that we have the epistemic freedom to trust God or not presupposes "that God has neither tampered with the evidence nor manipulated our thinking."[26] This worry is not unique to the cosmic conflict perspective but relates to standard cases in epistemology, such as Descartes's worry that a malignant genius or demon might be systematically deceiving him, leaving everything in doubt. Epistemologists generally recognize now that some decision regarding what one believes is an unavoidable starting point of any system of thought (including scientific inquiry). Whereas initial beliefs might be defeated via further inquiry, there is no neutral or indubitable starting point. To believe or know anything one must at least tentatively believe something or someone.[27] This is true not only regarding abstract epistemological concerns but also regarding our most cherished human relationships. How, for instance, could I know beyond the shadow of a doubt that my wife loves me? For a host of reasons, I am confident she does, but it's possible that she could be acting and deceiving me. Since I cannot read her mind, I am limited to external evidence, but I nevertheless trust that she does indeed love me, and I believe I have *excellent* reasons for doing so, reasons rooted in the experiences of our relationship. Nevertheless, for humans at

26. Rice, *Suffering and the Search for Meaning*, 86.
27. For a widely respected Christian epistemological perspective, see Plantinga, *Warranted Christian Belief*.

least, love inherently involves trust. Such trust can be strengthened or broken, sometimes irreparably, but there cannot be genuine love relationship without it.

Likewise, I am confident that I have excellent reasons for trusting that God is entirely loving and just, including the manifestation of the suffering God of the cross. If an all-powerful being intended to deceive me, that being could do so while avoiding the cross and other sufferings. Perhaps, one might object, the cross and other events were divinely orchestrated illusions.[28] However, if God is not actually loving, why would he care whether I think he is loving? Absent commitment to epistemic freedom, God could determine that everyone always thinks and does whatever God wants. There would be no need for any manifestation of God's character (e.g., Rom. 3:25–26; 5:8) or any other testimony (e.g., John 21:24), fabricated or otherwise. Our cognizance of the problem of evil itself, alongside the history of redemption, might be testimony that God is not manipulating or whitewashing our faculties.[29] The God of Scripture goes to great lengths to defend his character and patiently bring us into love relationship with him, which would be superfluous if God manipulated or controlled creatures' epistemic faculties.

Does This Model Work?

Some further questions might be raised with regard to the workability of this model. For example, some might question whether love is actually sufficient to account for the kind and amount of evil in this world. Further, even if this model provides a workable account relative to the evil in this world, additional questions regarding the apparent hiddenness of God remain. I will take up both of these issues in succession.

Is Love Sufficient to Account for the Evil in This World?

William Rowe contends that "there exist horrendous evils that an all-powerful, all-knowing, perfectly good being would have no justifying reason to permit." Further, he asks, "Is it rational to believe that each evil is such

---

28. On the view that we can have *some* knowledge of truth that does not depend on our mind (critical realism)—contra radical skepticism—there appear to be good historical reasons to believe Jesus rose from the dead. Consider Gary Habermas's minimal facts argument for the historicity of the resurrection in Habermas and Licona, *Case for the Resurrection*. Cf. Blomberg, *Historical Reliability of the Gospels*.

29. Further, some contend that even positing a problem of evil is inseparable from supposing some standard of goodness. This raises the problem of goodness—i.e., why there is any good at all. See Ganssle, "Evil as Evidence for Christianity," 214–23.

that were an all-powerful, all-knowing being to prevent it, he would have to forfeit some outweighing good?"[30] The force of Rowe's question trades on the intuition that there are evils in this world that the world would be better without, which seems correct. However, on this theodicy of love, only the possibility of evil is necessary for the greater good of love. No given event of evil is itself necessary for greater good. It would have been better had no event of evil ever occurred.

One might infer from this statement that God should prevent any such evils that do not in and of themselves bring about some greater good. However, to say that the world would be better without a given instance of evil is not the same as to say that *God should* prevent that instance of evil. There might be an overarching good that would be compromised if God did so, even if that instance of evil is not itself necessary for the overarching good. It might be that the world would be better if free creatures did not perpetrate some evil, but it also might be that *for God to prevent* such evil would (1) impinge on the extent of free will necessary for love, (2) be against the rules of engagement, or (3) otherwise lead to more deleterious results. If so, perhaps every evil that God permits is permitted because *for God to do otherwise* would damage the overarching good of the flourishing of love, without supposing that any specific instance of evil is itself necessary to achieve some outweighing good(s), or that specific instances of evil are themselves otherwise justified or justifiable.

This explanation would also apply to evils that are not directly attributable to the decisions of free creatures. It may well be against the rules of engagement for God to intervene to prevent certain instances of (so-called) natural evil.[31] God may wish to prevent all kinds of such evils—such as the suffering of Rowe's fawn and countless other instances of animal suffering—but it might be temporarily against the covenantal rules of engagement for him to do so.[32]

If love is the overarching greatest good, intrinsic to God's character and the highest value (see chap. 2), then it stands to reason that everlasting love between God and creatures is of immeasurable value. If so, and if God could not bring this about without permitting the evil in this world (because of creatures' free decisions and the rules of engagement), then it follows that love provides a morally sufficient reason for God to allow evil in this world.

30. Howard-Snyder, Bergmann, and Rowe, "Exchange on the Problem of Evil," 126.
31. On evil in nature, see chap. 4 of this book.
32. Ultimately, however, God will achieve nothing short of cosmic reconciliation (Rom. 8:20–22; cf. Eph. 1:10; Col. 1:19–20). Numerous Christians have posited that animals might receive eschatological compensation for suffering, which seems plausible to me. For more on the problem of animal suffering, see Murray, *Nature Red in Tooth and Claw*.

On this view, the alternative would require undermining love, which may not even be possible for God, who himself "is love" (1 John 4:8, 16).

What about Divine Hiddenness and the Appearance of Indifference?

Even if there are good reasons for God to permit the evil in this world, why does God sometimes appear to be hidden or silent? This presents both an existential and a cognitive problem. Regarding the latter, J. L. Schellenberg's hiddenness argument goes something like this: If a perfectly loving God exists, reasonable and a nonresistant nonbelief would not occur because such a God would make himself known to anyone capable of knowing him who does not resist. However, reasonable and nonresistant (or inculpable) nonbelief does occur. There are, in other words, nonresistant people who are apparently capable of knowing God who do not believe God exists. Thus, no perfectly loving God exists.[33]

Schellenberg uses the analogy of a child calling in the woods for his mother, who does not respond to the child's frantic calls. The child looks everywhere and keeps crying out to her, but there is no response. "Is she anywhere around? Would she fail to answer if she were around?"[34] Wouldn't any good parent respond to their child's distressed calls if she could? If a loving parent would not remain hidden from her distressed child, would not a perfectly loving God do at least this much?[35] Schellenberg's hiddenness argument has sparked a voluminous amount of engagement from theists and atheists, most of which cannot be adequately engaged here.[36] Two of the most prominent avenues in response are the suggestions that (1) Schellenberg's beliefs about what a perfectly loving God is like are mistaken,[37] and (2) some good reasons or impediments prevent God from making himself known to inculpable non-believers.[38] But even if one grants that a perfectly loving God would want to reveal himself to inculpable nonbelievers, it does not follow that such a God should do so in this world. God may have good reasons for remaining hidden,

---

33. See Schellenberg, *Divine Hiddenness and Human Reason*; Schellenberg, *Hiddenness Argument*.

34. Schellenberg, "Divine Hiddenness Justifies Atheism," 62.

35. See Louise Antony's claim that God is a "terrible" and "abusive parent" ("Does God Love Us?," 29–46) and Eleonore Stump's response ("Comments on 'Does God Love Us?,'" 47–53) in *Divine Evil?*, 29–57.

36. See, e.g., Green and Stump, *Hidden Divinity and Religious Belief*; Howard-Snyder and Moser, *Divine Hiddenness*; Rea, *Evil and the Hiddenness of God*.

37. See, e.g., Rea, "Hiddenness and Transcendence," 210–25; Rea, "Divine Hiddenness, Divine Silence," 161–64; Meister, "Evil and the Hiddenness of God," 149.

38. Another line of argument claims there are no *inculpable* nonbelievers. See, e.g., Spiegel, *Making of an Atheist*, 11.

including the requirements of epistemic freedom or the possibility that some individuals are in a state such that divine revelation would negatively impact them or have other deleterious consequences.[39]

In addition to these potential avenues for response, the hiddenness of God is precisely what we might expect in the midst of a primarily epistemic cosmic conflict with an enemy "ruler of this world." Scripture indicates that the sin in this world causes separation from divine presence as well as divine hiddenness (Isa. 59:2; cf. Gen. 3; Deut. 31:16–17). Moreover, the rules of engagement might further specify under what circumstances God may directly reveal himself to humans without obtaining an unfair advantage in the epistemic conflict. Even as God desires to prevent all kinds of evils, perhaps God wants to make himself known to humans more robustly but faces temporary impediments within the cosmic conflict that (morally) prevent him from doing so.[40]

A theodicy of love, then, might respond to the hiddenness argument in much the same way the problem of evil is met. It may be that God wishes to make himself known more robustly, especially to humans who are in distress, but doing so would (1) impinge on the extent of free will necessary for love, (2) be against the rules of engagement, or (3) otherwise lead to more deleterious results. Such an approach has the advantage of affirming that God does directly provide special revelation to humans in some cases, as depicted throughout Scripture (e.g., to Moses, Paul, and many others), while providing a framework that may help us understand why he does not do so more often.

A rules-of-engagement framework might be applied similarly in response to Paul Draper's hypothesis of indifference (HI), which posits that if supernatural beings exist, they are indifferent to human suffering and distress. Draper suggests that our experience in this world, particularly of pain and suffering, makes much more sense and is far less surprising on HI than on theism. Draper argues, further, that this provides a *prima facie* good reason for rejecting theism.[41] However, given a rules-of-engagement framework, wherein demonic agents work to increase the pain and suffering of God's creatures as much as they can (directly and indirectly), one would expect an enormous amount of suffering. As Rice puts it, "If the universe is populated by a host

39. See Meister, "Evil and the Hiddenness of God," 144–48.

40. Notably, a rules-of-engagement approach to the hiddenness argument appears to be effective relative to both why "God's reasons for permitting horrendous evil" might be "hidden from us" (hiddenness—level 1) *and* why God might hide "from us the fact that he has a reason for permitting horrendous evil and/or the fact that he exists or loves us and cares about us" (hiddenness—level 2). See Trakakis, "Skeptical Theist Response," 538.

41. Draper, "Pain and Pleasure," 181, 198, 182. See, conversely, van Inwagen, "Problem of Evil," 203–33. Cf. Plantinga, *Warranted Christian Belief*, 472–79.

of beings opposed to God and bent on wreaking death and destruction, it is hardly surprising that we suffer; it would be surprising if we didn't."[42]

Whereas Draper contends that God could grant humans free will "without permitting pain," such a view runs into problems if one affirms consequential freedom (see chap. 2). Further, it may not sufficiently account for the agency of malevolent celestial beings.[43] But even if freedom by itself could be disassociated from pain, it is hard to see how love could be disassociated from the possibility of (at least emotional) pain.[44] A rules-of-engagement framework can grant some of the intuitions that might motivate HI, such as the fact that God often does not appear to be present or intervene as we would expect if everything was up to him. At the same time, this approach suggests a framework for understanding why this might be so, namely, that divine action is temporarily and morally restricted. On this view, what Draper characterizes as indifference might result from God's commitments relative to love, including the rules of engagement that morally restrict him from eliminating evils he would otherwise eliminate or revealing himself more robustly. On the part of Satan and his cohorts, conversely, it does not seem at all surprising that they would remain hidden in contexts where most people believe they do not exist, while manifesting themselves in other contexts where there are widespread beliefs about and reports of supernatural activity. As the French poet Charles Baudelaire once put it, "The neatest trick of the devil is to persuade you that he does not exist."[45]

Does This Model Make Sense of Divine Action?

Additional questions may arise regarding whether this theodicy of love can make sense of divine action. Many have raised questions about the morality of God's behavior as depicted in Scripture. Further, there are questions relative to why God might act to prevent evil in some cases but not others. To these issues I now turn in succession.

What about the New Atheist Criticism of God's Behavior in the Bible?

The so-called new atheists and others have characterized the God of the Bible, particularly in the OT, as an immoral, bloodthirsty, and tyrannical deity who is not worthy of worship. A cosmic conflict theodicy of love, conversely,

---

42. Rice, *Suffering and the Search for Meaning*, 79.
43. Draper, "Pain and Pleasure," 191.
44. See Peckham, *Love of God*, 147–90.
45. Baudelaire, *Paris Spleen*, 60.

sheds some light on God's oft-misunderstood behavior in Scripture. First, there are significant differences between the new atheist characterizations of the God of the Bible and the actual depictions of God in Scripture. Whereas critics depict God as perpetually wrathful and continually executing judgment, Scripture describes God as exceedingly loving, compassionate, long-suffering, and patient with his people.[46] Although Scripture does include a number of instances of divine judgment and wrath, there are often long chronological gaps between them in history.

The prophets in particular depict God as the longsuffering, unrequited lover, who is repeatedly grieved by his people's spiritual adultery with foreign gods and other despicable practices (e.g., Ps. 78:58). This cycle of rebellion follows a pattern: God's people reject him repeatedly, unabashedly committing abhorrent atrocities (including child sacrifice); God withdraws according to their wishes; the people are oppressed by foreign nations; the people cry out for help; God graciously returns to deliver them; and then the people reject him again, more egregiously than before (see Ps. 78; Neh. 9).[47] Recall that God sustained his covenant people through famine, disaster, and destruction by surrounding enemies at nearly every turn. This relationship between God and his covenant people, including these special privileges, was governed by explicit covenant stipulations, with specific warnings of what would befall the people should they "go after other gods" (Deut. 8:19–20) or otherwise rupture relationship with God and reject his sustenance and protection (see, e.g., Lev. 26). Despite their repeated rebellions, God "being compassionate, forgave their iniquity and did not destroy them; / And often He restrained His anger / And did not arouse all His wrath" (Ps. 78:38).

God rightly hates evil because evil inevitably harms his children, even if it is self-inflicted. Yet God's wrath is far exceeded by his compassion. Whereas God's "anger is but for a moment, / His favor is for a lifetime" (Ps. 30:5). Wrath is not an essential attribute of God, but God's wrath is the appropriate and temporary response of love against evil. Where there is no evil, there is no wrath. Moreover, God "does not afflict willingly" (Lam. 3:33) and has "no pleasure in the death of anyone" (Ezek. 18:32; cf. 33:11). When God finally brings or allows judgment, it is because "there [is] no remedy" (2 Chron. 36:16; cf. Isa. 5:1–7). Even in such instances as the destruction of Jerusalem by Babylon, God provided a way of escape for those who would listen, instructing people through the prophet Jeremiah that those who remained in the city would die but those who surrendered to Babylon would live (Jer. 38:2).

46. See, e.g., Richard Dawkins, *God Delusion*, 51.
47. See the discussion in Peckham, *Love of God*; Peckham, *Concept of Divine Love*.

Further, many judgments that Scripture depicts as brought about by God are elsewhere explained as instances where God—in accordance with the people's own decisions to forsake God and serve the gods of the nations (Judg. 10:6–16; cf. Deut. 29:24–26)—"gives" them over to their enemies,[48] the nations around them ruled by demons masquerading as gods (Deut. 32:8, 17).

Although at places in the OT God is depicted as having withdrawn his protection and thus having given his people over to nations such as Babylon (Ezra 5:12), perhaps as required by the rules of engagement, elsewhere in the OT he is depicted as lamenting the excessive amount of devastation Babylon caused and judges Babylon and its gods (Jer. 51:24–25, 44). This is because while God "was only a little angry, they made the disaster worse" (Zech. 1:15 NRSV)[49] and thus "have engaged in conflict with the LORD" (Jer. 50:24). The destruction of Jerusalem by Babylon therefore appears to be an explicit instance of weak actualization. In one sense, God does bring the judgment against Judah by withdrawing from Jerusalem (Ezek. 11:23)—albeit reticently (cf. Hosea 11:8–9; Matt. 23:37), in accordance with covenant parameters. In another sense, God neither causes nor controls what Babylon freely does, for which he holds them morally responsible.

Such weak actualization is not limited to foreign incursions. In many instances, including those noted in chapter 2, God appears to take a circuitous route to his objective. Consider the oft-cited case of Joseph, who says to his brothers about their choice to sell him into slavery, "You meant evil against me, but God meant it for good in order to bring about this present result, to preserve many people alive" (Gen. 50:20). Given God's omnipotence (and absent other impediments), God could have preserved people from famine in several more direct ways without Joseph being sold into slavery, which itself led to Israel being enslaved in Egypt for centuries.[50] For instance, God might have simply prevented the famine or provided manna from heaven. If God was working within the constraints of creaturely freedom and the rules of engagement, perhaps these and other avenues were unavailable or otherwise undesirable. Here God appears to navigate around many unseen factors and impediments.[51]

Further, consider the narrative of the bronze serpent, when "the LORD sent fiery serpents among the people" (Num. 21:6). Although this seems to be a

---

48. See, e.g., Judg. 2:13–14; Ezra 5:12; Neh. 9:30; Ps. 106:41–42; Jer. 38:18; cf. Ps. 81:12.

49. Cf. Isa. 47:6; Jer. 25:12–14; 50–51.

50. One might respond that, had Israel not been enslaved, God's glory would not have been manifested in the exodus. However, absent other factors or impediments, there would be more direct ways for God to manifest his glory.

51. This "circuitous route" motif of Scripture is apparent in the very route of the exodus. Consider also the many instances of covenant jeopardy in Israel's history, including God's circuitous route of blessing Israel *in order to* bless all nations (Gen. 12:3).

straightforward account of God strongly actualizing judgment, Deuteronomy 8:15 speaks as if the fiery serpents were already present: "He led you through the great and terrible wilderness, with its fiery serpents and scorpions and thirsty ground where there was no water" (cf. Isa. 30:6). This verse suggests that God was protecting and sustaining the people from what otherwise would have been certain death, and in Numbers 21 God withdrew that protection.[52] This is not to say that all divine judgments are brought about by weak actualization but that many appear to be so. In such instances, insofar as God withdraws or gives the people over to their decisions, it is no longer up to God just what happens to them.

Even in instances where God strongly actualizes judgment, which I believe occurs in the final, eschatological judgment, God does so because there is no preferable alternative available (cf. Lam. 3:32–33). Sometimes God might strongly actualize discipline to prevent the people from straying so far from him that he could not (in keeping with the rules of engagement) continue to sustain and protect them. When God disciplines his people, he does so for their good (Deut. 8:16) as a good father disciplines his beloved child (Prov. 3:12; cf. Heb. 12:6).

Whereas some might view God's discipline as harsh, it is important to remember that the people had no chance of survival without God's protection. If they strayed completely away from God, they would surely perish (cf. Deut. 8:19–20). Similar to the way the consequences for breaking some laws aboard an airplane are far more serious than for doing so elsewhere because of the increased dangers to all concerned, so God's laws and governance of his covenant people were aimed at preventing their total destruction by surrounding nations, which would occur without his protection. God did everything he could to call his people back to him so they could remain in his care (Isa. 5:1–7). Whereas love is popularly viewed as licentious, in Scripture genuine love requires (eventual) justice. God would not be loving if he did not eventually eradicate evil. As omniscient and omnibenevolent, knowing and desiring what is best for all concerned, God is uniquely positioned to pass and execute just judgment. God always takes the most loving action he can for all concerned.

Thus far we have been considering God's actions toward the Israelites, but there is still the question about the purported genocide of the Canaanites. Again, I cannot do justice to this complex issue here. Doing so would require at least a book-length treatment of its own, which has been offered by

---

52. Further, whereas Scripture depicts God as setting up kings (Dan. 2:21), God did not want Israel to have a king and laments, "They have set up kings, but not by Me" (Hosea 8:4).

others. In this regard, I believe Paul Copan and Matthew Flannagan make a largely compelling case that, according to Scripture itself, God did not actually command genocide and did not intend the total destruction of all the Canaanites.[53] Rather, after centuries of probation while the "iniquity" of the nations was "not yet complete" (Gen. 15:16), God commanded that Israel completely drive out the Canaanites from the Promised Land because of the heinous "wickedness of these nations" (Deut. 9:4–5)—including child sacrifice to their "gods" (Lev. 18; Deut. 12:29–31; cf. 2 Kings 3:27). This command to Israel required that only those who obstinately refused to flee be destroyed.[54] Even given this understanding, many questions remain. However, Copan and Flannagan show that there are numerous more satisfying lines of thought in this regard than many people believe.[55]

For now, I wish to highlight that God's commands relative to driving out the Canaanites and destroying those who refused to flee are (1) directly related to the broader cosmic conflict framework and (2) specifically restricted to the context of safely settling Israel after their enslavement in Egypt.[56] Recall again

---

53. See Copan and Flannagan, *Did God Really Command Genocide?*

54. Copan and Flannagan argue that the "biblical command to 'utterly destroy' cannot refer to anything like 'absolute extermination' since there are an even greater number of commands or descriptions related to 'dispossession' or 'driving out' the Canaanites (Exod. 23:27–31; Num. 21:32; 33:51–56; Deut. 7:17–23 [cf. Deut. 9:1; 11:23; 18:12–14; 19:2]). The expectation is that the Canaanites would be driven out gradually" (Exod. 23:29–33), aided by the "fear of Israel and Israel's God" going before them (Josh. 2:9, 24; 9:24), providing opportunity to flee (Exod. 23:27–31). Copan and Flannagan, *Did God Really Command Genocide?*, 82. Although some texts speak of utter destruction *of those who remained in a particular location* (e.g., Josh. 10:28–30), other "texts make clear that not all the Canaanites were anywhere near destroyed" but only those who remained were destroyed as in, e.g., Josh. 23:7 and Judg. 1–2 (92). Anticipating this situation, God commands that Israel "make no covenant with [the Canaanites] or with their gods" and that the Canaanites "shall not live in [the Israelites'] land, because they will make [Israel] sin against" God and "serve their gods" (Exod. 23:32–33; cf. Deut. 7:1–6). As such, Copan and Flannagan make a strong case that God's "intent" was "not to destroy" the "Canaanite peoples but to put an end to their pernicious [evil] criminal influence" (136). They argue, "If the Canaanites had chosen to flee from the land, none of them would have been killed at all. Most of them in all likelihood did flee" (83). Cf. the case of Rahab (Josh. 2:1–22; 6:25). See further Barna Magyarosi's case that the conquest aimed at dispossession rather than annihilation and that God offered a way of escape for Canaanites analogous to that later offered to inhabitants of Jerusalem before the Babylonian conquest. Magyarosi, *Holy War and Cosmic Conflict*, 112–24.

55. See especially Copan and Flannagan, *Did God Really Command Genocide?*, 76–83.

56. As such, however one interprets the conquest, no command relative to driving out the Canaanites is valid for Christians—or anyone else—today. Such commands were specific to Israel and the Promised Land *at that time*; Israel was "prohibited from attacking neighboring nations such as Moab, Ammon, and Edom" (Deut. 2:4, 9, 19; 23:7) and received different instructions for other warfare contexts (see Deut. 20). Copan and Flannagan, *Did God Really Command Genocide?*, 60.

that the Canaanite nations were beholden to patron gods—that is, demons who wanted to destroy Israel and thus cut off God's allotted conduit to redeem the world (Deut. 32:8–9, 17). A major emphasis in God's instructions is that, if God's people fail to drive the Canaanites out of the land, they would fall into the worship of the false gods and the atrocious practices associated with it (cf. Exod. 23:31–33; Deut. 7:4–6). This would eventually cut them off from God's protection, leave them to be crushed by God's enemies (cf. Deut. 8:19), and cut off the allotted conduit of divine blessing and redemption for all peoples (cf. Gen. 12:3). As such, Copan rightly sets this in the framework of "cosmic warfare between Yahweh and the dark powers opposed to his rule."[57]

This broader framework does not answer all our questions relative to the conquest or otherwise. We do not possess sufficient information to know precisely what avenues were (morally) available to God, given the rules of engagement, or what the long-term consequences of such avenues would entail. One need not claim that what actually occurred was itself good in order to recognize the possibility that all the alternatives available to God might have been worse. Despite our limited knowledge in this regard, we have good reasons to trust that the God who willingly suffered at the cross for us knows and does what is right, loves all people, and abhors evil far more than we do.

Does God Selectively Intervene in Response to Prayers?

Another question for this model regards why God sometimes intervenes but other times appears not to do so. In particular, why does God appear to respond to some prayers but not others? Just as I do not claim that this model provides knowledge of why God permits specific events of evil, neither do I claim that it provides God's specific reasons for acting as he does. However, this rules-of-engagement framework does posit that when God does not respond to our prayers as we might hope, doing so might have been against the rules of engagement, subverted creaturely freedom, or resulted in greater evil.

We might wonder how prayer could have any impact at all. After all, would not God do what is best anyway, given his morally perfect nature? As noted previously, some texts seem to indicate that divine activity is tied somehow to belief and prayer such that at least some impediments on divine action are dynamically related to these factors.[58] Indeed, prayer may grant God jurisdiction to intervene in ways that otherwise would not be available.[59] Whereas

57. Copan, *Is God a Moral Monster?*, 167.
58. See Matt. 17:20; Mark 9:23–29; 11:22–24; cf. 2 Chron. 7:14.
59. I put forward no theory regarding just *how* this works. I am wary of positions regarding spiritual warfare that make claims regarding the inner workings of the spiritual realm that go far

prayer may open avenues for God within the rules of engagement that were not otherwise (morally) available, there are many other factors and constraints beyond our perception such that prayer and faith do not open every avenue. This understanding entails that when our prayers are not answered as we had hoped, we should not assume that we did something wrong, did not pray hard enough, or did not have enough faith (cf. Matt. 26:39; Luke 22:32).

Christians often pray as if every outcome is strictly up to God, without any recognition that even God faces impediments, given his commitments to love and the rules of engagement. This assumption might cause severe dissonance when prayer for a loved one to be delivered from cancer appears to have no effect. It may be that God deeply wanted to cure that loved one, but that avenue was not (morally) available to him given the totality of other factors involved. As discussed in chapter 2, God often does not get what he wants. Here, Christ's prayer in Gethsemane is especially instructive. "If it is possible," Christ prayed, "let this cup pass from Me; yet not as I will, but as You will" (Matt. 26:39; cf. 6:10). The qualification "if it is possible" indicates that some avenues are not available to God, given his commitments and goals. In this case, God could not accomplish his greater desire of saving humans without Christ enduring the cross. Further, it affirms that God's (remedial) will is the optimal avenue available.

Perhaps believers, particularly in times of great distress, should adopt such a framework for prayer, not only praying that God's "will be done" but also praying, "If it is possible, let this cup pass," in explicit recognition that not every outcome is morally available to God. However one decides to pray, the cosmic conflict framework exposes that there are far more factors involved relative to divine action and apparent inaction than we could fathom. We might fervently pray for divine intervention and even cry out to God that we feel forsaken (Matt. 27:46) while trusting in God's unwavering benevolence (cf. Ps. 22; Dan. 3:17–18).

Some Advantages of This Model

Much more could be said about the questions discussed above. However, my hope is that by considering how a theodicy of love might address these questions, one might begin to see how this model offers helpful avenues to advance the discussion. To this end, we now turn to a survey of some advantages this model offers for approaching the problem of evil.[60]

---

beyond what Scripture reveals. For a balanced discussion of spiritual warfare, see Arnold, *3 Crucial Questions about Spiritual Warfare*. Cf. Beilby and Eddy, *Understanding Spiritual Warfare*.

60. The avenues engaged below warrant further discussion. This brief treatment aims at providing only a basic evaluation.

Exhaustive Definite Foreknowledge

While upholding the core commitments of the traditional Christian view that God is omnibenevolent, omniscient, and omnipotent, the theodicy of love model also upholds the core commitments of the sovereignty defender and free will defender alike. Specifically, this approach affirms the sovereignty defender's commitment to a robust conception of God's providence while also affirming the free will defender's commitment to the indeterministic free will of creatures. While doing so, this model affirms exhaustive definite foreknowledge (EDF). However, some open theists claim that the denial of EDF holds significant advantages such as (1) relieving God from culpability for evils he could not foresee and (2) affirming the biblical testimony that God experiences genuine emotions responsive to creaturely decisions and actions. Regarding the first claim, as briefly noted earlier, denying EDF does not help to explain why God permits evil. Even if God lacks exhaustive foreknowledge, given omnipotence, God could still anticipate and prevent any evil just before it would occur.

With regard to the second claim, it does not follow that divine foreknowledge would prevent God from experiencing genuinely responsive emotions such as grief or joy. Even as people might be emotionally moved by reading a book they had read before, there does not seem to be any necessary relationship between surprise and the kinds of emotions attributed to God in Scripture.[61] This model can consistently affirm the suffering God of Scripture who delights in goodness, is grieved by evil, remains sovereign, and will finally eradicate evil. Conversely, open theism and other approaches that deny EDF have difficulty accounting for long-term prophecies without claiming that God selectively determined creaturely wills in some instances.[62] If God can

---

61. Open theists claim that some texts attribute surprise to God. However, consistently taking such texts as indicative of divine surprise would require not only that God lacks EDF but also that he lacks present knowledge, denying omniscience. For instance, taking God's declaration to Abraham "Now I know that you fear God" (Gen. 22:12) to mean that God did not already know Abraham's heart denies not merely foreknowledge but also omniscience of the present state of Abraham's mind. Cf. God's questioning of Adam and Eve in Gen. 3:9–13, which I take to be (informal) covenant trials within the cosmic courtroom drama—perhaps for the benefit of the heavenly council. Likewise, claims that attributions of *naham* (sometimes translated "repent") indicate that God lacks foreknowledge are unpersuasive, since *naham* in such contexts may indicate divine sorrow about what has occurred because of the decisions of others without any regret regarding divine action. For instance, it would be a mistake to take Genesis 6:6—"the Lord was sorry [*naham*] that He had made man on the earth"—to mean that God regretted creating humans, particularly given God's following action to save the human race in the ark and later send the Son to die for humanity on the cross. On displays of divine emotion as analogical, see Peckham, *Love of God*, 147–89.

62. See the discussion in Peckham, *Doctrine of God* (forthcoming).

selectively determine creaturely wills without undermining love, however, why would he not do so to prevent all kinds of horrendous moral evils?

Further, those who reject EDF struggle to account for God's promises that evil will not continue forever or arise again sometime in the future.[63] If God does not actually know how things will turn out, his plans and commands might ultimately be unsuccessful or allow far more evil than would have been preferable had he known better. Might God have chosen not to create humans had he known what we would do? Did Christ really choose to die for *us*? Did he even know for sure we would be born?

Whereas open theism struggles to address such questions, this theodicy of love contends that God chose to create a world that includes us while knowing full well the unfathomable cost to himself. Further, given his foreknowledge, God knows that the manifestation of God's character in this cosmic conflict will effectively inoculate the universe against evil such that, while creatures continue to possess consequential freedom for eternity, God is epistemologically certain that evil will never arise again. As Paul puts it, "The sufferings of this present time are not worthy to be compared with the glory that is to be revealed" (Rom. 8:18; cf. 2 Cor. 4:17).

Special Divine Action and Power to Eliminate Evil

Beyond affirming EDF, the theodicy of love model offers a consistent avenue toward accounting for the kind and amount of evil in this world without claiming that God lacks the power to prevent evil (as in finitist models) or that God is, by nature, incapable of preventing the evils in this world because he is love.[64] In this vein, Thomas Jay Oord's essential kenosis approach is

---

63. The open theist might affirm that redeemed humans reach a state that Kevin Timpe describes as "perfected freedom," wherein they have formed a character by their own previous choices (absent external divine causation) such that they *cannot* sin in the eschaton. Timpe, *Free Will in Philosophical Theology*, 83–101. Greg Boyd affirms something like this in Boyd, *Satan and the Problem of Evil*, 190–91. Elsewhere, Boyd maintains that "the purpose of libertarian freedom is provisional, intended eventually to lead us to a much greater, eternally solidified form of compatibilistic freedom." Boyd, "God Limits His Control," 194. However, given open theism, God could not know with certainty whether any humans *will* form such a character, especially prior to the eschaton (if it is even possible). Those who died without "perfected freedom" might be transformed (glorification), but this group would not have formed "perfect freedom" apart from external divine causation. To avoid this conclusion, Timpe suggests purgatory as the means to bridge the gap. Timpe, *Free Will in Philosophical Theology*, 98–101. Cf. Boyd's openness to postmortem opportunity for some in Boyd, *Satan and the Problem of Evil*, 381–85.

64. David Ray Griffin contends, "We must fully surrender" the "traditional doctrine of divine omnipotence" in order to maintain that God "is unambiguously loving." Griffin, "Critique of the Free Will Defense," 96.

largely aimed at assuaging "the problem of selective miracles"—that is, the problem that arises "if God sometimes voluntarily acts miraculously but not at other times."[65] Oord addresses this problem by arguing that (1) control and coercion are unloving, and thus God is incapable of control or coercion, and (2) all genuine evils are such that God could not prevent or eliminate them without coercion.[66] God is, by nature (ontologically) incapable of preventing or eliminating genuine evils and therefore cannot be held responsible for failing to do so.

Conversely, Oord contends, if God does not "prevent genuinely evil occurrences while having the power to do so, God is not love."[67] In this regard, Oord strongly criticizes the view of John Sanders, who believes that God allows some evils because he chooses to respect free will.[68] However, this criticism appears to be invalid. The salient point that some ways of intervening are intrinsically unloving works just as well for the free will theist who says God chooses not to act unlovingly as it does for Oord, who says God cannot do so. Claiming otherwise entails that God should choose to do something unloving if he could, as long as doing so would prevent evil. This position would require affirming the inconsistent claims that (1) the only way to prevent some specific evil would be unloving, and (2) it would be unloving not to prevent that specific evil. Further, approaches like Oord's may come at the high cost of a less than robust account of divine sovereignty and providence. Specifically, such accounts may be unable to adequately account for the kind of special divine action depicted in Scripture and may raise significant problems for Christian eschatology.

With regard to the former, it is not clear how Oord's model can adequately account for the biblical depictions of special divine action without falling prey to his own problem of "selective miracles." Here, part of the problem for Oord is what counts as coercion or as unloving. If Oord is to coherently affirm the biblical miracles, it must be that such miracles did not require

65. Oord, *Uncontrolling Love of God*, 192. Elsewhere Oord contends that "God does not essentially possess all power" and is thus not responsible for evil. Oord, "Matching Theology and Piety," 314.

66. As Oord puts it, "Love by definition is noncoercive" and "love never controls others entirely." As such, "God cannot coerce" because "God loves necessarily." Oord, *Uncontrolling Love of God*, 181. Griffin has similarly argued that the issue is not the amount but "the *kind* of power God has." He contends, "Divine power should be thought of not as coercive power, but as persuasive power, the power of love." Griffin, "Rejoinder," 139 (emphasis his). Bruce R. Reichenbach contends that the God of process theology "could exercise his persuasive causation to a greater extent to limit horrendous evils." Reichenbach, "Evil, Omnipotence, and Process Thought," 323.

67. Oord, "Matching Theology and Piety," 345.

68. See Sanders, *God Who Risks*.

divine coercion and are not otherwise unloving.[69] However, if the kinds of things Jesus is depicted as doing in Scripture—turning water into wine, healing (withered hands, blindness, a chronic flow of blood), calming storms, exponentially multiplying food for hungry crowds, raising the dead, and so on—do not require coercion and are not otherwise unloving, then God is manifestly capable of doing many things that would eliminate many (if not all) of the genuine evils in this world. Even strategic warnings alone could greatly mitigate evil. If God warned Pharaoh of impending famine in a way that was not coercive or unloving, it could not be in and of itself unloving for God to warn humans today of any number of impending disasters. Insofar as Oord affirms the biblical miracle accounts, his own approach does not alleviate the problem of selective miracles.[70]

Conversely, this theodicy of love addresses the problem of selective miracles by suggesting there are some evils that God cannot (morally) prevent, while denying that some permanent restriction (ontological or otherwise) prevents God from eliminating evil in cases he does not do so.[71] In other words, while God is ontologically capable of eliminating such kinds of evils, God may be temporarily restricted (morally) from doing so, given the covenantal parameters of the cosmic conflict. Such a framework further accounts for those evils that it seems God would not be prevented from mitigating or eliminating out of his respect for free will alone (in the free will defense) or his restraint from doing anything unloving (in the essential kenosis model). Here, the problem of selective miracles is addressed by recognizing that there is a broader matrix of factors at work in the cosmic conflict such that God is temporarily (morally) restricted from eliminating evil but will finally eradicate it without in any way compromising his utter goodness and love.

Conversely, if God is permanently incapable of preventing or eliminating the evils in this world, then it seems God would be incapable of strongly actualizing or otherwise ensuring an eschaton without suffering and death.[72]

69. Oord attests: "I know of no miracles described in the Bible . . . that require God to coerce." Oord, *Uncontrolling Love of God*, 201.

70. This "problem" is embedded in biblical narratives themselves, such as when Jesus healed the man by the pool of Bethesda (John 5:8–9) but did not heal others of the "multitude of those who were sick" (v. 3). Cf. John 11:37.

71. On Oord's view, "God cannot unilaterally prevent suffering caused by" the "malfunction" of "simple entities" in our bodies, leading to "debilitating condition[s]," because "God cannot withdraw, override or fail to provide agency and self-organization to any simple organism or entity that causes genuine evil." Rather, "God necessarily provides agency and self-organization to the entities and organs of our bodies." Oord, *Uncontrolling Love of God*, 172.

72. Griffin has claimed that the "Christian hope" for "life beyond death is fully supportable in terms of persuasive divine power." Griffin, "Creation out of Nothing," 125. He admits that whether "God will be effectual in bringing about this new form of civilization will depend on

This theodicy of love, however, can coherently affirm that God has morally sufficient reasons for temporarily allowing the evils in this world and that God can and will finally and permanently "wipe away every tear" so that "there will no longer be any death; there will no longer be any mourning, or crying, or pain" (Rev. 21:4).

What about Felix Culpa?

A similar advantage appears relative to *felix culpa* and other accounts that posit some evil as necessary for some greater good.[73] If some evil is deemed to be constitutive of some greater good, then, in order for that greater good to exist in the eschaton, whatever evil is constitutive of it must also continue.[74] This seems to contradict the traditional Christian eschatological view that evil will be eradicated.[75] Perhaps, however, some evils are necessary for greater goods in a developmental rather than a constitutive fashion.[76] Perhaps some process that requires evil is an antecedent condition of creaturely flourishing—maybe in order for free, effective creaturely choice to be developed or requisite to the process of soul-making.[77]

---

whether we respond to this call." Griffin, "Critique of a Theodicy of Protest," 28. Stephen T. Davis criticizes this view, saying that one "can only hope that God will emerge victorious." S. Davis, "Critique of Process Theodicy," 136.

73. E.g., Swinburne's higher-order goods defense. Swinburne, *Providence and the Problem of Evil*. Here, whereas Swinburne argues that goods such as compassion would not be possible without suffering, one wonders whether there might be comparable or better expressions of the love that grounds compassion in a world without evil.

74. Recognizing this implication, Swinburne believes that the world to come "lacks a few goods which our world contains, including the good of being able to reject the good." Swinburne, "Some Major Strands of Theodicy," 260–61. If paradise lacks such goods, one wonders whether they really are so valuable. Further, it is not at all clear that most of the evils, particularly natural evils, are necessary for higher-order goods. See, in this regard, the rebuttal of Swinburne's view in Stump, "Knowledge, Freedom, and the Problem of Evil," 459–72.

75. Some claim that law-like or nomic regularity (NR) is itself necessary for the flourishing of creation and that NR includes the necessity of suffering and death. However, it is not clear why suffering or death should be a necessary by-product of NR, absent some other factor(s). Christians have traditionally believed (in accordance with texts like Rev. 21:4) that a perfect realm without suffering awaits the redeemed. If so, either a perfect realm does not require NR or NR does not (by itself) require suffering or death. Consider the important distinction between logical and physical necessity, the latter referring to that which is necessary *given* the physical laws of *this world*. If God is the volitional source of this world's "physical necessities," then God could have created different physical or other laws. Tracy, "Lawfulness of Nature," 162.

76. Cf. the distinction between "good-harm analyses" (GHAs) of constitutive and developmental necessity relationships in Southgate and Robinson, "Varieties of Theodicy," 70. Cf. their third category, "property-consequence GHAs," which would apply to my model, in which "a consequence of the existence of a good" is *only the possibility* of its causing harm (70).

77. For an argument regarding free, effective choice, see Murray, *Nature Red in Tooth and Claw*, 139–40. Cf. Meister, *Evil*, 40.

Even if such greater goods are sufficiently outweighing, we might ask whether there is a condition of developmental necessity between such goods and *all* the evil in the history of this world.[78] Why should we believe, for instance, that an all-powerful God could not create humans with free, effective choice by fiat?[79] Why should we believe that an all-powerful God would need all the evil in this world in order to develop human souls?[80] In this regard, John Hick claims that "God must [initially] set man at a distance from Himself, from which he can then voluntarily come to God"; otherwise there could not be "authentic personal [love] relationship with Him."[81] Indeed, Hick believes that in order for authentic relationship to be possible, the world must be "as if there were no God."[82] David Ray Griffin avers, however, that "Hick's entire theodicy" thus "involves deception by making the world seem as if there were no God."[83]

Moreover, such a degree of epistemic distance does not appear to be necessary for authentic love relationship. Children, for instance, can love their parents without being set at such a distance first. Further, Stephen Davis comments, "Surely an omnipotent being . . . could have made us grow and learn in a much less painful, harsh, and destructive world."[84] J. L. Schellenberg adds, "There must remain an infinite number of ways of growing into wholeness and fulfillment in God" without the "horrors" of this world.[85] Additionally, some have noted that soul-making approaches face the significant problem that humans do not seem to be developing in a positive fashion at all; quite the opposite. As Chad Meister observes, "To make matters worse, some evils seem to be character-destroying rather than character-building."[86] Hick responds

78. As Daniel Speak writes, "Even if some suffering is needed for the project of shaping our characters, do we really need it in the full plenitude of kinds and amounts we find?" Speak, "Free Will and Soul-Making Theodicies," 219.

79. See, e.g., Mats Wahlberg's arguments that a "doppelgänger created" by fiat would be just as "free" and "self-conscious" as a "molecule-for-molecule identical" creature who was produced by a free process of evolution. Wahlberg, "Was Evolution the Only Possible Way?," 41. The success of this objection does not require the view that such a doppelgänger would be the same in *every* significant respect (e.g., history of free decisions) but only requires the claim that the doppelgänger would have sufficiently similar *capacities*.

80. The Bible does maintain that suffering *may* assist in building character and strengthening reliance on God (e.g., Rom. 5:3–4; 1 Pet. 4:12–14; cf. 2 Cor. 12:8–10). However, such instances presuppose a fallen world wherein humans are depraved, are in need of reconciliation, and face the enemy's attacks. The theodicy of love suggests there is no *intrinsic necessity* that humans build character by experiencing evil.

81. Hick, *Evil and the God of Love*, 317, 311.

82. Hick, *Evil and the God of Love*, 317.

83. Griffin, "Critique of Irenaean Theodicy," 54.

84. S. Davis, "Critique of Irenaean Theodicy," 60.

85. Schellenberg, "Stalemate and Strategy," 165.

86. Meister, *Evil*, 37.

by claiming that development continues in the eschaton; the "progress made by each individual in the course of this life goes with that individual into the next" but "does not accumulate from generation to generation" and thus "does not show in" this world.[87] If this is so, either the eschaton includes all the kinds of evils that Hick posits as necessary for soul-making or such evils are not necessary for soul-making.

Further, this concept of soul-making by virtue of one's free choices in the midst of struggle runs counter to the view that God will resurrect humans and transform their natures, "in the twinkling of an eye," at glorification (1 Cor. 15:52; cf. vv. 53–55; Phil. 3:20–21). If God cannot create humans by such direct special divine action without compromising some greater goods in the first place, it is difficult to see how he could do so without compromising such goods in the end. Even if these difficulties can be effectively answered, perhaps the biggest problem is that, given such *felix culpa* views, every evil would be an instrumental good.[88] As Davis states, "Those theists who hold that all evil helps lead to a greater good deny that 'genuine evil' exists. They implicitly affirm that all evil is only apparent."[89] Further, Karl Barth comments, if "sin is understood positively" as "counterbalanc[ing] grace" and "indispensable to it, it is not real sin."[90] If so, Kevin Diller adds, "we can no longer condemn evil and injustice as wholly antithetical to what is good."[91]

Indeed, if every instance of evil is permitted by God because that evil is necessary for some greater good, then human action to prevent any evil would

87. Hick, "Rejoinder," 68. John B. Cobb Jr. replies that Hick's "hypothesis that this growth occurs in other worlds after death is too ad hoc" and "has no biblical warrant." Cobb, "Problem of Evil and the Task of Ministry," 183.

88. Hick himself "reluctantly" admits that this involves "some kind of instrumental view of evil." Hick, *Evil and the God of Love*, 239.

89. S. Davis, "Critique of Process Theodicy," 134.

90. K. Barth, *CD* III/3:333.

91. Diller, "Are Sin and Evil Necessary?," 402. Diller argues against Plantinga's *felix culpa* theodicy, which suggests that "any world with incarnation and atonement is a better world than any without it—or at any rate better than any world in which God does nothing comparable to incarnation and atonement." Plantinga, "Supralapsarianism or 'O Felix Culpa,'" 10. Further, Plantinga argues that "a necessary condition of atonement is sin and evil" (12). As such, "suffering is itself of instrumental value" (19). However, Diller and others argue that Christ might have become incarnate anyway, even without evil, and it seems questionable whether the good of atonement is an *intrinsic* good that would outweigh all the evil in this world. Diller, "Are Sin and Evil Necessary?," 396, 403. Even if atonement is an incomparably great good, it seems that the atonement could have taken place in a world with far less suffering. Michael Peterson maintains that "God could have carried out his original wonderful plan for humanity in worlds that do not contain sin and Atonement. So, it was always possible, and always more desirable, not to sin." Peterson, "Christian Theism and the Evidential Argument," 179.

reduce the goodness of the world. As Swinburne states, affirming a *felix culpa* approach, "each evil or possible evil removed takes away one more actual good."[92] This position is not only problematic relative to human morality; it also runs counter to Paul's rejection of the view, "Let us do evil that good may come" (Rom. 3:8; cf. 6:1). If evil is never gratuitous, why should evil ever be prevented? Indeed, if every evil brings some greater good, why not propagate more evil?

This theodicy of love, conversely, contends that things would be better had no evil ever occurred.[93] Whereas the possibility of evil is necessary for the flourishing of love, the actualization of evil is not.[94] God can bring good out of some evils and appears to permit some instances because there is no preferable alternative available (e.g., Gen. 50:20). As Rice puts it, "While in themselves [evils] have no benefit, God can respond even to life's greatest losses in ways that bless and benefit us."[95] However, this possibility does not entail that every instance of evil brings about some greater good that could not have been achieved without it.[96] Whereas it may be morally necessary that God refrains from preventing some evils because doing so might negate the kind of freedom necessary for love, be against the rules of engagement, or lead to more deleterious results, it does not follow that the evils themselves are necessary for some greater good.[97] This theodicy of love thus holds the advantages of not instrumentalizing evil and of being able to forthrightly call all people to do whatever they can to prevent evil.

92. Swinburne, "Some Major Strands of Theodicy," 258.

93. This position is contra claims that all evil in this world is necessary for God's glory (the divine glory defense/theodicy) or some other great good. See Johnson, "Calvinism and the Problem of Evil," 43–48. See also chap. 2 in the present volume.

94. As Diller explains, "In a free will theodicy it is the permission of evil that is essential to the greater good that God intends, but in the *Felix Culpa* theodicy it is the evil itself that is essential to the greater good." Diller, "Are Sin and Evil Necessary?," 402.

95. Rice, *Suffering and the Search for Meaning*, 152.

96. T. F. Torrance maintains that evil is "an outrage against the love of God" and that we should not "regard evil and disorder in the universe as in any way intended or as given a direct function by God in the development of His creation," though "even these enormities can be made to serve His final end for the created order." Torrance, *Divine and Contingent Order*, 139.

97. On the oft-misunderstood text of Rom. 8:28, "God causes all things to work together for good to those who love God," Rice notes, "This does not mean that everything is ultimately good. Nothing makes it good that bad things happen. What it means is that God works for good, no matter what happens." Rice, *Suffering and the Search for Meaning*, 99. Cf. Eleonore Stump's approach (which she attributes to Aquinas), which maintains that union with God is the greatest possible good for any human and lack of such union "is the worst thing that can happen to a person" such that "attaining this union is of greater value for a person than avoiding suffering." Stump, *Wandering in the Darkness*, 394.

Beyond Inscrutability

One might nevertheless argue that, for all we know, there is some necessity relationship between *all* the evil in this world and some greater good. Perhaps we should be skeptical of our ability to render judgment on such matters. Just because one cannot conceive of how the evils of this world could be necessary for good does not mean that it could not be so.[98] However, even *if* such an appeal to inscrutability is technically successful, which remains the subject of considerable debate, it may not be very satisfying or helpful to someone who is struggling with doubt about God's goodness.[99] God has revealed significant information regarding evil, and while we should stop short of claiming to have sufficient data or cognitive ability to make final judgments, the Christian theist should make the best case for God's goodness that can be made, given the data available to us.[100] While recognizing that we should be humble about and skeptical of our own judgments, this theodicy of love goes beyond appeals to divine inscrutability toward providing a robust, canonical framework for addressing the problem of evil.

Protesting and Resisting Evil

John K. Roth claims that theodicy itself is problematic and requires justifying evil, and he is rightly concerned that evil not merely be thought of instrumentally.[101] In many ways, I resonate with such concerns.[102] Whatever we say about the problem of evil, we should be careful not to trivialize it or in any way minimize the horrendous sufferings that people have endured and continue to endure. As Russell puts it, "Any decent religion must face" the enormity of evil "squarely."[103] Indeed, one of the reasons I refuse to accept that evil is necessary for good is because in my view that amounts to a denial of genuine evil.

At the same time, I do not think every theodicy must be problematic in the way Roth contends. This theodicy of love articulates an overarching

---

98. See the discussion of skeptical theism and noseeum arguments in chap. 5 of the present volume.

99. Bart Ehrman, for instance, claims that appeal to "mystery" amounts to "an admission that there is no answer." Ehrman, *God's Problem*, 13.

100. As Murray puts it, "How much better if the theist could go beyond arguing that our ignorance makes it unreasonable to" claim that God could have no sufficient reason(s) for permitting evils "to supplying suitable reasons that might explain God's permission of actual evils?" Murray, *Nature Red in Tooth and Claw*, 35.

101. Roth believes that "most theodicies" actually "legitimate evil." Roth, "Theodicy of Protest," 17.

102. However, I strongly disagree with Roth's position that God is not entirely *good*.

103. Russell, *Mephistopheles*, 300.

framework in which one might make sense of God's allowance of evil broadly (for the sake of love) but makes no attempt to explain every specific instance of evil and explicitly denies that every instance of evil is, in and of itself, necessary for some greater good. Further, this theodicy does not justify any evil but contends that it would have been better had no evil ever occurred. Neither this nor any other theodicy should "still our anger, hostility, and sadness."[104]

This cosmic conflict theodicy of love contends that God himself abhors evil and does not desire that evil occur but deeply desires to eliminate evil altogether. Further, it contends that one day God will utterly eradicate evil forevermore. In the meantime, this theodicy maintains that "an enemy has done this" (Matt. 13:28). It is not supposed to be this way and will not always be this way because the suffering God of the cross has made a way to redeem this world while defeating and finally destroying evil forevermore.

This perspective does not assuage our suffering or explain it away, and it does not intend to do so. It recognizes evil as the heinous enemy that it is and as stemming from the ruthless malice of demonic forces that work against God's (ideal) will. Nevertheless, in the midst of great suffering, all theodicies ring hollow. This is not a shortcoming of theodicy per se but stems from the sheer *evilness* of evil. Whatever else we say, we should never even imply that any evil, such as the dying of children, is not that bad after all. It is worse than that bad. It is diabolical. The suffering God of the cross himself took on death in order to destroy it, and he will indeed destroy death and the enemy who has its power (Heb. 2:14). In the meantime, we can maintain faith in the goodness of this God of love while raging against the (temporary) "dying of the light."[105]

Our "anger, hostility, and sadness" should be directed not against the God who took on our suffering and gave himself for us on the cross but against the enemy of love and his minions and against the evil that resides in the human heart. As C. S. Lewis maintains, "Enemy-occupied territory—that is what this world is. Christianity is the story of how the rightful king has landed, you might say landed in disguise, and is calling us all to take part in a great campaign of sabotage."[106] Those of us who recognize there is a real conflict between forces of good and evil cannot remain silent in the face of evil or resign ourselves to it as God's (ideal) will; we must turn and fight against darkness with light—that is, in a way that imitates Christ's own form of resistance against evil, even as we await the (apocalyptic) solution from outside, which alone will be sufficient.

104. Roth, "Theodicy of Protest," 18.
105. Dylan Thomas, "Do not go gentle into that good night," in *Poems of Dylan Thomas*, 239.
106. Lewis, *Mere Christianity*, 46.

Conclusion

This final chapter has addressed the viability and advantages of this theodicy of love in light of potential objections and other approaches. This treatment has not fully bridged the gap between the biblical trajectory of a cosmic conflict theodicy of love and contemporary questions. Still, I believe this approach, despite its limitations, offers numerous helpful ways forward while recognizing the need for humility regarding one's understanding of God and one's interpretation of the world around us.

Whatever is said about this specific approach, I am confident that the God of love depicted in Scripture is wholly good, loving, righteous, and just. Even as prospective answers to specific evils are less than fully satisfying, my hope and confidence are in the suffering God of the cross *and* of the resurrection, the God who gave himself for this world in order to defeat evil and provide the ultimate manifestation of his righteousness and love, the almighty God who will finally destroy evil once and for all.

> Worthy is the Lamb that was slain to receive power and riches and wisdom and might and honor and glory and blessing. . . .
>
> To Him who sits on the throne, and to the Lamb, be blessing and honor and glory and dominion forever and ever. (Rev. 5:12–13)

Bibliography

Adams, Marilyn McCord. *Horrendous Evils and the Goodness of God*. Ithaca, NY: Cornell University Press, 1999.

Adams, Marilyn McCord, and Robert Merrihew Adams, eds. *The Problem of Evil*. New York: Oxford University Press, 1990.

Adams, Robert Merrihew. "Middle Knowledge and the Problem of Evil." In Adams and Adams, *Problem of Evil*, 110–25.

———. "Must God Create the Best?" In Rowe, *God and the Problem of Evil*, 24–37.

Alden, Robert L. *Job*. NAC. Nashville: Broadman & Holman, 1993.

Alter, Robert. *The Wisdom Books: Job, Proverbs, and Ecclesiastes*. New York: Norton, 2010.

Andersen, Frances I. *Job*. Nottingham, UK: Inter-Varsity, 1976.

Ante-Nicene Fathers, The. Edited by Alexander Roberts and James Donaldson. 10 vols. Buffalo: Christian Literature Company, 1885–87.

Antony, Louise. "Does God Love Us?" In Bergman, Murray, and Rea, *Divine Evil?*, 29–46.

———. "Reply to Stump." In Bergmann, Murray, and Rea, *Divine Evil?*, 54–56.

Archer, Gleason L. "Daniel." In *Daniel and the Minor Prophets*, edited by F. E. Gaebelein, 3–160. Expositor's Bible Commentary 7. Grand Rapids: Zondervan, 1986.

Arnold, Clinton E. *Powers of Darkness: Principalities and Powers in Paul's Letters*. Downers Grove, IL: IVP Academic, 1992.

———. "Principalities and Powers." *ABD* 5:467.

———. *3 Crucial Questions about Spiritual Warfare*. Grand Rapids: Baker, 1997.

Aune, David E. *Revelation 1–5:14*. WBC. Dallas: Word, 1997.

———. *Revelation 6–16*. WBC. Dallas: Word, 1998.

Baggett, David, and Jerry L. Walls. *Good God: The Theistic Foundations of Morality.* New York: Oxford University Press, 2011.

Balthasar, Hans Urs von. *The Action.* Vol. 4 of *Theo-Drama: Theological Dramatic Theory.* San Francisco: Ignatius, 1994.

Balz, H., and G. Schneider, eds. *Exegetical Dictionary of the New Testament.* 3 vols. Grand Rapids: Eerdmans, 1990–93.

Barnett, Paul. *The Second Epistle to the Corinthians.* NICNT. Grand Rapids: Eerdmans, 1997.

Barth, Karl. *Church Dogmatics (CD).* Edited by Geoffrey W. Bromiley and T. F. Torrance. 14 vols. Edinburgh: T&T Clark, 1936–69.

Barth, Markus. *Ephesians 1–3.* AB. New Haven: Yale University Press, 2008.

Bauckham, Richard J. *2 Peter, Jude.* WBC. Dallas: Word, 1990.

———. *The Theology of the Book of Revelation.* Cambridge, UK: Cambridge University Press, 1993.

Baudelaire, Charles. *Paris Spleen: Little Poems in Prose.* Translated by Keith Waldrop. Middletown, CT: Wesleyan University Press, 2009.

Bauer, W., F. W. Danker, W. F. Arndt, and F. W. Gingrich, eds. *Greek-English Lexicon of the New Testament and Other Early Christian Literature.* 2nd ed. Chicago: University of Chicago Press, 1979.

Beale, G. K. *Revelation.* NIGTC. Grand Rapids: Eerdmans, 1999.

Beilby, James K., and Paul Rhodes Eddy, eds. *Understanding Spiritual Warfare.* Grand Rapids: Baker Academic, 2012.

Bergmann, Michael, and Daniel Howard-Snyder. "Reply to Rowe." In Rowe, *God and the Problem of Evil*, 137–40.

Bergmann, Michael, Michael J. Murray, and Michael C. Rea, eds. *Divine Evil? The Moral Character of the God of Abraham.* New York: Oxford University Press, 2011.

Bertoluci, Jose M. "The Son of the Morning and the Guardian Cherub in the Context of the Controversy between Good and Evil." ThD diss., Berrien Springs: Andrews University, 1985.

Blenkinsopp, Joseph. *Isaiah 1–39.* AB. New Haven: Yale University Press, 2008.

———. *Isaiah 40–55.* AB. New Haven: Yale University Press, 2008.

Blocher, Henri. *Evil and the Cross.* Downers Grove, IL: IVP, 1994.

Block, Daniel I. *The Book of Ezekiel: Chapters 1–24.* NICOT. Grand Rapids: Eerdmans, 1997.

———. *The Gods of the Nations: Studies in Ancient Near Eastern National Theology.* 2nd ed. Grand Rapids: Baker Academic, 2000.

Blomberg, Craig. *The Historical Reliability of the Gospels.* 2nd ed. Downers Grove, IL: IVP Academic, 2007.

Boda, Mark J. *The Book of Zechariah*. NICOT. Grand Rapids: Eerdmans, 2016.

Bonhoeffer, Dietrich. *Letters and Papers from Prison*. Vol. 8 of *Dietrich Bonhoeffer Works*, edited by John W. de Gruchy. Minneapolis: Fortress, 2009.

Borchert, Gerald L. *John 1–11*. NAC. Nashville: Broadman & Holman, 2001.

Bovon, François. *Luke 1:1–9:50*. Hermeneia. Minneapolis: Fortress, 2002.

Boyd, Gregory A. *God at War: The Bible and Spiritual Conflict*. Downers Grove, IL: IVP Academic, 1997.

———. "God Limits His Control." In Jowers, *Four Views on Divine Providence*, 183–208.

———. *Satan and the Problem of Evil: Constructing a Trinitarian Warfare Theodicy*. Downers Grove, IL: IVP Academic, 2001.

Brown, Colin, ed. *New International Dictionary of New Testament Theology*. Grand Rapids: Zondervan, 1986.

Brown, Derek R. *The God of This Age: Satan in the Churches and Letters of the Apostle Paul*. Tübingen: Mohr Siebeck, 2015.

Brown, Raymond E. *The Epistles of John*. AB. New Haven: Yale University Press, 2008.

Bruce, F. F. *Colossians, Philemon, and Ephesians*. NICNT. Grand Rapids: Eerdmans, 1984.

———. *Hebrews*. NICNT. Grand Rapids: Eerdmans, 1990.

———. *Romans*. Downers Grove, IL: IVP, 1985.

Brümmer, Vincent. *The Model of Love: A Study in Philosophical Theology*. Cambridge, UK: Cambridge University Press, 1993.

Bultmann, Rudolf. *New Testament Mythology and Other Basic Writings*. Philadelphia: Fortress, 1984.

Burns, Charlene P. E. *Christian Understandings of Evil: The Historical Trajectory*. Minneapolis: Fortress, 2016.

Calvin, John. *Calvin's Calvinism: Treatises on the Eternal Predestination of God and the Secret Providence of God*. Translated by Henry Cole. 2 vols. London: Wertheim & Macintosh, 1856–57.

———. *Commentaries on the Catholic Epistles*. Grand Rapids: Eerdmans, 1948.

———. "Defence of the Secret Providence of God." In Calvin, *Calvin's Calvinism*, 2:3–133.

Chesterton, G. K. *The Man Who Was Thursday: A Nightmare*. New York: Dodd, Mead, 1912.

Christensen, Duane L. *Deuteronomy 21:10–34:12*. WBC. Dallas: Word, 2002.

Clements, Ronald E. "Deuteronomy." *NIB* 2:269–538.

Clines, David J. A. *Job 1–20*. WBC. Dallas: Word, 2002.

Cobb, John B., Jr. "The Problem of Evil and the Task of Ministry." In S. Davis, *Encountering Evil*, 181–90.

Cogan, Mordechai. *1 Kings*. AB. New Haven: Yale University Press, 2001.

Collins, Adela Yarbro. *The Apocalypse*. Collegeville, MN: Liturgical Press, 1979.

Collins, John J. *Daniel*. Hermeneia. Minneapolis: Fortress, 1993.

Cooper, Lamar Eugene, Sr. *Ezekiel*. NAC. Nashville: Broadman & Holman, 1994.

Copan, Paul. *Is God a Moral Monster?* Grand Rapids: Baker Books, 2011.

Copan, Paul, and Matthew Flannagan. *Did God Really Command Genocide?* Grand Rapids: Baker Books, 2014.

Cowan, Steven B., and James S. Spiegel. *The Love of Wisdom: A Christian Introduction to Philosophy*. Nashville: B&H, 2009.

Craig, William Lane. "Response to Boyd." In Jowers, *Four Views on Divine Providence*, 224–30.

Craigie, Peter C. *The Book of Deuteronomy*. NICOT. Grand Rapids: Eerdmans, 1976.

Creegan, Nicola Hoggard. *Animal Suffering and the Problem of Evil*. New York: Oxford University Press, 2013.

Crenshaw, James L. *Defending God: Biblical Responses to the Problem of Evil*. New York: Oxford University Press, 2005.

———, ed. *Theodicy in the Old Testament*. London: SPCK, 1983.

Crisp, Oliver. *Deviant Calvinism: Broadening Reformed Theology*. Minneapolis: Fortress, 2014.

———. *Saving Calvinism: Expanding the Reformed Tradition*. Downers Grove, IL: IVP Academic, 2016.

Date, Christopher M., Gregory B. Stump, and Joshua W. Anderson, eds. *Rethinking Hell: Readings in Evangelical Conditionalism*. Eugene, OR: Cascade, 2014.

Davids, Peter H. *The Letters of 2 Peter and Jude*. PNTC. Grand Rapids: Eerdmans, 2006.

Davidson, Richard M. "The Divine Covenant Lawsuit Motif in Canonical Perspective." *Journal of the Adventist Theological Society* 21, nos. 1–2 (2010): 45–84.

Davies, W. D., and Dale C. Allison Jr. *Matthew 8–18*. International Critical Commentary. New York: T&T Clark, 1991.

Davis, R. Dean. *The Heavenly Court Judgment of Revelation 4–5*. Lanham, MD: University Press of America, 1992.

Davis, Stephen T. "Critique of Irenaean Theodicy." In S. Davis, *Encountering Evil*, 58–62.

———. "Critique of Process Theodicy." In S. Davis, *Encountering Evil*, 133–37.

———, ed. *Encountering Evil: Live Options in Theodicy*. New ed. Louisville: Westminster John Knox, 2001.

———. "Free Will and Evil." In S. Davis, *Encountering Evil*, 73–89.

———. "Introduction." In S. Davis, *Encountering Evil*, vii–xiii.

———. "Rejoinder." In S. Davis, *Encountering Evil*, 101–7.

Dawkins, Richard. *The God Delusion*. New York: Houghton Mifflin, 2006.

Day, Peggy L. *An Adversary in Heaven: Satan in the Hebrew Bible*. Atlanta: Scholars Press, 1988.

Day, Peggy L., and C. Breytenbach. "Satan." In van der Toorn, Becking, and van der Horst, *DDD*, 726–31.

De La Torre, Miguel A., and Albert Hernández. *The Quest for the Historical Satan*. Minneapolis: Fortress, 2011.

DeWeese, Garrett. "Natural Evil: A 'Free Process' Defense." In Meister and Dew, *God and Evil*, 53–64.

Diller, Kevin. "Are Sin and Evil Necessary for a Really Good World?" In Peterson, *Problem of Evil*, 2nd ed., 390–409.

Dougherty, Trent, and Justin P. McBrayer, eds. *Skeptical Theism: New Essays*. New York: Oxford University Press, 2014.

Draper, Paul. "Pain and Pleasure: An Evidential Problem for Theists." In Rowe, *God and the Problem of Evil*, 180–202.

Dunn, James D. G. *The Epistles to the Colossians and to Philemon*. NIGTC. Grand Rapids: Eerdmans, 1996.

———. *Romans 9–16*. WBC. Dallas: Word, 2002.

Edwards, David L., and John R. W. Stott. *Evangelical Essentials: A Liberal-Evangelical Dialogue*. Downers Grove, IL: IVP, 1989.

Ehrman, Bart D. *God's Problem: How the Bible Fails to Answer Our Most Important Question—Why We Suffer*. New York: HarperOne, 2008.

Ekstrom, Laura W. "A Christian Theodicy." In McBrayer and Howard-Snyder, *Blackwell Companion to the Problem of Evil*, 266–80.

———. "Event-Causal Libertarianism." In Timpe, Griffith, and Levy, *Routledge Companion to Free Will*, 62–71.

Erickson, Millard. *Christian Theology*. 3rd ed. Grand Rapids: Baker Academic, 2013.

Fee, Gordon D. *The First Epistle to the Corinthians*. NICNT. Grand Rapids: Eerdmans, 1987.

Feinberg, John S. *The Many Faces of Evil: Theological Systems and the Problems of Evil*. Rev. ed. Wheaton: Crossway, 2004.

Ferdinando, Keith. *The Triumph of Christ in African Perspective: A Study of Demonology and Redemption in the African Context*. Carlisle, UK: Paternoster, 1999.

Flint, Thomas P. *Divine Providence: The Molinist Account*. Ithaca, NY: Cornell University Press, 1998.

France, R. T. *Matthew*. NICNT. Grand Rapids: Eerdmans, 2007.

Frankfurt, Harry. "Alternate Possibilities and Moral Responsibility." *Journal of Philosophy* 66, no. 23 (1969): 829–39.

Freedman, David Noel, ed. *The Anchor Bible Dictionary*. 6 vols. New York: Doubleday, 1996.

Fretheim, Terence E. "The Book of Genesis." *NIB* 1:319–676.

Fuchs, Eric, and Pierre Reymond. *La deuxième Épitre de Saint Pierre. L'épitre de Saint Jude*. Neuchâtel, Switzerland: Delachaux & Niestlé, 1980.

Fudge, Edward. *The Fire That Consumes: A Biblical and Historical Study of the Doctrine of Final Punishment*. 3rd ed. Eugene, OR: Cascade, 2011.

Gane, Roy. *Cult and Character: Purification Offerings, Day of Atonement, and Theodicy*. Winona Lake, IN: Eisenbrauns, 2005.

Ganssle, Gregory E. "Evil as Evidence for Christianity." In Meister and Dew, *God and Evil*, 214–23.

Ganssle, Gregory E., and Yena Lee. "Evidential Problems of Evil." In Meister and Dew, *God and Evil*, 15–25.

Garrett, Susan R. *The Demise of the Devil*. Minneapolis: Fortress, 1990.

Gatumu, Kabiro wa. *The Pauline Concept of Supernatural Powers: A Reading from the African Worldview*. Paternoster Biblical Monographs. Milton Keynes, UK: Paternoster, 2008.

Gavrilyuk, Paul L. "An Overview of Patristic Theodicies." In *Suffering and Evil in Early Christian Thought*, edited by Nonna Verna Harrison and David G. Hunter, 1–6. Grand Rapids: Baker Academic, 2016.

Gilmore, George W., and Walter Caspari. "Renunciation of the Devil in the Baptismal Rite." In *The New Schaff-Herzog Encyclopedia of Religious Knowledge*, edited by Samuel Macauley Jackson, 9:488–89. Grand Rapids: Baker, 1953.

Ginet, Carl. "In Defense of the Principle of Alternative Possibilities: Why I Don't Find Frankfurt's Argument Convincing." In Widerker and McKenna, *Moral Responsibility and Alternative Possibilities*, 53–57.

Goldingay, John E. *Daniel*. WBC. Dallas: Word, 1989.

———. *Israel's Faith*. Vol. 2 of *Old Testament Theology*. Downers Grove, IL: IVP Academic, 2006.

Gowan, Donald E. *From Eden to Babel: A Commentary on the Book of Genesis 1–11*. International Theological Commentary. Grand Rapids: Eerdmans, 1988.

Grabiner, Steven. *Revelation's Hymns: Commentary on the Cosmic Conflict*. Library of New Testament Studies. New York: T&T Clark, 2015.

Green, Adam, and Eleonore Stump, eds. *Hidden Divinity and Religious Belief*. New York: Cambridge University Press, 2015.

Green, Joel B. *The Gospel of Luke*. NICNT. Grand Rapids: Eerdmans, 1997.

Gregg, Brian Han. *What Does the Bible Say about Suffering?* Downers Grove, IL: IVP Academic, 2016.

Griffin, David Ray. "Creation out of Nothing, Creation of Chaos, and the Problem of Evil." In S. Davis, *Encountering Evil*, 108–25.

———. "Critique of a Theodicy of Protest." In S. Davis, *Encountering Evil*, 25–28.

———. "Critique of Irenaean Theodicy." In S. Davis, *Encountering Evil*, 52–56.

———. "Critique of the Free Will Defense." In S. Davis, *Encountering Evil*, 93–97.

———. "Rejoinder." In S. Davis, *Encountering Evil*, 137–44.

Griffith, Meghan. "Agent Causation." In Timpe, Griffith, and Levy, *Routledge Companion to Free Will*, 72–85.

Habermas, Gary R., and R. Michael Licona. *The Case for the Resurrection of Jesus*. Grand Rapids: Kregel, 2004.

Hagner, Donald A. *Matthew 1–13*. WBC. Dallas: Word, 2002.

Hamilton, Victor P. *The Book of Genesis: Chapters 1–17*. NICOT. Grand Rapids: Eerdmans, 1990.

———. "Satan." *ABD* 5:985–89.

Hanson, Paul D. *Isaiah 40–66*. Interpretation. Louisville: Westminster John Knox, 1995.

Harkins, Angela Kim, Kelley Coblentz Baunch, and John C. Endres, eds. *The Watchers in Jewish and Christian Traditions*. Minneapolis: Fortress, 2014.

Harris, Murray J. *The Second Epistle to the Corinthians*. NIGTC. Grand Rapids: Eerdmans, 2005.

Hart, David Bentley. *The Doors of the Sea: Where Was God in the Tsunami?* Grand Rapids: Eerdmans, 2005.

———. "Providence and Causality: On Divine Innocence." In *The Providence of God*, edited by Francesca Aran Murphy and Philip G. Ziegler, 34–56. New York: T&T Clark, 2009.

Hartley, John E. *The Book of Job*. NICOT. Grand Rapids: Eerdmans, 1988.

Hartman, Louis F., and Alexander Di Lella. *Daniel*. AB. New Haven: Yale University Press, 2008.

Hartshorne, Charles. *Reality as Social Process*. New York: Hafner, 1971.

Hasker, William. *The Triumph of God over Evil: Theodicy for a World of Suffering*. Downers Grove, IL: IVP Academic, 2008.

Heiser, Michael S. "Deuteronomy 32:8 and the Sons of God." *Bibliotheca Sacra* 158 (2001): 52–74.

———. "Deuteronomy 32:8–9 and the Old Testament Worldview." In *Faithlife Study Bible*, edited by John D. Barry, Michael R. Grigoni, et al. Bellingham, WA: Logos, 2012.

———. "Divine Council." In *The Lexham Bible Dictionary*, edited by John D. Barry et al. Bellingham, WA: Lexham, 2016.

———. *The Unseen Realm: Recovering the Supernatural Worldview of the Bible*. Bellingham, WA: Lexham, 2015.

Helm, Paul. "God, Compatibilism, and the Authorship of Sin." *Religious Studies* 46, no. 1 (2010): 115–24.

Helseth, Paul Kjoss. "God Causes All Things." In Jowers, *Four Views on Divine Providence*, 25–52.

Hick, John. *Evil and the God of Love*. London: Macmillan, 1966.

———. "An Irenaean Theodicy." In S. Davis, *Encountering Evil*, 38–52.

———. "Rejoinder." In S. Davis, *Encountering Evil*, 65–72.

———. "Soul-Making Theodicy." In Rowe, *God and the Problem of Evil*, 265–81.

Highfield, Ron. "God Controls by Liberating." In Jowers, *Four Views on Divine Providence*, 141–64.

———. "Response to Paul Kjoss Helseth." In Jowers, *Four Views on Divine Providence*, 63–68.

Horton, Michael. *Lord and Servant: A Covenant Christology*. Louisville: Westminster John Knox, 2005.

Hossfeld, Frank-Lothar, and Erich Zenger. *Psalms 2: A Commentary on Psalms 51–100*. Hermeneia. Minneapolis: Fortress, 2005.

Howard-Snyder, Daniel, Michael Bergmann, and William L. Rowe. "An Exchange on the Problem of Evil." In Rowe, *God and the Problem of Evil*, 124–58.

Howard-Snyder, Daniel, and Paul K. Moser, eds. *Divine Hiddenness: New Essays*. Cambridge, UK: Cambridge University Press, 2002.

Hume, David. *Dialogues concerning Natural Religion*. Edinburgh: Blackwood & Sons, 1907.

Johnson, Daniel M. "Calvinism and the Problem of Evil: A Map of the Territory." In *Calvinism and the Problem of Evil*, edited by David E. Alexander and Daniel M. Johnson, 19–55. Eugene, OR: Pickwick, 2016.

Jowers, Dennis, ed. *Four Views on Divine Providence*. Grand Rapids: Zondervan, 2011.

Kane, Robert. *A Contemporary Introduction to Free Will*. New York: Oxford University Press, 2005.

———, ed. *The Oxford Handbook of Free Will*. 2nd ed. Oxford: Oxford University Press, 2011.

Keck, Leander E., ed. *The New Interpreter's Bible*. 12 vols. Nashville: Abingdon, 1994.

Keener, Craig. *Miracles: The Credibility of the New Testament Accounts*. 2 vols. Grand Rapids: Baker Academic, 2011.

Kidner, Derek. *Psalms 73–150*. Nottingham, UK: Inter-Varsity, 1975.

Kittel, Gerhard, and Gerhard Friedrich, eds. *Theological Dictionary of the New Testament*. 10 vols. Grand Rapids: Eerdmans, 1964–76.

Klein, George L. *Zechariah*. NAC. Nashville: B&H, 2008.

Koehler, Ludwig, Walter Baumgartner, and Johann Jacob Stamm. *The Hebrew and Aramaic Lexicon of the Old Testament*. Translated and edited under the supervision of M. E. J. Richardson. 4 vols. Leiden: Brill, 1994–99.

Köstenberger, Andreas J. *A Theology of John's Gospel and Letters*. Grand Rapids: Zondervan, 2009.

Kraus, H. *Psalms 60–150*. CC. Minneapolis: Fortress, 1993.

Laato, Anti, and Johannes C. de Moor, eds. *Theodicy in the World of the Bible*. Leiden: Brill, 2003.

Ladd, G. E. *A Commentary on the Revelation of John*. Grand Rapids: Eerdmans, 1972.

Lewis, C. S. "Christianity and Culture." In *Christian Reflections*, edited by Walter Hooper, 12–36. Grand Rapids: Eerdmans, 1967.

———. *The Lion, the Witch, and the Wardrobe*. New York: Scholastic, 1987.

———. *Mere Christianity*. New York: HarperOne, 2001.

———. *The Problem of Pain*. New York: HarperOne, 2001.

Lincoln, Andrew T. *Ephesians*. WBC. Dallas: Word, 2002.

———. *Truth on Trial: The Lawsuit Motif in the Fourth Gospel*. Peabody, MA: Hendrickson, 2000.

Lloyd, Michael. "Are Animals Fallen?" In *Animals on the Agenda*, edited by Andrew Linzey and Dorothy Yamamoto, 147–60. Chicago: University of Illinois Press, 1998.

Löfstedt, Torsten. "The Ruler of This World." *Svenska exegetiska sällskapet* 74 (2009): 55–79.

Longman, Tremper, III. *Daniel*. NIVAC. Grand Rapids: Zondervan, 1999.

Longman, Tremper, III, and Daniel G. Reid. *God Is a Warrior*. Grand Rapids: Zondervan, 1995.

Louw, J. P., and E. A. Nida. *Greek-English Lexicon of the New Testament: Based on Semantic Domains*. 2nd ed. New York: UBS, 1989.

Mackie, J. L. "Evil and Omnipotence." In Adams and Adams, *Problem of Evil*, 25–37.

Magyarosi, Barna. *Holy War and Cosmic Conflict in the Old Testament*. Berrien Springs, MI: ATS Publications, 2010.

Manis, R. Zachary. "Could God Do Something Evil? A Molinist Solution to the Problem of Divine Freedom." *Faith and Philosophy* 28, no. 2 (2011): 209–23.

Marcus, Joel. *Mark 1–8*. AB. New Haven: Yale University Press, 2008.

Marshall, I. Howard. *The Epistles of John*. NICNT. Grand Rapids: Eerdmans, 1978.

———. *The Gospel of Luke*. NIGTC. Grand Rapids: Eerdmans, 1978.

———. "The New Testament Does Not Teach Universal Salvation." In *Universal Salvation? The Current Debate*, edited by Robin Parry and Christopher Partridge, 55–76. Grand Rapids: Eerdmans, 2003.

Mathews, Kenneth A. *Genesis 1–11:26*. NAC. Nashville: Broadman & Holman, 1995.

Mays, James L. *Psalms*. Interpretation. Louisville: Westminster John Knox, 1994.

McBrayer, Justin P., and Daniel Howard-Snyder, eds. *The Blackwell Companion to the Problem of Evil*. Malden, MA: Wiley-Blackwell, 2013.

McCall, Thomas H. "I Believe in Divine Sovereignty." *Trinity Journal* 29, no. 2 (2008): 205–26.

———. *An Invitation to Analytic Christian Theology*. Downers Grove, IL: IVP Academic, 2015.

———. "We Believe in God's Sovereign Goodness: A Rejoinder to John Piper." *Trinity Journal* 29, no. 2 (2008): 235–46.

McCann, J. Clinton, Jr. "Psalms." *NIB* 4:639–1280.

Meister, Chad. *Evil: A Guide for the Perplexed*. New York: Bloomsbury Academic, 2012.

———. "Evil and the Hiddenness of God." In Meister and Dew, *God and Evil*, 138–51.

Meister, Chad, and James K. Dew Jr., eds. *God and Evil: The Case for God in a World Filled with Pain*. Downers Grove, IL: IVP, 2013.

Merrill, Eugene H. *Deuteronomy*. NAC. Nashville: Broadman & Holman, 1994.

Meyers, Carol, and Eric Meyers. *Haggai, Zechariah 1–8*. AB. New Haven: Yale University Press, 2008.

Miller, Patrick D. *Deuteronomy*. Interpretation. Louisville: Westminster John Knox, 1990.

Miller, Stephen R. *Daniel*. NAC. Nashville: Broadman & Holman, 1994.

Moltmann, Jürgen. *The Crucified God*. New York: Harper & Row, 1974.

Moo, Douglas J. *The Letters to the Colossians and to Philemon*. PNTC. Grand Rapids: Eerdmans, 2008.

———. *Romans*. NICNT. Grand Rapids: Eerdmans, 1996.

———. *2 Peter and Jude*. NIVAC. Grand Rapids: Zondervan, 1996.

Morris, Leon. *John*. NICNT. Grand Rapids: Eerdmans, 1995.

Moses, Robert Ewusie. *Practices of Power: Revisiting the Principalities and Powers in the Pauline Letters*. Minneapolis: Fortress, 2014.

Mullen, E. T., Jr. "Divine Assembly." *ABD* 2:214–17.

———. *The Divine Council in Canaanite and Early Hebrew Literature*. Harvard Semitic Monographs 24. Chico, CA: Scholars Press, 1980.

Muller, Richard A. *Divine Will and Human Choice: Freedom, Contingency, and Necessity in Early Modern Reformed Thought*. Grand Rapids: Baker Academic, 2017.

Murray, Michael. *Nature Red in Tooth and Claw: Theism and the Problem of Animal Suffering*. New York: Oxford University Press, 2008.

Newsom, Carol A. "Job." *NIB* 4:317–637.

Noll, Stephen F. "Angels, Doctrine of." *DTIB*, 45–48.

———. *Angels of Light, Powers of Darkness: Thinking Biblically about Angels, Satan, and Principalities*. Downers Grove, IL: IVP, 1998.

Nolland, John. *Luke 1:1–9:20*. WBC. Dallas: Word, 2002.

———. *Matthew*. NIGTC. Grand Rapids: Eerdmans, 2005.

Oden, Thomas C. *Classic Christianity: A Systematic Theology*. New York: Harper-Collins, 2009.

Olson, Roger. "Response to Thomas Jay Oord's *The Uncontrolling Love of God*." Paper presented at AAR, San Antonio, November 2016.

Oord, Thomas Jay. "Matching Theology and Piety: An Evangelical Process Theology of Love." PhD diss., Claremont Graduate University, 1999.

———. *The Nature of Love*. St. Louis: Chalice, 2010.

———. *The Uncontrolling Love of God: An Open and Relational Account of Providence*. Downers Grove, IL: IVP Academic, 2015.

Ortlund, Gavin. "On the Fall of Angels and the Fallenness of Nature: An Evangelical Hypothesis Regarding Natural Evil." *Evangelical Quarterly* 87, no. 2 (2015): 114–36.

Osborne, Grant R. *Matthew*. ECNT. Grand Rapids: Zondervan, 2010.

Oswalt, John N. *The Book of Isaiah: Chapters 40–66*. NICOT. Grand Rapids: Eerdmans, 1998.

Page, Sydney H. T. *Powers of Evil: A Biblical Study of Satan and Demons*. Grand Rapids: Baker, 1995.

Pannenberg, Wolfhart. *Systematic Theology*. 3 vols. Grand Rapids: Eerdmans, 1994.

Peckham, John C. *Canonical Theology: The Biblical Canon*, Sola Scriptura, *and Theological Method*. Grand Rapids: Eerdmans, 2016.

———. *The Concept of Divine Love in the Context of the God-World Relationship*. New York: Peter Lang, 2014.

———. *The Doctrine of God: Introducing the Big Questions*. London: T&T Clark, forthcoming.

———. *The Love of God: A Canonical Model*. Downers Grove, IL: IVP Academic, 2015.

Perszyk, Ken, ed. *Molinism: The Contemporary Debate*. New York: Oxford University Press, 2011.

Peterson, Michael L. "Christian Theism and the Evidential Argument from Evil." In Peterson, *Problem of Evil*, 2nd ed., 166–92.

———, ed. *The Problem of Evil: Selected Readings*, 1st ed. Notre Dame, IN: University of Notre Dame Press, 1992.

———, ed. *The Problem of Evil: Selected Readings*, 2nd ed. Notre Dame, IN: University of Notre Dame Press, 2016.

Phillips, D. Z. "Critique of the Free Will Defense." In Davis, *Encountering Evil*, 89–91.

Pike, Nelson. "Divine Omniscience and Voluntary Action." *Philosophical Review* 74 (1965): 27–46.

Piper, John. "Are There Two Wills in God?" In *Still Sovereign: Contemporary Perspectives on Election, Foreknowledge, and Grace*, edited by Thomas R. Schreiner and Bruce A. Ware, 107–32. Grand Rapids: Baker, 2000.

———. "How Does a Sovereign God Love? Reply to Thomas Talbott." *Reformed Journal* 33, no. 4 (1983): 9–13.

Plantinga, Alvin. "Ad Walls." In Peterson, *Problem of Evil*, 1st ed., 335–38.

———. *God, Freedom, and Evil*. Grand Rapids: Eerdmans, 1977.

———. *The Nature of Necessity*. Oxford: Clarendon, 1974.

———. "Reply to the Basingers on Divine Omnipotence." *Process Studies* 11, no. 1 (1981): 25–29.

———. "Self-Profile." In *Alvin Plantinga*, edited by James E. Tomberlin and Peter van Inwagen, 3–97. Dordrecht: D. Riedel, 1985.

———. "Supralapsarianism or 'O Felix Culpa.'" In *Christian Faith and the Problem of Evil*, edited by Peter van Inwagen, 1–25. Grand Rapids: Eerdmans, 2004.

———. *Warranted Christian Belief*. New York: Oxford University Press, 2000.

Pope, Marvin H. *Job*. AB. New Haven: Yale University Press, 2008.

Pritchard, James B., ed. *Ancient Near Eastern Texts Relating to the Old Testament*. 3rd ed. Princeton: Princeton University Press, 1969.

Rea, Michael. "Divine Hiddenness, Divine Silence." In Rea, *Evil and the Hiddenness of God*, 156–65.

———, ed. *Evil and the Hiddenness of God*. Stamford, CT: Cengage, 2015.

———. "Hiddenness and Transcendence." In Green and Stump, *Hidden Divinity and Religious Belief*, 210–25.

Reese, David George. "Demons: New Testament." *ABD* 2:140–42.

Reichenbach, Bruce R. *Divine Providence: God's Love and Human Freedom*. Eugene, OR: Cascade, 2016.

———. "Evil, Omnipotence, and Process Thought." In Peterson, *Problem of Evil*, 2nd ed., 301–26.

———. *Evil and a Good God*. New York: Fordham University Press, 1982.

Reid, Daniel G. "Principalities and Powers." In *Dictionary of Paul and His Letters*, edited by Gerald F. Hawthorne, Ralph P. Martin, and Daniel G. Reid, 746–52. Downers Grove, IL: IVP, 1993.

Rice, Richard. *Suffering and the Search for Meaning*. Downers Grove, IL: IVP Academic, 2014.

Roth, John K. "A Theodicy of Protest." In S. Davis, *Encountering Evil*, 1–20.

Routledge, Robin. "'An Evil Spirit from the Lord'—Demonic Influence or Divine Instrument?" *Evangelical Quarterly* 70, no. 1 (1998): 3–22.

Rowe, William L., ed. *God and the Problem of Evil*. Malden, MA: Blackwell, 2001.

———. "Introduction to Part II: The Logical Problem of Evil." In Rowe, *God and the Problem of Evil*, 75–76.

Russell, Jeffrey Burton. *The Devil: Perceptions of Evil from Antiquity to Primitive Christianity*. Ithaca, NY: Cornell University Press, 1977.

———. *Mephistopheles: The Devil in the Modern World*. Ithaca, NY: Cornell University Press, 1990.

———. *The Prince of Darkness*. Ithaca, NY: Cornell University Press, 1993.

———. *Satan: The Early Christian Tradition*. Ithaca, NY: Cornell University Press, 1981.

Sanders, John. *The God Who Risks*. Rev. ed. Downers Grove, IL: IVP Academic, 2007.

Sarna, Nahum M. *Genesis*. JPS Commentary. Philadelphia: JPS, 1989.

Schellenberg, J. L. *Divine Hiddenness and Human Reason*. Ithaca, NY: Cornell University Press, 1993.

———. "Divine Hiddenness Justifies Atheism." In Rea, *Evil and the Hiddenness of God*, 61–70.

———. *The Hiddenness Argument*. New York: Oxford University Press, 2015.

———. "A New Logical Problem of Evil." In McBrayer and Howard-Snyder, *Blackwell Companion to the Problem of Evil*, 34–48.

———. "Stalemate and Strategy: Rethinking the Evidential Argument from Evil." In Rowe, *God and the Problem of Evil*, 159–79.

Schreiner, Thomas R. *1, 2 Peter, Jude*. NAC. Nashville: B&H, 2007.

Silva, Moisés, ed. *New International Dictionary of New Testament Theology and Exegesis*. 5 vols. Grand Rapids: Zondervan, 2014.

Smith, Ralph L. *Micah–Malachi*. WBC. Dallas: Word, 1998.

Smith-Christopher, Daniel L. "Daniel." *NIB* 7:17–152.

Southgate, Christopher, and Andrew Robinson. "Varieties of Theodicy: An Exploration of Responses to the Problem of Evil Based on a Typology of Good-Harm Analyses." In *Physics and Cosmology: Scientific Perspectives on the Problem of Natural Evil*, edited by Nancey Murphy, Robert John Russell, and William R. Stoeger, 67–90. Vatican City: Vatican Observatory, 2007.

Speak, Daniel. "Free Will and Soul-Making Theodicies." In McBrayer and Howard-Snyder, *Blackwell Companion to the Problem of Evil*, 205–21.

Spiegel, James S. *The Making of an Atheist: How Immorality Leads to Unbelief*. Chicago: Moody, 2010.

Sprinkle, Preston, ed. *Four Views on Hell*. 2nd ed. Grand Rapids: Zondervan, 2016.

Stackhouse, John G., Jr. *Can God Be Trusted? Faith and the Challenge of Evil*. New York: Oxford University Press, 1998.

———. "Terminal Punishment." In Sprinkle, *Four Views on Hell*, 61–81.

Stefanović, Ranko. *Revelation of Jesus Christ*. Berrien Springs, MI: Andrews University Press, 2002.

Stott, John R. W. *The Cross of Christ*. Downers Grove, IL: IVP, 2006.

Stuckenbruck, Loren T. *The Myth of Rebellious Angels: Studies in Second Temple Judaism and New Testament Texts*. Grand Rapids: Eerdmans, 2017.

Stump, Eleonore. "Augustine on Free Will." In *The Cambridge Companion to Augustine*, edited by Eleonore Stump and Norman Kretzmann, 124–47. Cambridge, UK: Cambridge University Press, 2006.

———. "Comments on 'Does God Love Us?'" In Bergmann, Murray, and Rea, *Divine Evil?*, 47–53.

———. "Knowledge, Freedom, and the Problem of Evil." In Peterson, *Problem of Evil*, 2nd ed., 459–72.

———. *Wandering in the Darkness: Narrative and the Problem of Suffering*. New York: Oxford University Press, 2010.

Swinburne, Richard. *The Coherence of Theism*. Rev. ed. Oxford: Clarendon, 1993.

———. *Is There a God?* Rev. ed. New York: Oxford University Press, 2010.

———. *Providence and the Problem of Evil*. Oxford: Clarendon, 1998.

———. "Some Major Strands of Theodicy." In Rowe, *God and the Problem of Evil*, 240–64.

Tanner, Beth LaNeel. "Book Three of the Psalter: Psalms 73–89." In *The Book of Psalms*, edited by Nancy deClaissé-Walford, Rolf A. Jacobson, and Beth LaNeel Tanner, 581–684. NICOT. Grand Rapids: Eerdmans, 2014.

Tate, Marvin E. *Psalms 51–100*. WBC. Dallas: Word, 2002.

Thiselton, Anthony C. *The Two Horizons: New Testament Hermeneutics and Philosophical Description*. Grand Rapids: Eerdmans, 1980.

Thomas, Dylan. *The Poems of Dylan Thomas*, edited by Daniel Jones. New York: New Directions, 2003.

Thompson, J. A. *Deuteronomy*. Nottingham, UK: Inter-Varsity, 1974.

Tigay, Jeffrey H. *Deuteronomy*. JPS Commentary. Philadelphia: JPS, 1996.

Timpe, Kevin. *Free Will in Philosophical Theology*. New York: Bloomsbury Academic, 2014.

———. *Free Will: Sourcehood and Its Alternatives*. 2nd ed. New York: Bloomsbury Academic, 2013.

———. "Leeway vs. Sourcehood Conceptions of Free Will." In Timpe, Griffith, and Levy, *Routledge Companion to Free Will*, 213–24.

Timpe, Kevin, Meghan Griffith, and Neil Levy, eds. *The Routledge Companion to Free Will*. New York: Routledge, 2017.

Tonstad, Sigve K. *God of Sense and Traditions of Nonsense*. Eugene, OR: Wipf & Stock, 2016.

———. *Saving God's Reputation: The Theological Function of* Pistis Iesou *in the Cosmic Narratives of Revelation*. Library of New Testament Studies. New York: T&T Clark, 2006.

———. "Theodicy and the Theme of Cosmic Conflict in the Early Church." Andrews University Seminary Studies 42, no. 1 (2004): 169–202.

Tooley, Michael. "The Problem of Evil." In *Stanford Encyclopedia of Philosophy*. Fall 2015. Accessed November 4, 2016. http://plato.stanford.edu/archives/fall2015/entries/evil.

Torrance, T. F. *The Christian Doctrine of God: One Being, Three Persons*. New York: T&T Clark, 1996.

————. *Divine and Contingent Order*. Oxford: Oxford University Press, 1981.

Towner, W. Sibley. *Daniel*. Interpretation. Louisville: Westminster John Knox, 1984.

Tracy, Thomas F. "The Lawfulness of Nature and the Problem of Evil." In *Physics and Cosmology: Scientific Perspectives on the Problem of Natural Evil*, edited by Nancey Murphy, Robert John Russell, and William R. Stoeger, 153–78. Vatican City: Vatican Observatory, 2007.

Trakakis, Nick. "The Skeptical Theist Response to Rowe's Evidential Argument from Evil." In Peterson, *Problem of Evil*, 2nd ed., 530–52.

Trites, Alison A. *The New Testament Concept of Witness*. Cambridge, UK: Cambridge University Press, 1977.

van der Toorn, Karen, Bob Becking, and Pieter W. van der Horst, eds. *Dictionary of Deities and Demons in the Bible*. 2nd ed. Grand Rapids: Eerdmans, 1999.

VanGemeren, Willem A., ed. *New International Dictionary of Old Testament Theology and Exegesis*. 4 vols. Grand Rapids: Zondervan, 1997.

Vanhoozer, Kevin J. *The Drama of Doctrine: A Canonical-Linguistic Approach to Christian Theology*. Louisville: Westminster John Knox, 2005.

————. *Faith Speaking Understanding: Performing the Drama of Doctrine*. Louisville: Westminster John Knox, 2014.

Vanhoozer, Kevin J., Craig G. Bartholomew, Daniel J. Treier, and N. T. Wright, eds. *Dictionary for Theological Interpretation of the Bible*. Grand Rapids: Baker Academic, 2005.

Van Inwagen, Peter. *An Essay on Free Will*. Oxford: Clarendon, 1983.

————. "The Problem of Evil, the Problem of Air, and the Problem of Silence." In Rowe, *God and the Problem of Evil*, 203–33.

Vögtle, Anton. *Der Judasbrief, der zweite Petrusbrief*. EKK Studienausgabe 22. Düsseldorf: Benziger Verlag, 1994.

Wahlberg, Mats. "Was Evolution the Only Possible Way for God to Make Autonomous Creatures? Examination of an Argument in Evolutionary Theodicy." *International Journal for Philosophy of Religion* 77 (2015): 37–51.

Walls, Jerry L. "Why No Classical Theist, Let Alone Orthodox Christian, Should Ever Be a Compatibilist." *Philosophia Christi* 13, no. 1 (2011): 75–104.

————. "Why Plantinga Must Move from Defense to Theodicy." In Peterson, *Problem of Evil*, 1st ed., 331–34.

Walton, John H. *Covenant: God's Purpose, God's Plan*. Grand Rapids: Zondervan, 1994.

Wenham, Gordon J. *Genesis 1–15*. WBC. Waco: Word, 1987.

Westermann, Claus. *Genesis 1–11*. CC. Minneapolis: Fortress, 1994.

Widerker, David. "Libertarianism and Frankfurt's Attack on the Principle of Alternative Possibilities." *Philosophical Review* 104 (1995): 247–61.

Widerker, David, and Michael McKenna, eds. *Moral Responsibility and Alternative Possibilities: Essays on the Importance of Alternative Possibilities*. Burlington, VT: Ashgate, 2003.

Wiesel, Elie. *Night*. Translated by Marion Wiesel. New York: Hill & Wang, 2006.

Wilson, Lindsay. *Job*. Two Horizons Old Testament Commentary. Grand Rapids: Eerdmans, 2015.

Wink, Walter. *Walter Wink: Collected Readings*. Edited by Henry French. Minneapolis: Fortress, 2013.

Wolterstorff, Nicholas. *Lament for a Son*. Grand Rapids: Eerdmans, 1987.

———. "Suffering Love." In *Augustine's Confessions: Critical Essays*, edited by William E. Mann, 107–46. Oxford: Rowman & Littlefield, 2006.

Wright, N. T. *The Day the Revolution Began*. New York: HarperOne, 2016.

———. *Evil and the Justice of God*. Downers Grove, IL: IVP, 2006.

———. *Matthew for Everyone, Part 1: Chapters 1–15*. London: SPCK, 2004.

Wykstra, Stephen J. "Rowe's Noseeum Arguments from Evil." In *The Evidential Argument from Evil*, edited by Daniel Howard-Snyder, 126–50. Bloomington: Indiana University Press, 1996.

Yandell, Keith. "Divine Necessity and Divine Goodness." In *Divine and Human Action: Essays in the Metaphysics of Theism*, edited by Thomas V. Morris, 313–34. Ithaca, NY: Cornell University Press, 1988.

Scripture Index

Author Index

Subject Index

Printed and bound by CPI Group (UK) Ltd, Croydon, CR0 4YY

13/04/2025

14656457-0004